Persia Blues

Persia Blues

volume 2
Love and War

Dara Naraghi
Brent Bowman

ISBN 978-1-56163-977-9
© 2015 Dara Naraghi & Brent Bowman
Library of Congress Control Number 2013938100
Translation of Rumi poems graciously provided by, and
used with the permission of, www.RumiOnFire.com
1st printing December 2015

Comicslit is an imprint
and trademark of

NANTIER · BEALL · MINOUSTCHINE
Publishing inc.
new york

Everyday I meditate upon this, and every night I groan
Why is my own existence to myself the least known?
Whence have I come, why this coming here?
Where to must I go, when will my home to me be shown?
--Rumi

AS SEEN IN VOLUME 1

HERE

MINOO SHIRAZI

ADVENTURER

TYLER CLARKE

MINOO'S COMPANION

AHURA MAZDA

SUPREME CREATOR

(ZOROASTRIANISM)

AHRIMAN

DESTRUCTIVE SPIRIT

(ZOROASTRIANISM)

EMPRESS PURANDOKHT

RULER OF THE PERSIAN EMPIRE

THE GRIFFON

MYSTIC MESSENGER/ GUIDE

THERE

MINOO SHIRAZI

ARCHITECTURAL STUDENT

BIJAN SHIRAZI

MINOO'S FATHER

MANIJEH SHIRAZI

MINOO'S MOTHER

RAMIN SHIRAZI

MINOO'S OLDER BROTHER

Our Story Thus Far

Minoo Shirazi, a smart, confident, headstrong young Iranian woman, leads an improbable double-life. In an ancient Persia infused with elements of mythology ("Here"), she's a free-spirited adventurer, while in modern Iran ("There"), she is a recent college graduate, forging a path through life under an oppressive government and an overbearing father.

Here

Minoo is informed by a dying Zoroastrian priest that her destiny lies in Persepolis, the ancient capital city of the Persian Empire. This prophecy is also confirmed by a mystical griffon, who sets Minoo and her boyfriend, Tyler, on the path to adventure. During their journey, they are set upon by Ahriman, the Zoroastrian personification of evil and destruction. However, the duo is ultimately saved by the timely appearance of Ahura Mazda, the sole god and creator. Upon their arrival at Persepolis, they find the city under attack by an army of Ahriman's man-beasts. Minoo rushes into the fray, helping the Immortal Army to a victory over the monsters. Minoo is presented to Empress Purandokht, ruler of the Persian Empire, who reveals that she is Minoo's real mother.

There

Jumping back and forth through time, we witness key moments in Minoo's life: confrontations with Iran's Morality Police, family tragedies, struggles with young love, and her love/hate relationship with her father, Bijan. Although loving and nurturing in his own way, he is also a great source of frustration for Minoo. His stubborn nature, inflexible principles, and staunch nationalism leads him to clash with the ruling theocracy as well as his own family, culminating in the breakup of his marriage to Minoo's mother, Manijeh. Years later, Minoo loses her mother to cancer, while an unspoken tragedy robs her of Ramin, her older brother, protector, and best friend. Ultimately, Bijan uses his academic contacts in the US to help Minoo secure admission to The Ohio State University, where she intends to pursue her graduate studies in architecture.

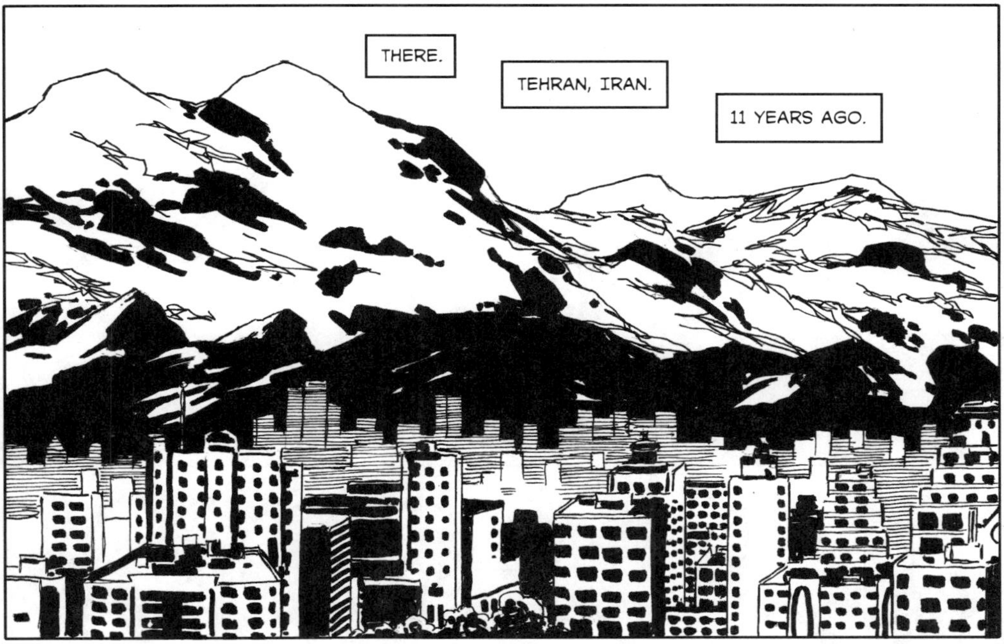
THERE.
TEHRAN, IRAN.
11 YEARS AGO.

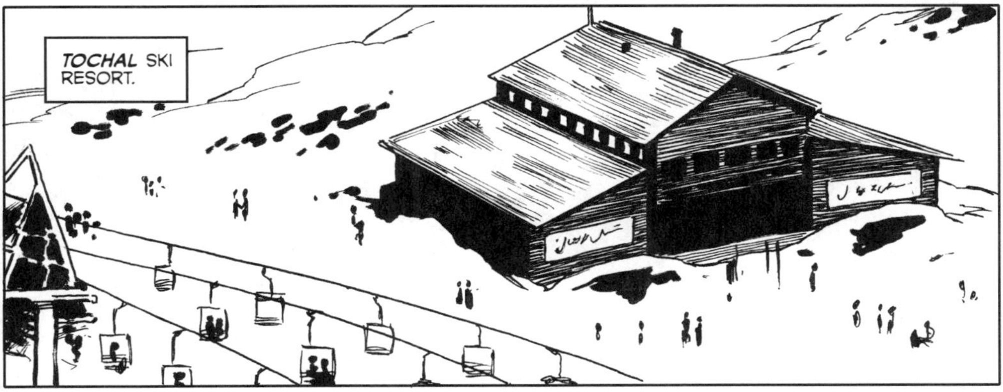
TOCHAL SKI RESORT.

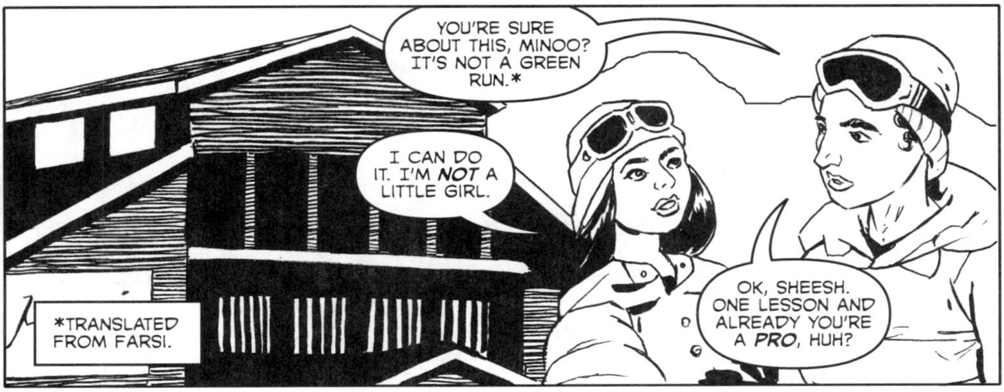
YOU'RE SURE ABOUT THIS, MINOO? IT'S NOT A GREEN RUN.*
I CAN DO IT. I'M NOT A LITTLE GIRL.
OK, SHEESH. ONE LESSON AND ALREADY YOU'RE A PRO, HUH?
*TRANSLATED FROM FARSI.

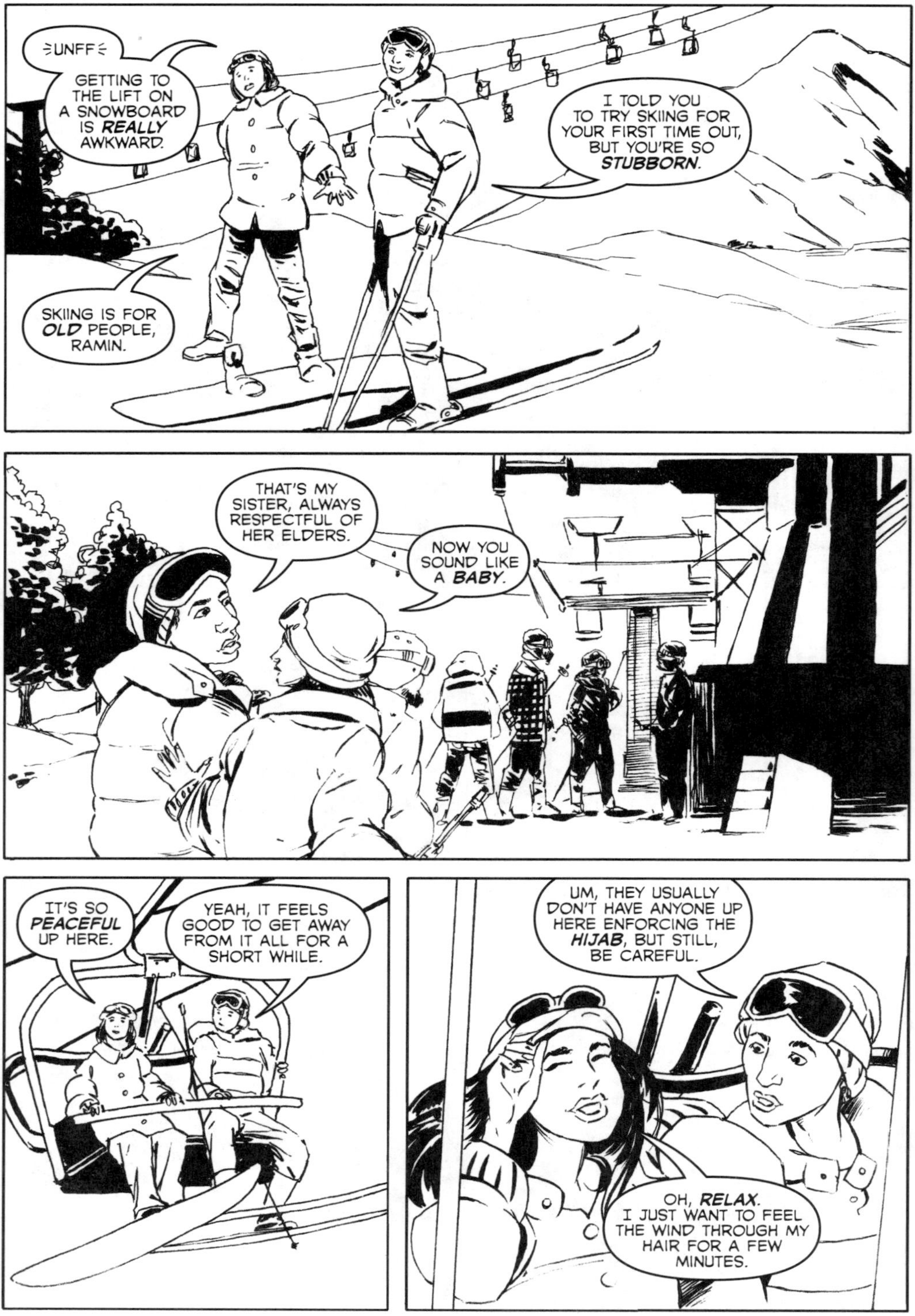
UNFF
GETTING TO THE LIFT ON A SNOWBOARD IS **REALLY** AWKWARD.
I TOLD YOU TO TRY SKIING FOR YOUR FIRST TIME OUT, BUT YOU'RE SO **STUBBORN**.
SKIING IS FOR **OLD** PEOPLE, RAMIN.
THAT'S MY SISTER, ALWAYS RESPECTFUL OF HER ELDERS.
NOW YOU SOUND LIKE A **BABY**.
IT'S SO **PEACEFUL** UP HERE.
YEAH, IT FEELS GOOD TO GET AWAY FROM IT ALL FOR A SHORT WHILE.
UM, THEY USUALLY DON'T HAVE ANYONE UP HERE ENFORCING THE **HIJAB**, BUT STILL, BE CAREFUL.
OH, **RELAX**. I JUST WANT TO FEEL THE WIND THROUGH MY HAIR FOR A FEW MINUTES.

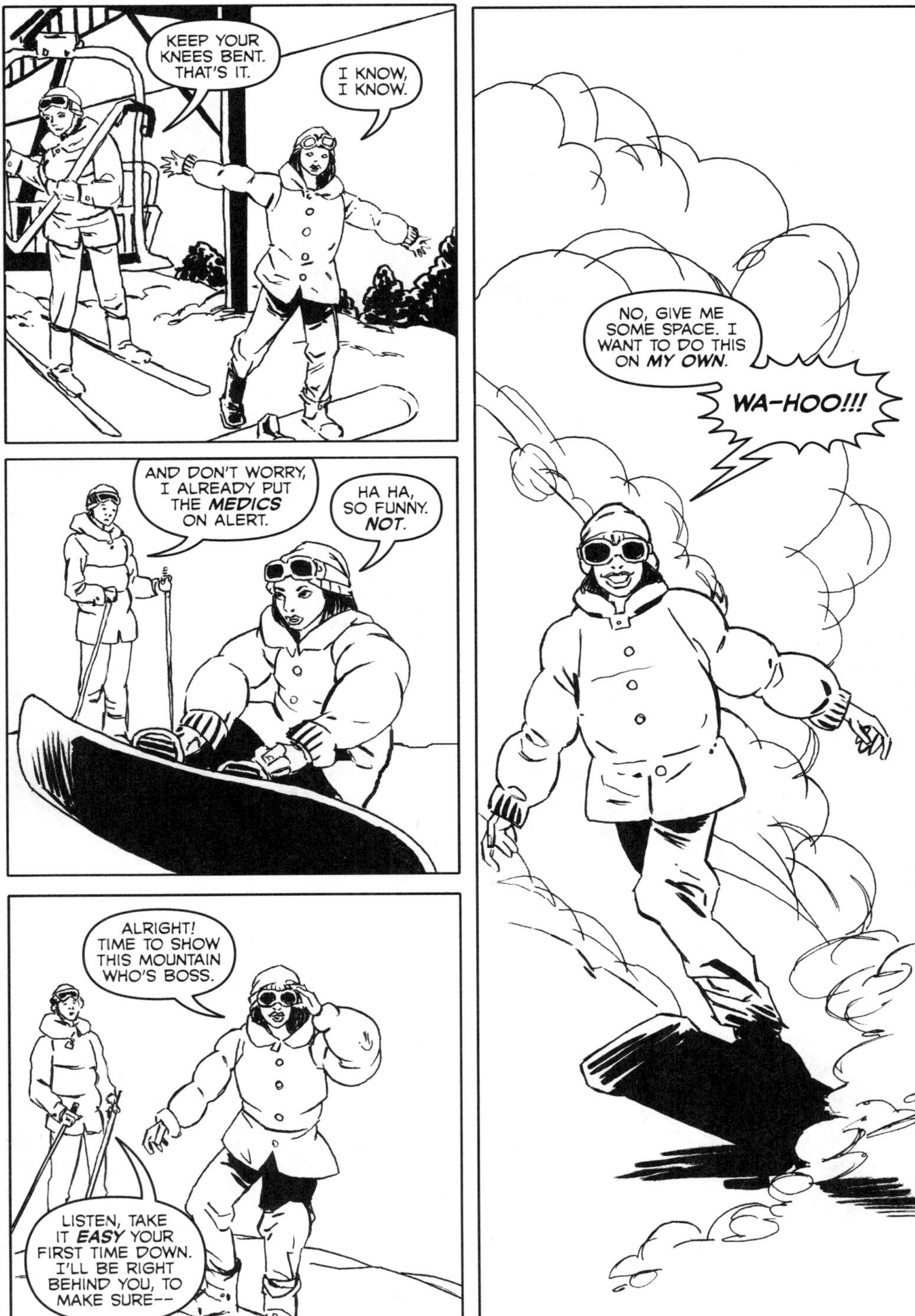
KEEP YOUR KNEES BENT. THAT'S IT.
I KNOW, I KNOW.
AND DON'T WORRY, I ALREADY PUT THE *MEDICS* ON ALERT.
HA HA, SO FUNNY. *NOT*.
ALRIGHT! TIME TO SHOW THIS MOUNTAIN WHO'S BOSS.
LISTEN, TAKE IT *EASY* YOUR FIRST TIME DOWN. I'LL BE RIGHT BEHIND YOU, TO MAKE SURE--
NO, GIVE ME SOME SPACE. I WANT TO DO THIS ON *MY OWN*.
WA-HOO!!!

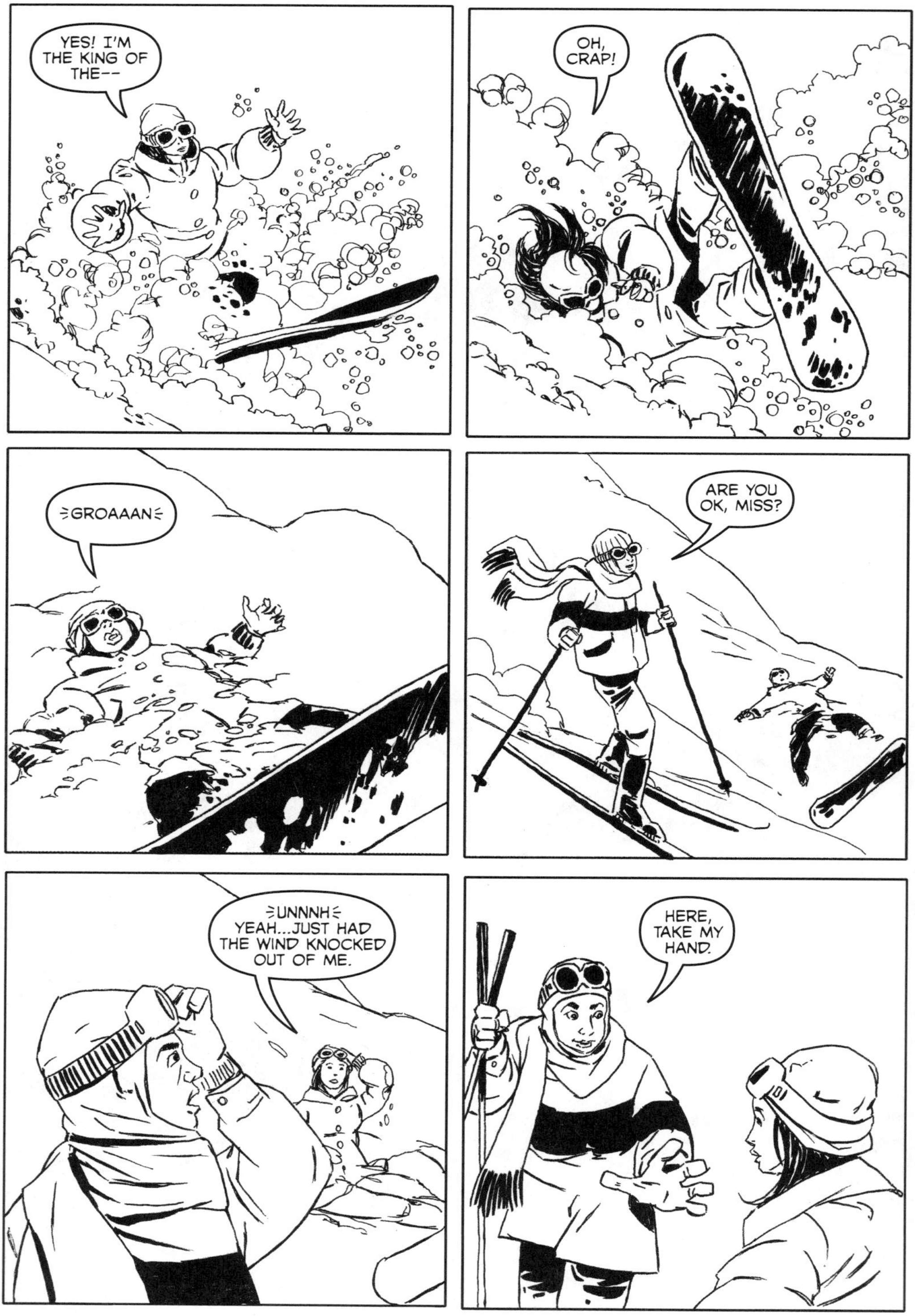
YES! I'M THE KING OF THE--
OH, CRAP!
GROAAAN
ARE YOU OK, MISS?
UNNNH YEAH...JUST HAD THE WIND KNOCKED OUT OF ME.
HERE, TAKE MY HAND.

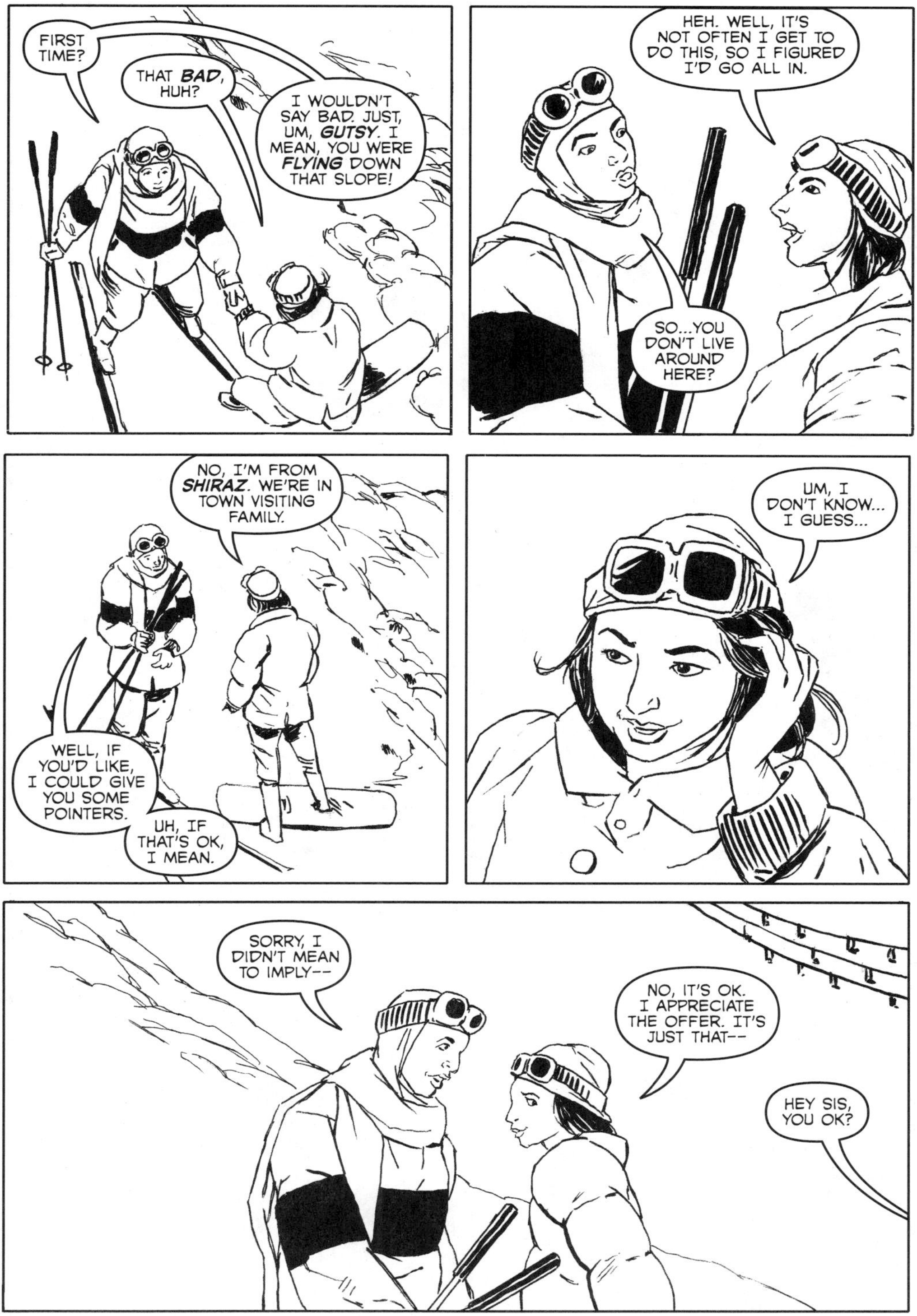
FIRST TIME?
THAT **BAD**, HUH?
I WOULDN'T SAY BAD. JUST, UM, ***GUTSY***. I MEAN, YOU WERE ***FLYING*** DOWN THAT SLOPE!
HEH. WELL, IT'S NOT OFTEN I GET TO DO THIS, SO I FIGURED I'D GO ALL IN.
SO...YOU DON'T LIVE AROUND HERE?
NO, I'M FROM ***SHIRAZ***. WE'RE IN TOWN VISITING FAMILY.
WELL, IF YOU'D LIKE, I COULD GIVE YOU SOME POINTERS.
UH, IF THAT'S OK, I MEAN.
UM, I DON'T KNOW... I GUESS...
SORRY, I DIDN'T MEAN TO IMPLY--
NO, IT'S OK. I APPRECIATE THE OFFER. IT'S JUST THAT--
HEY SIS, YOU OK?

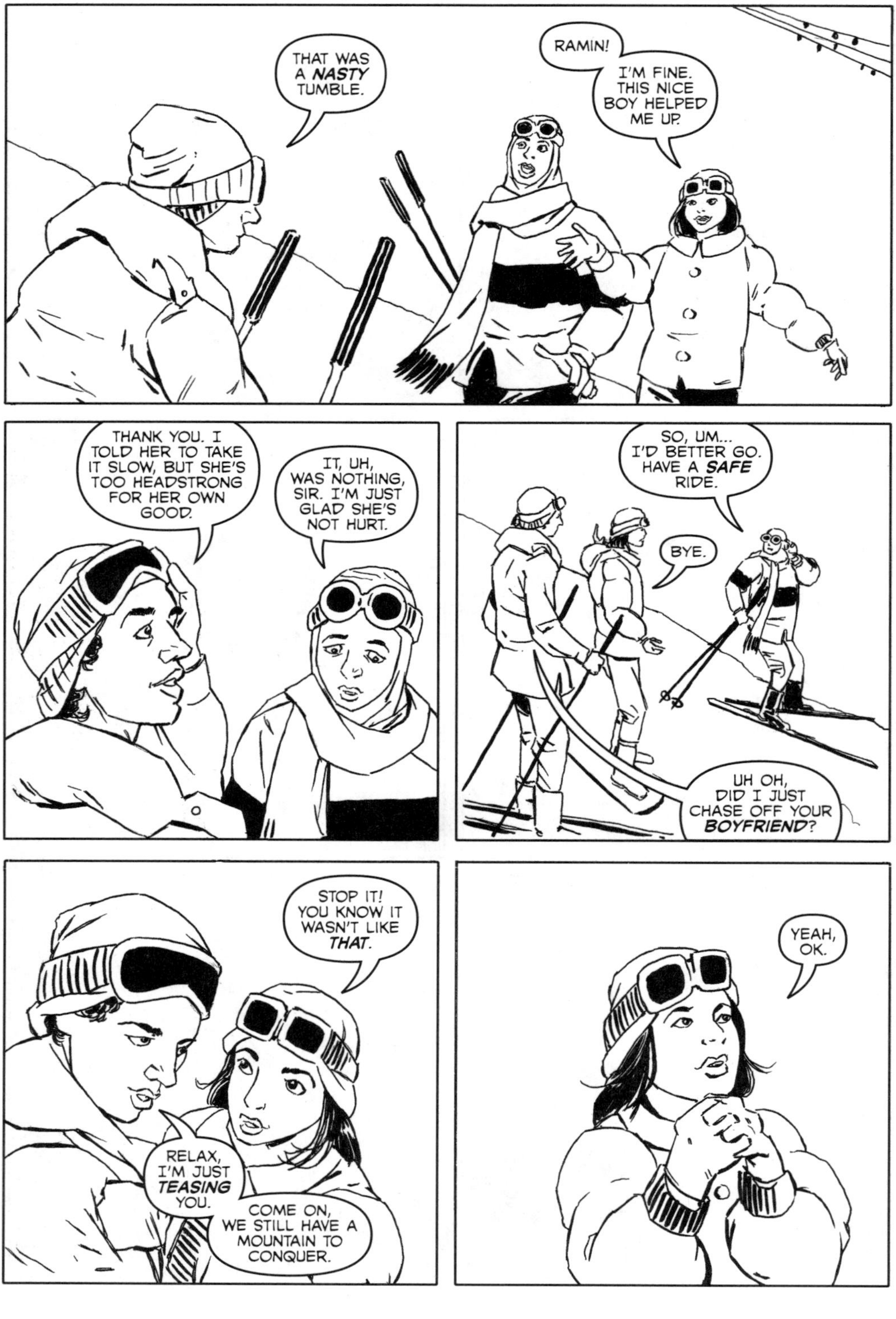

THAT WAS A NASTY TUMBLE.
RAMIN!
I'M FINE. THIS NICE BOY HELPED ME UP.
THANK YOU. I TOLD HER TO TAKE IT SLOW, BUT SHE'S TOO HEADSTRONG FOR HER OWN GOOD.
IT, UH, WAS NOTHING, SIR. I'M JUST GLAD SHE'S NOT HURT.
SO, UM... I'D BETTER GO. HAVE A SAFE RIDE.
BYE.
UH OH, DID I JUST CHASE OFF YOUR BOYFRIEND?
STOP IT! YOU KNOW IT WASN'T LIKE THAT.
RELAX, I'M JUST TEASING YOU.
COME ON, WE STILL HAVE A MOUNTAIN TO CONQUER.
YEAH, OK.

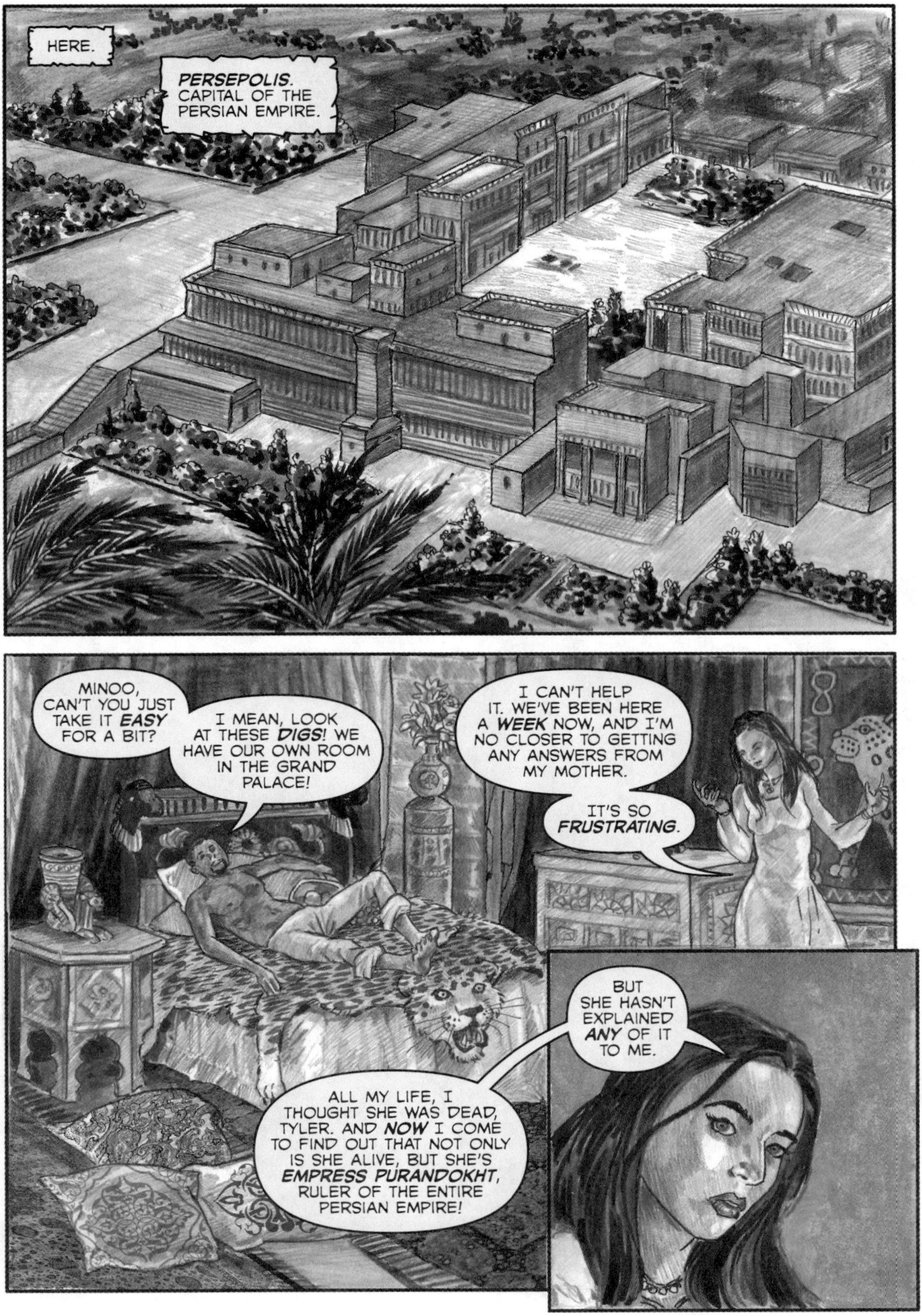
HERE.
PERSEPOLIS. CAPITAL OF THE PERSIAN EMPIRE.
MINOO, CAN'T YOU JUST TAKE IT *EASY* FOR A BIT?
I MEAN, LOOK AT THESE *DIGS!* WE HAVE OUR OWN ROOM IN THE GRAND PALACE!
I CAN'T HELP IT. WE'VE BEEN HERE A *WEEK* NOW, AND I'M NO CLOSER TO GETTING ANY ANSWERS FROM MY MOTHER.
IT'S SO *FRUSTRATING.*
ALL MY LIFE, I THOUGHT SHE WAS DEAD, TYLER. AND *NOW* I COME TO FIND OUT THAT NOT ONLY IS SHE ALIVE, BUT SHE'S *EMPRESS PURANDOKHT,* RULER OF THE ENTIRE PERSIAN EMPIRE!
BUT SHE HASN'T EXPLAINED *ANY* OF IT TO ME.

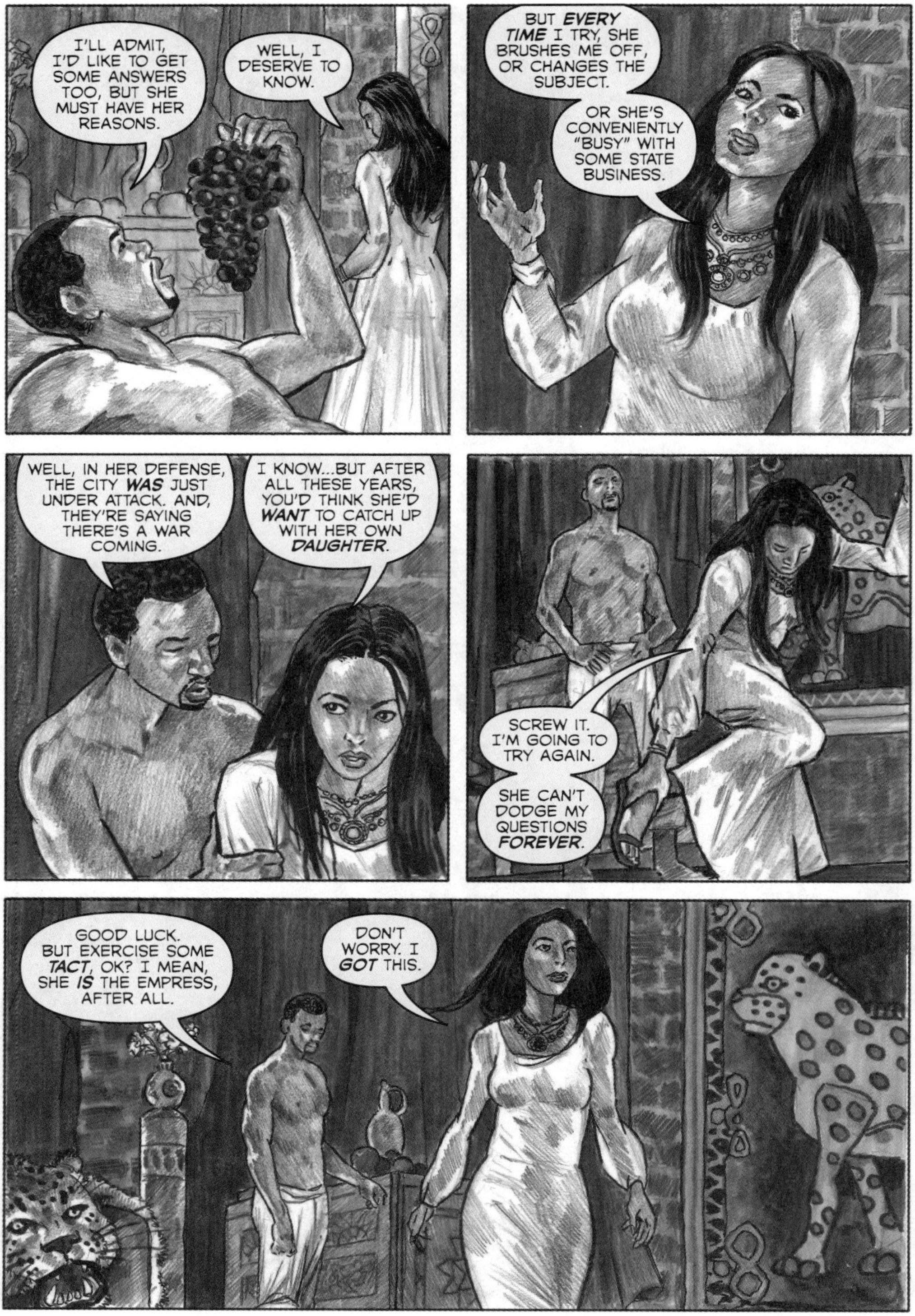
I'LL ADMIT, I'D LIKE TO GET SOME ANSWERS TOO, BUT SHE MUST HAVE HER REASONS.
WELL, I DESERVE TO KNOW.
BUT EVERY TIME I TRY, SHE BRUSHES ME OFF, OR CHANGES THE SUBJECT.
OR SHE'S CONVENIENTLY "BUSY" WITH SOME STATE BUSINESS.
WELL, IN HER DEFENSE, THE CITY WAS JUST UNDER ATTACK. AND, THEY'RE SAYING THERE'S A WAR COMING.
I KNOW...BUT AFTER ALL THESE YEARS, YOU'D THINK SHE'D WANT TO CATCH UP WITH HER OWN DAUGHTER.
SCREW IT. I'M GOING TO TRY AGAIN.
SHE CAN'T DODGE MY QUESTIONS FOREVER.
GOOD LUCK. BUT EXERCISE SOME TACT, OK? I MEAN, SHE IS THE EMPRESS, AFTER ALL.
DON'T WORRY. I GOT THIS.

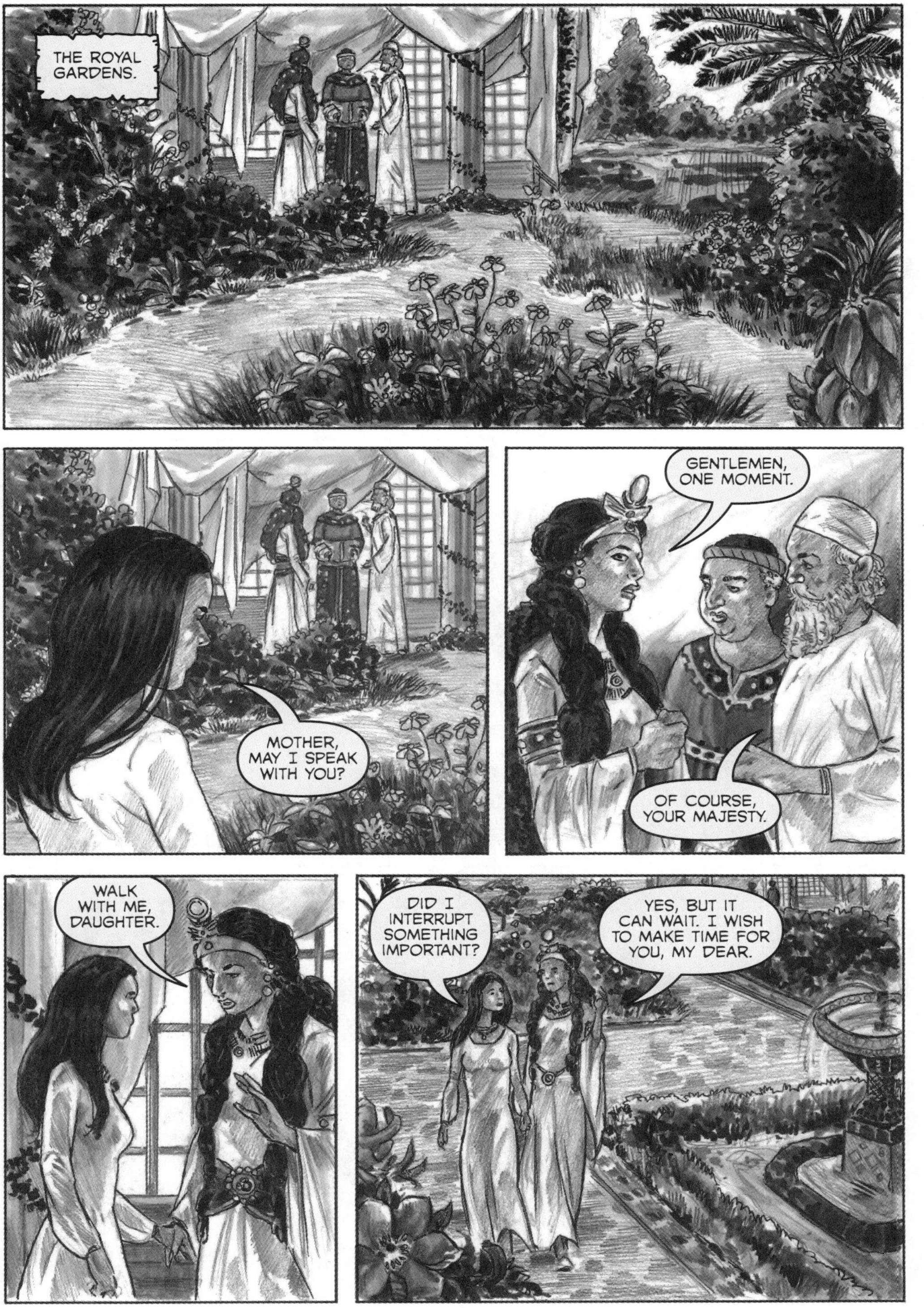
THE ROYAL GARDENS.
MOTHER, MAY I SPEAK WITH YOU?
GENTLEMEN, ONE MOMENT.
OF COURSE, YOUR MAJESTY.
WALK WITH ME, DAUGHTER.
DID I INTERRUPT SOMETHING IMPORTANT?
YES, BUT IT CAN WAIT. I WISH TO MAKE TIME FOR YOU, MY DEAR.

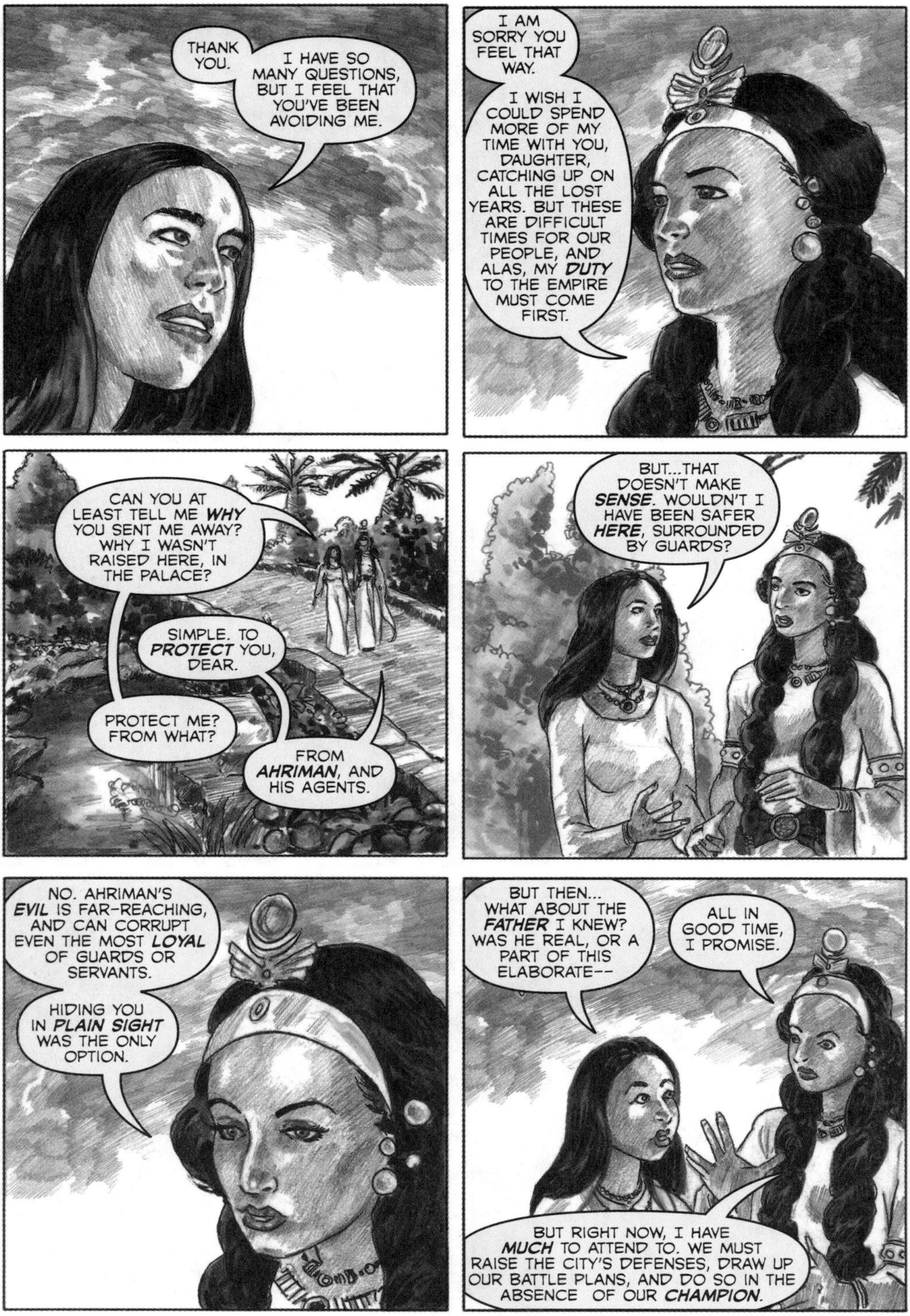
THANK YOU.
I HAVE SO MANY QUESTIONS, BUT I FEEL THAT YOU'VE BEEN AVOIDING ME.
I AM SORRY YOU FEEL THAT WAY.
I WISH I COULD SPEND MORE OF MY TIME WITH YOU, DAUGHTER, CATCHING UP ON ALL THE LOST YEARS. BUT THESE ARE DIFFICULT TIMES FOR OUR PEOPLE, AND ALAS, MY DUTY TO THE EMPIRE MUST COME FIRST.
CAN YOU AT LEAST TELL ME WHY YOU SENT ME AWAY? WHY I WASN'T RAISED HERE, IN THE PALACE?
SIMPLE. TO PROTECT YOU, DEAR.
PROTECT ME? FROM WHAT?
FROM AHRIMAN, AND HIS AGENTS.
BUT...THAT DOESN'T MAKE SENSE. WOULDN'T I HAVE BEEN SAFER HERE, SURROUNDED BY GUARDS?
NO. AHRIMAN'S EVIL IS FAR-REACHING, AND CAN CORRUPT EVEN THE MOST LOYAL OF GUARDS OR SERVANTS.
HIDING YOU IN PLAIN SIGHT WAS THE ONLY OPTION.
BUT THEN... WHAT ABOUT THE FATHER I KNEW? WAS HE REAL, OR A PART OF THIS ELABORATE--
ALL IN GOOD TIME, I PROMISE.
BUT RIGHT NOW, I HAVE MUCH TO ATTEND TO. WE MUST RAISE THE CITY'S DEFENSES, DRAW UP OUR BATTLE PLANS, AND DO SO IN THE ABSENCE OF OUR CHAMPION.

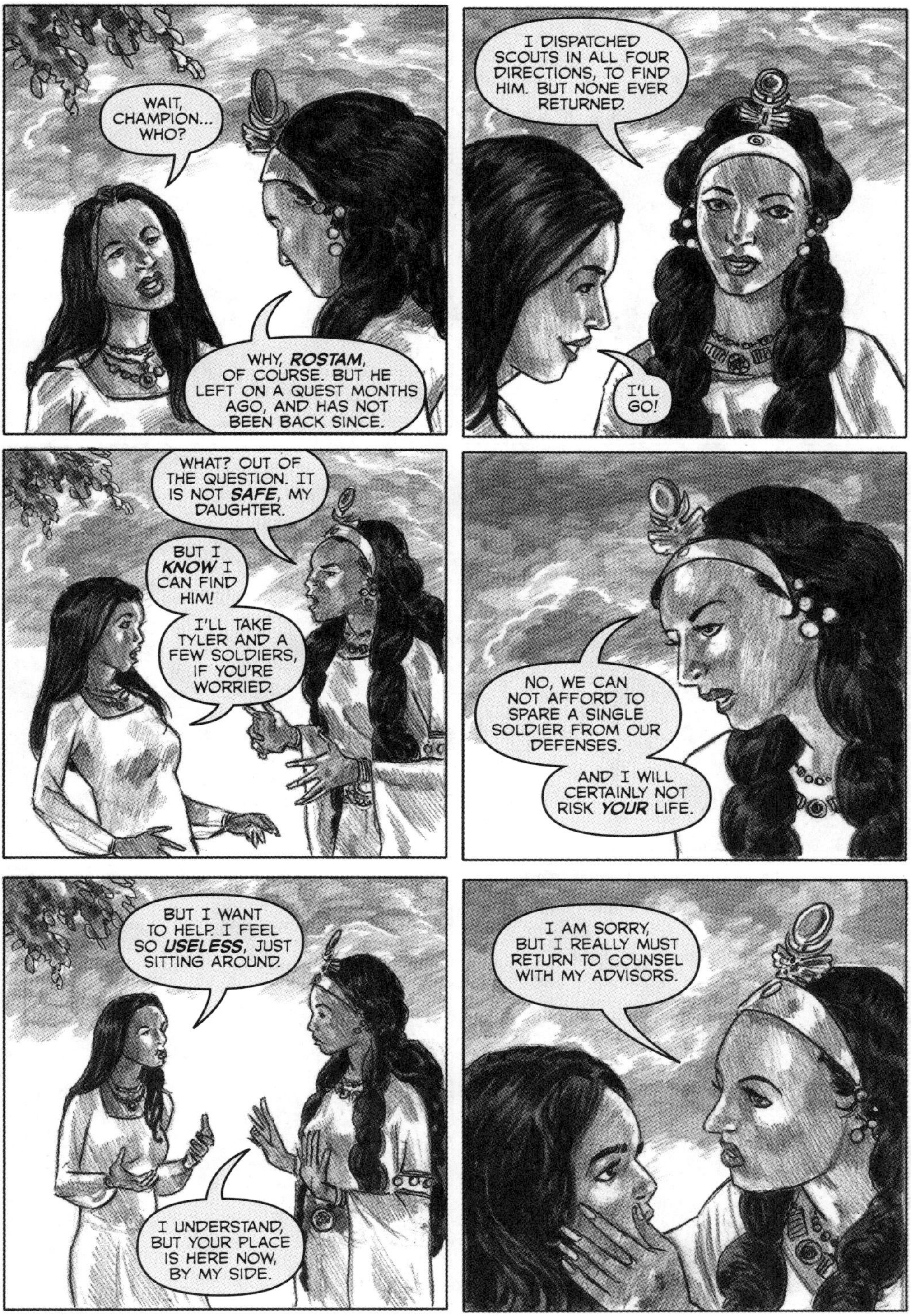
WAIT, CHAMPION... WHO?
WHY, ROSTAM, OF COURSE. BUT HE LEFT ON A QUEST MONTHS AGO, AND HAS NOT BEEN BACK SINCE.
I DISPATCHED SCOUTS IN ALL FOUR DIRECTIONS, TO FIND HIM. BUT NONE EVER RETURNED.
I'LL GO!
WHAT? OUT OF THE QUESTION. IT IS NOT SAFE, MY DAUGHTER.
BUT I KNOW I CAN FIND HIM!
I'LL TAKE TYLER AND A FEW SOLDIERS, IF YOU'RE WORRIED.
NO, WE CAN NOT AFFORD TO SPARE A SINGLE SOLDIER FROM OUR DEFENSES.
AND I WILL CERTAINLY NOT RISK YOUR LIFE.
BUT I WANT TO HELP. I FEEL SO USELESS, JUST SITTING AROUND.
I UNDERSTAND, BUT YOUR PLACE IS HERE NOW, BY MY SIDE.
I AM SORRY, BUT I REALLY MUST RETURN TO COUNSEL WITH MY ADVISORS.

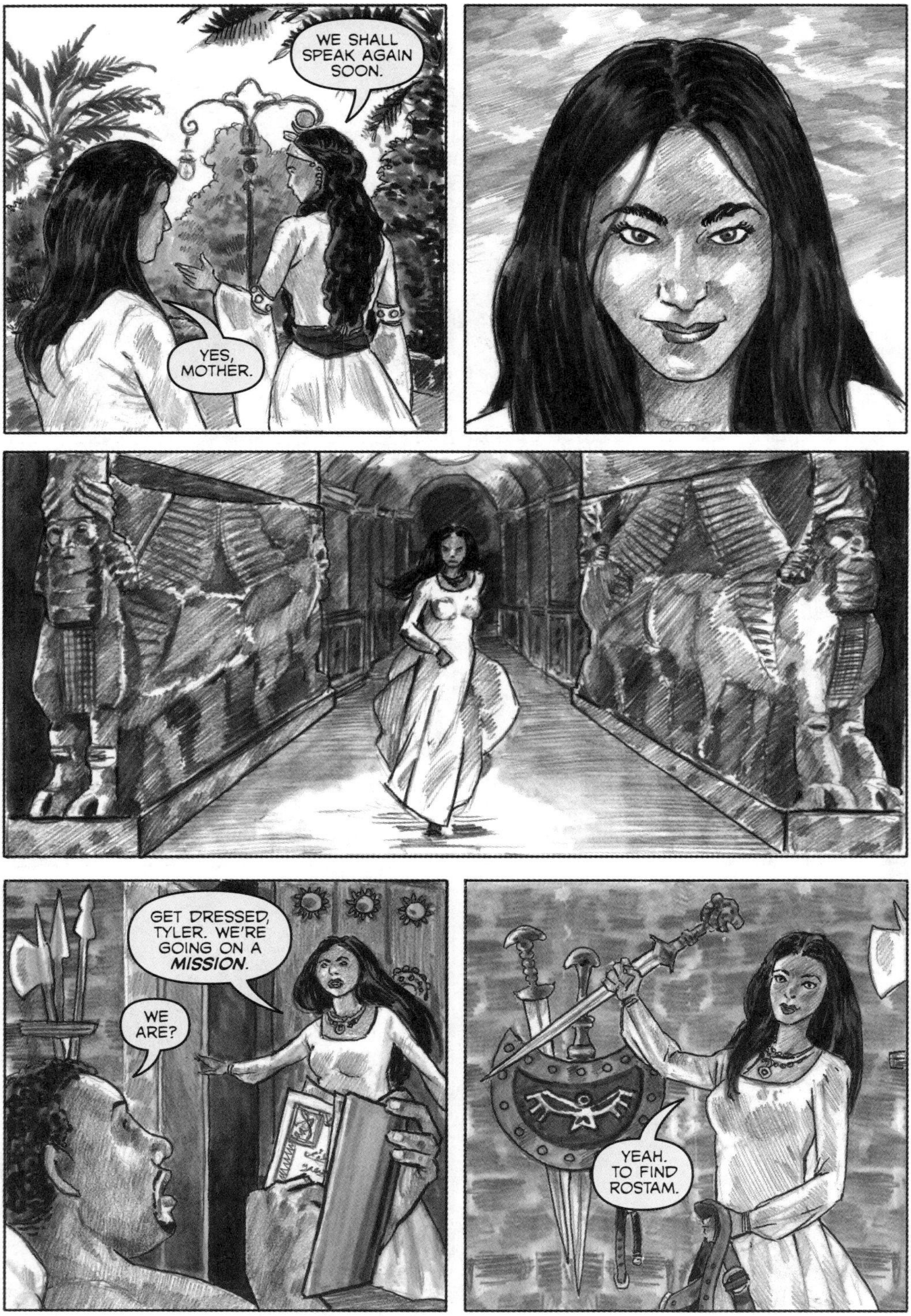
WE SHALL SPEAK AGAIN SOON.
YES, MOTHER.
GET DRESSED, TYLER. WE'RE GOING ON A *MISSION*.
WE ARE?
YEAH. TO FIND ROSTAM.

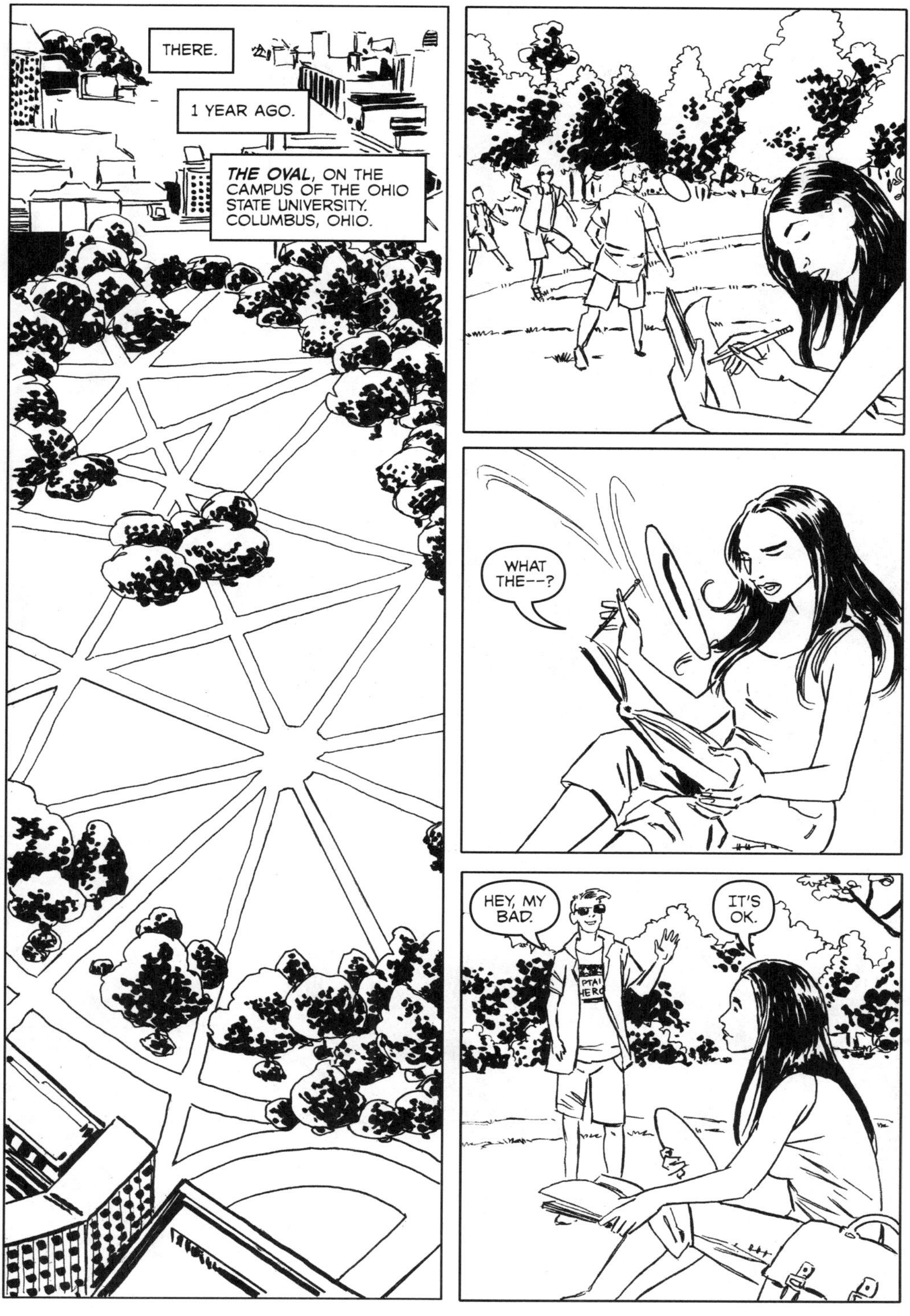
THERE.
1 YEAR AGO.
THE OVAL, ON THE CAMPUS OF THE OHIO STATE UNIVERSITY. COLUMBUS, OHIO.
WHAT THE--?
HEY, MY BAD.
IT'S OK.

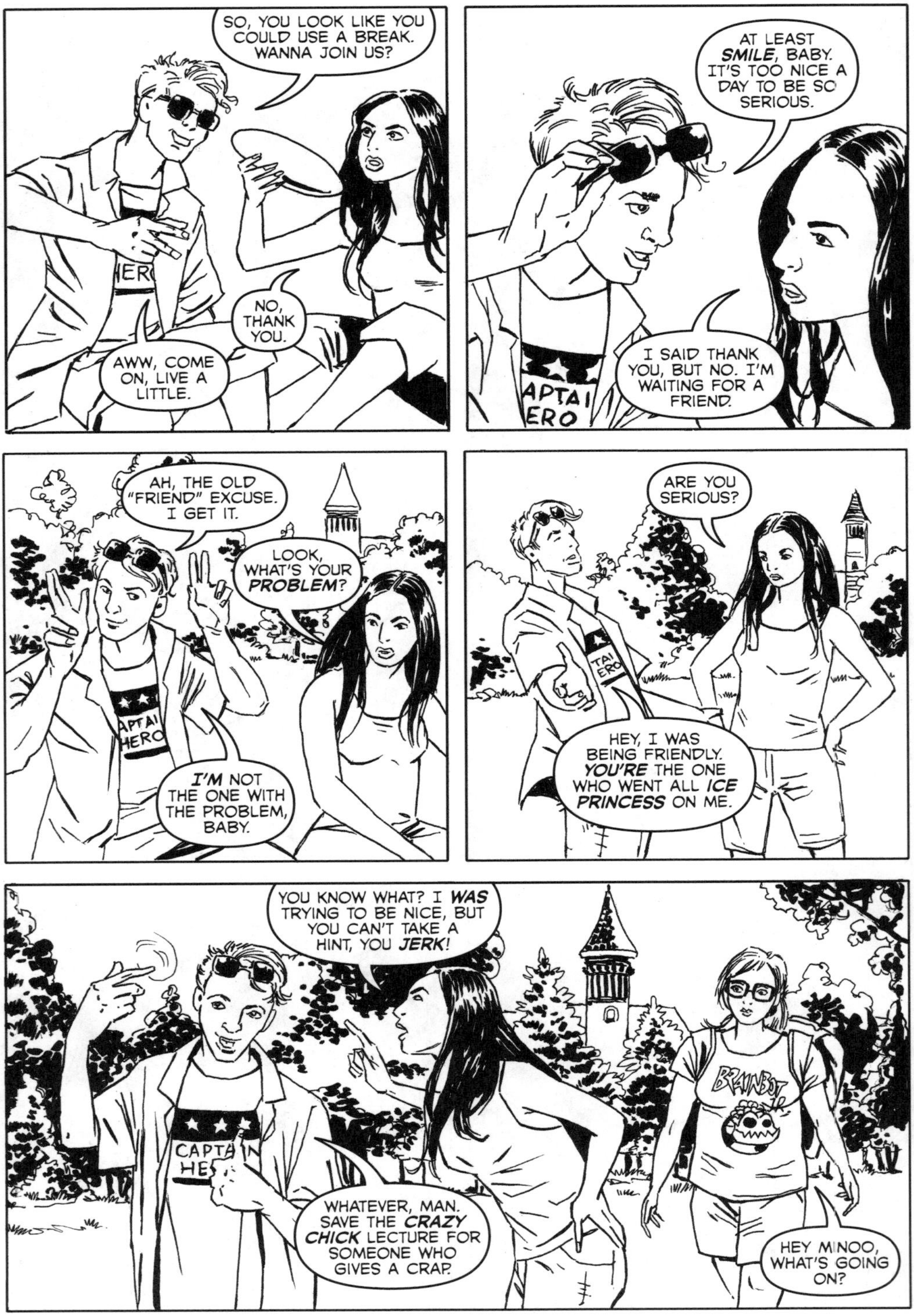
SO, YOU LOOK LIKE YOU COULD USE A BREAK. WANNA JOIN US?
NO, THANK YOU.
AWW, COME ON, LIVE A LITTLE.
AT LEAST *SMILE*, BABY. IT'S TOO NICE A DAY TO BE SO SERIOUS.
I SAID THANK YOU, BUT NO. I'M WAITING FOR A FRIEND.
AH, THE OLD "FRIEND" EXCUSE. I GET IT.
LOOK, WHAT'S YOUR *PROBLEM*?
I'M NOT THE ONE WITH THE PROBLEM, BABY.
ARE YOU SERIOUS?
HEY, I WAS BEING FRIENDLY. *YOU'RE* THE ONE WHO WENT ALL *ICE PRINCESS* ON ME.
YOU KNOW WHAT? I *WAS* TRYING TO BE NICE, BUT YOU CAN'T TAKE A HINT, YOU *JERK*!
WHATEVER, MAN. SAVE THE *CRAZY CHICK* LECTURE FOR SOMEONE WHO GIVES A CRAP.
HEY MINOO, WHAT'S GOING ON?

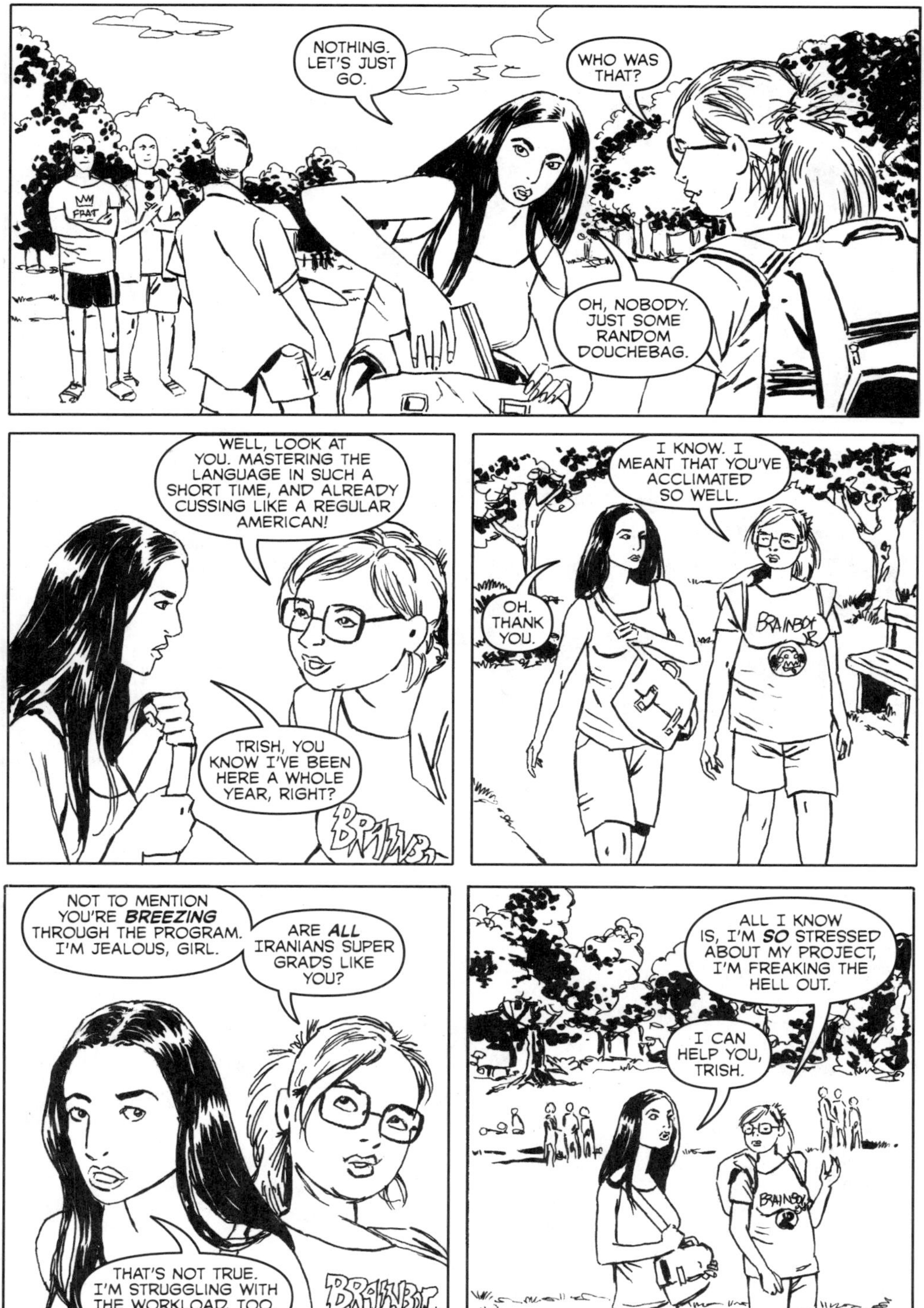
NOTHING. LET'S JUST GO.
WHO WAS THAT?
FRAT
OH, NOBODY. JUST SOME RANDOM DOUCHEBAG.
WELL, LOOK AT YOU. MASTERING THE LANGUAGE IN SUCH A SHORT TIME, AND ALREADY CUSSING LIKE A REGULAR AMERICAN!
TRISH, YOU KNOW I'VE BEEN HERE A WHOLE YEAR, RIGHT?
I KNOW. I MEANT THAT YOU'VE ACCLIMATED SO WELL.
OH. THANK YOU.
NOT TO MENTION YOU'RE **BREEZING** THROUGH THE PROGRAM. I'M JEALOUS, GIRL.
ARE **ALL** IRANIANS SUPER GRADS LIKE YOU?
THAT'S NOT TRUE. I'M STRUGGLING WITH THE WORKLOAD, TOO.
ALL I KNOW IS, I'M **SO** STRESSED ABOUT MY PROJECT, I'M FREAKING THE HELL OUT.
I CAN HELP YOU, TRISH.

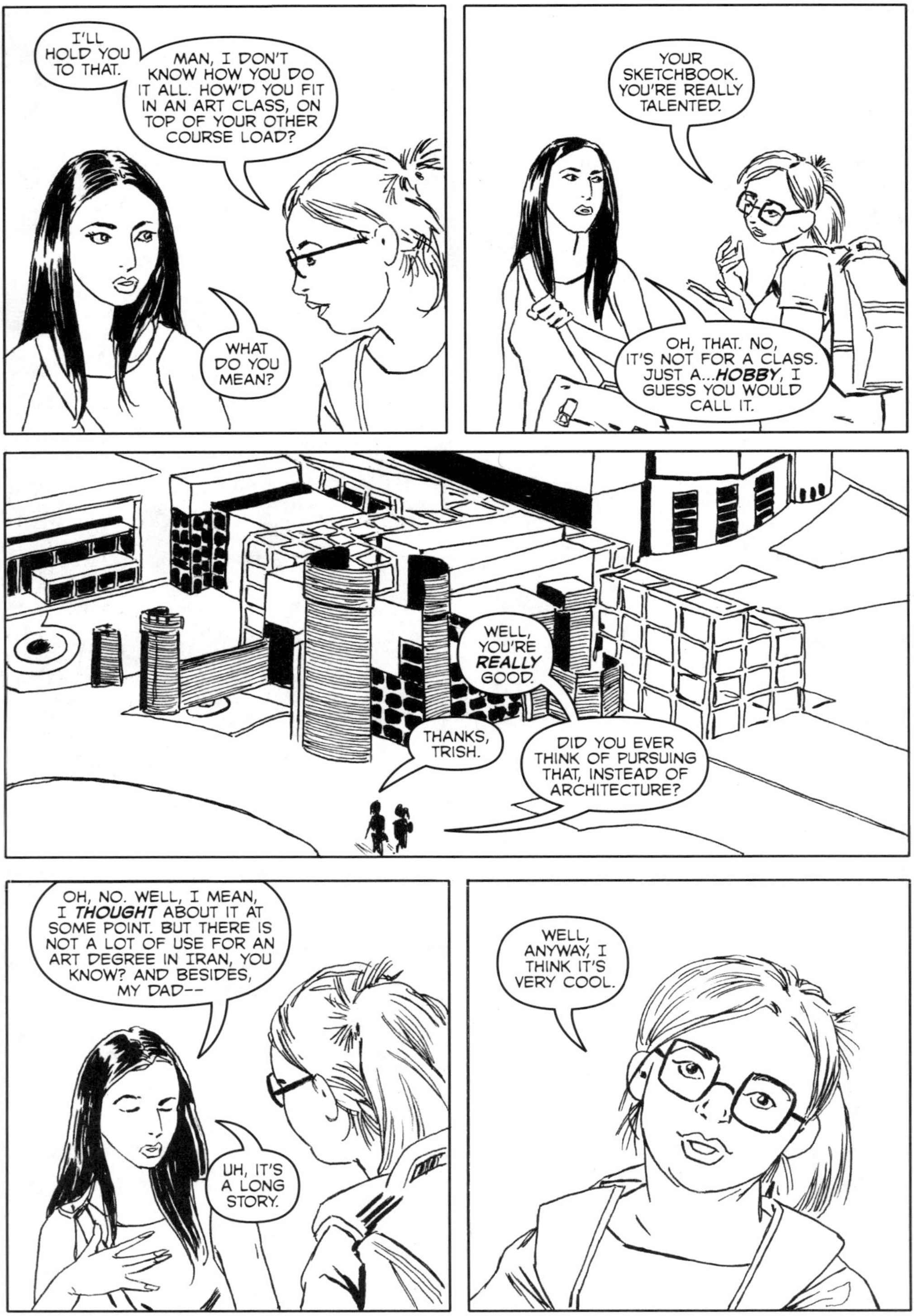

I'LL HOLD YOU TO THAT.
MAN, I DON'T KNOW HOW YOU DO IT ALL. HOW'D YOU FIT IN AN ART CLASS, ON TOP OF YOUR OTHER COURSE LOAD?
WHAT DO YOU MEAN?
YOUR SKETCHBOOK. YOU'RE REALLY TALENTED.
OH, THAT. NO, IT'S NOT FOR A CLASS. JUST A...*HOBBY*, I GUESS YOU WOULD CALL IT.
WELL, YOU'RE *REALLY* GOOD.
THANKS, TRISH.
DID YOU EVER THINK OF PURSUING THAT, INSTEAD OF ARCHITECTURE?
OH, NO. WELL, I MEAN, I *THOUGHT* ABOUT IT AT SOME POINT. BUT THERE IS NOT A LOT OF USE FOR AN ART DEGREE IN IRAN, YOU KNOW? AND BESIDES, MY DAD--
UH, IT'S A LONG STORY.
WELL, ANYWAY, I THINK IT'S VERY COOL.

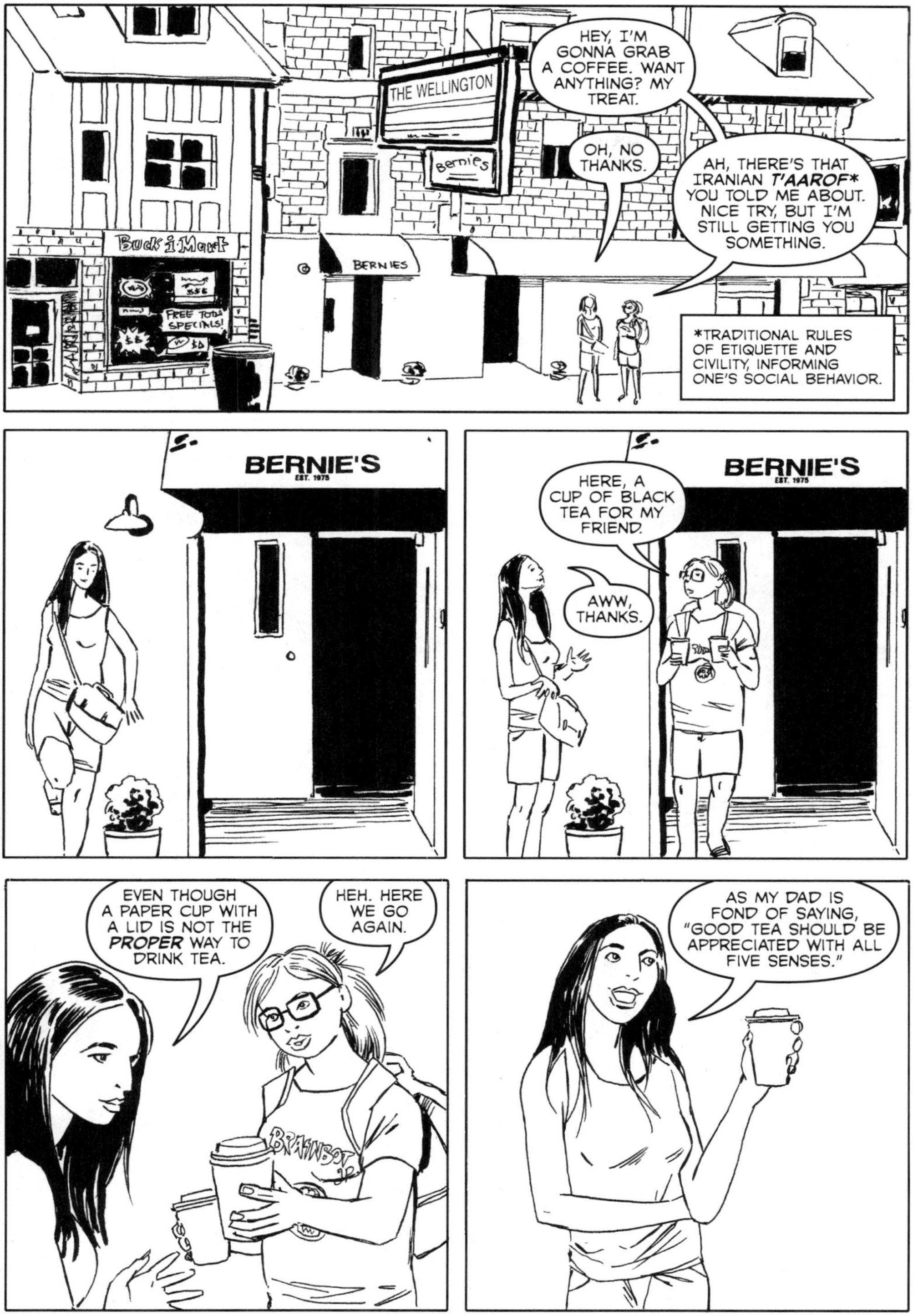
THE WELLINGTON
BERNIES
HEY, I'M GONNA GRAB A COFFEE. WANT ANYTHING? MY TREAT.
OH, NO THANKS.
AH, THERE'S THAT IRANIAN *T'AAROF** YOU TOLD ME ABOUT. NICE TRY, BUT I'M STILL GETTING YOU SOMETHING.
*TRADITIONAL RULES OF ETIQUETTE AND CIVILITY, INFORMING ONE'S SOCIAL BEHAVIOR.
BERNIE'S
EST. 1975
BERNIE'S
EST. 1975
HERE, A CUP OF BLACK TEA FOR MY FRIEND.
AWW, THANKS.
EVEN THOUGH A PAPER CUP WITH A LID IS NOT THE ***PROPER*** WAY TO DRINK TEA.
HEH. HERE WE GO AGAIN.
AS MY DAD IS FOND OF SAYING, "GOOD TEA SHOULD BE APPRECIATED WITH ALL FIVE SENSES."

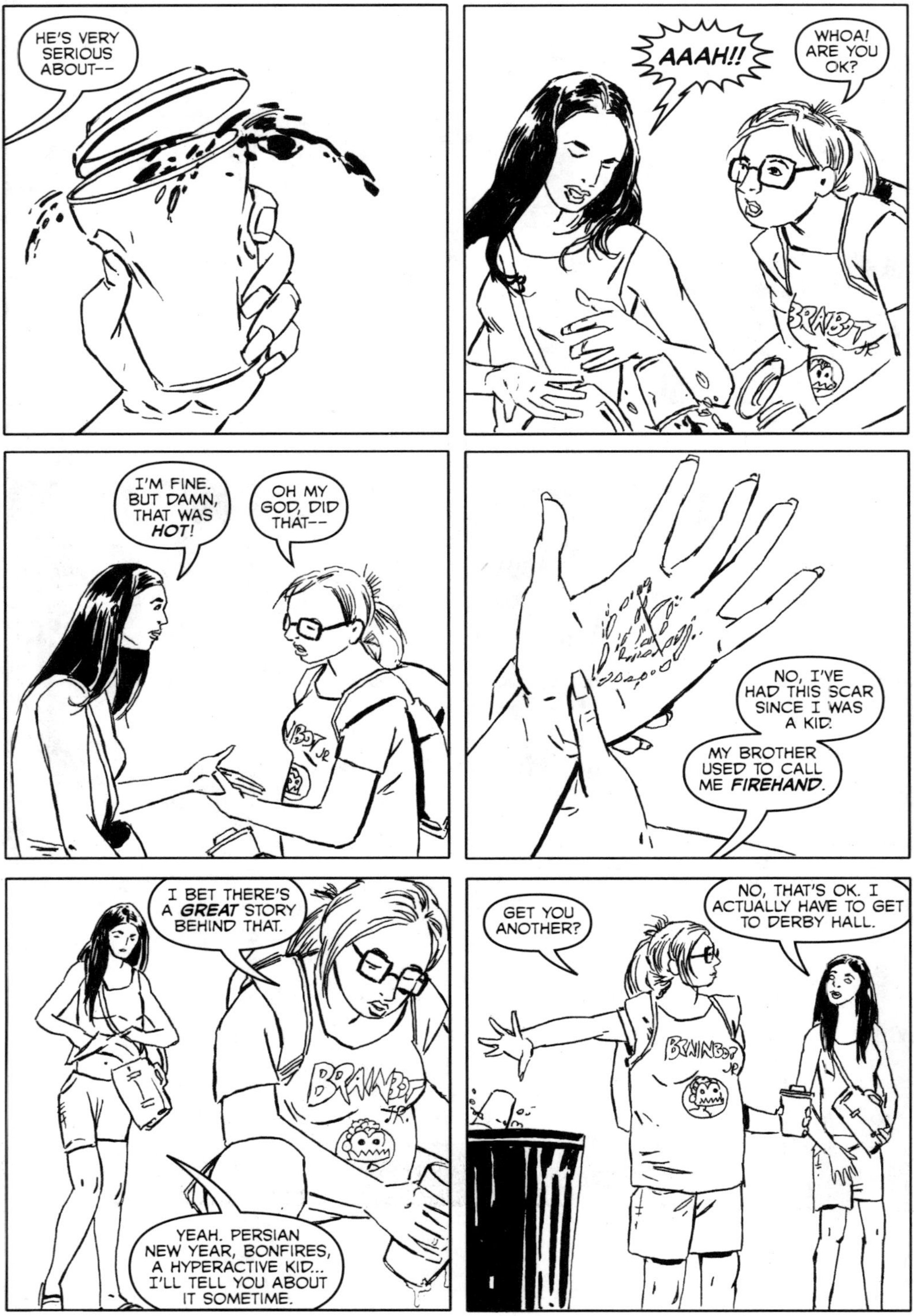
HE'S VERY SERIOUS ABOUT--
AAAH!!
WHOA! ARE YOU OK?
I'M FINE. BUT DAMN, THAT WAS HOT!
OH MY GOD, DID THAT--
NO, I'VE HAD THIS SCAR SINCE I WAS A KID.
MY BROTHER USED TO CALL ME FIREHAND.
I BET THERE'S A GREAT STORY BEHIND THAT.
YEAH. PERSIAN NEW YEAR, BONFIRES, A HYPERACTIVE KID... I'LL TELL YOU ABOUT IT SOMETIME.
GET YOU ANOTHER?
NO, THAT'S OK. I ACTUALLY HAVE TO GET TO DERBY HALL.

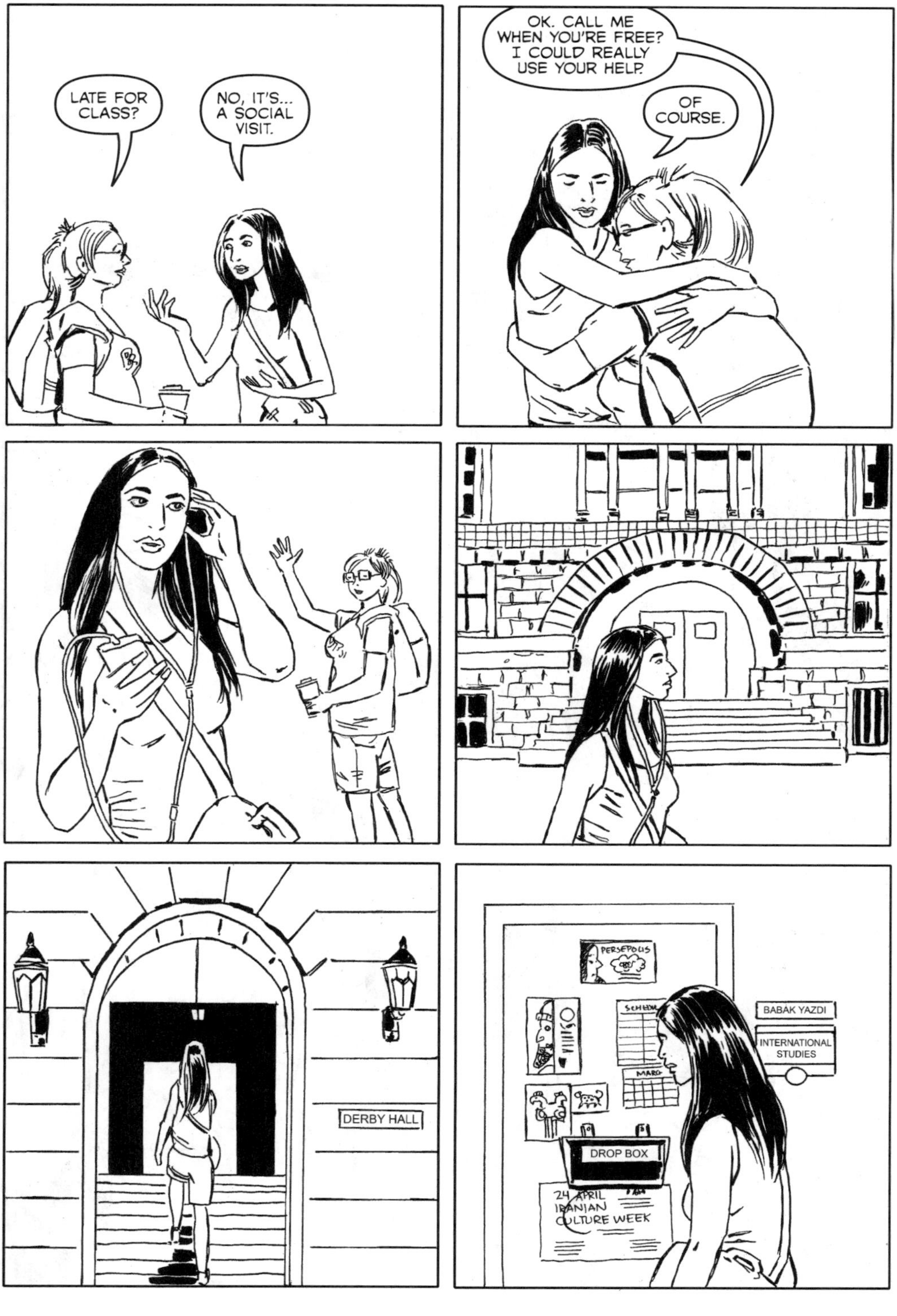
LATE FOR CLASS?
NO, IT'S... A SOCIAL VISIT.
OK. CALL ME WHEN YOU'RE FREE? I COULD REALLY USE YOUR HELP.
OF COURSE.
DERBY HALL
PERSEPOLIS
BABAK YAZDI
INTERNATIONAL STUDIES
DROP BOX
24 APRIL
IRANIAN
CULTURE WEEK

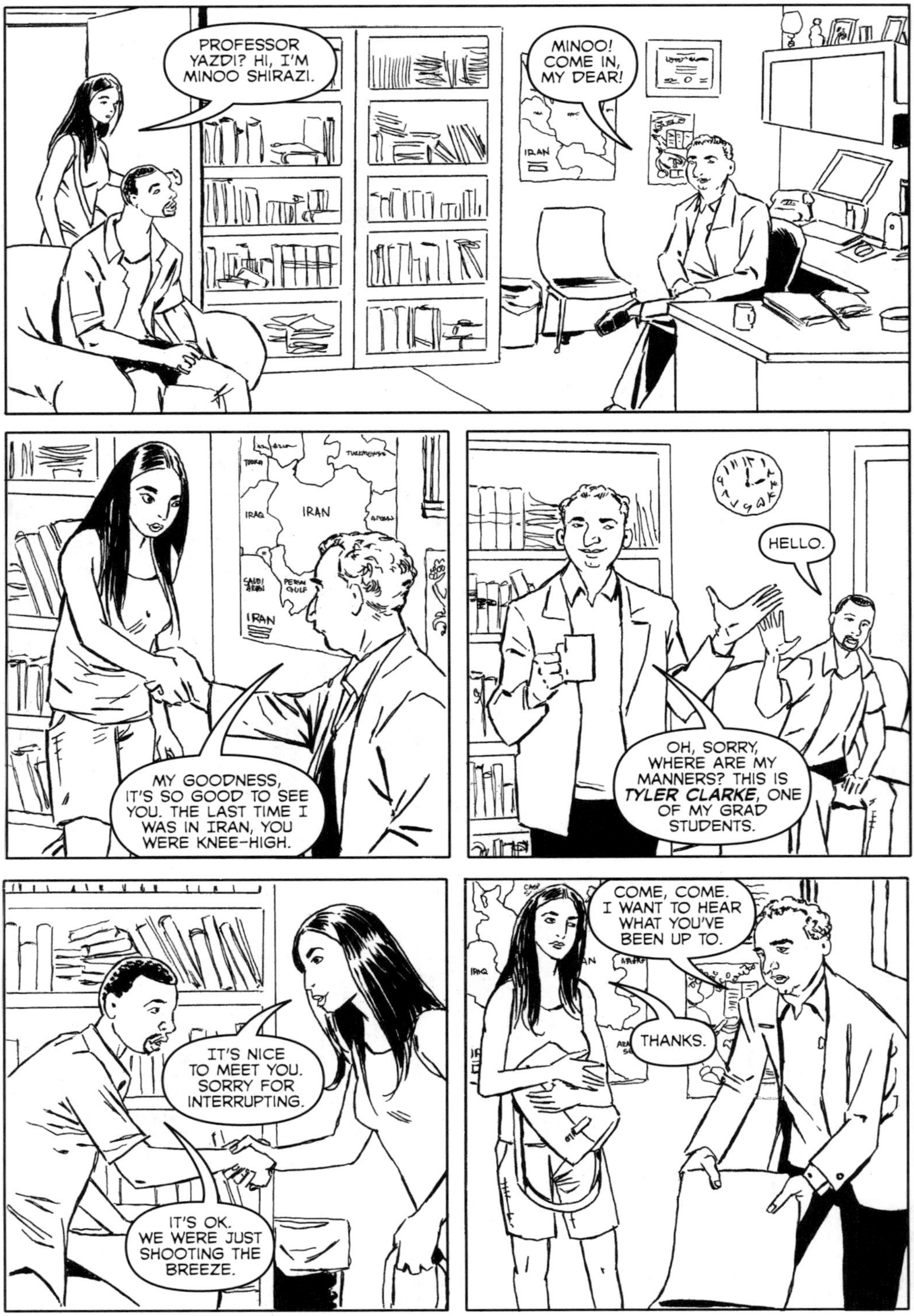
PROFESSOR YAZDI? HI, I'M MINOO SHIRAZI.
MINOO! COME IN, MY DEAR!
IRAN
IRAN
IRAN
MY GOODNESS, IT'S SO GOOD TO SEE YOU. THE LAST TIME I WAS IN IRAN, YOU WERE KNEE-HIGH.
HELLO.
OH, SORRY, WHERE ARE MY MANNERS? THIS IS *TYLER CLARKE*, ONE OF MY GRAD STUDENTS.
IT'S NICE TO MEET YOU. SORRY FOR INTERRUPTING.
IT'S OK. WE WERE JUST SHOOTING THE BREEZE.
COME, COME. I WANT TO HEAR WHAT YOU'VE BEEN UP TO.
THANKS.

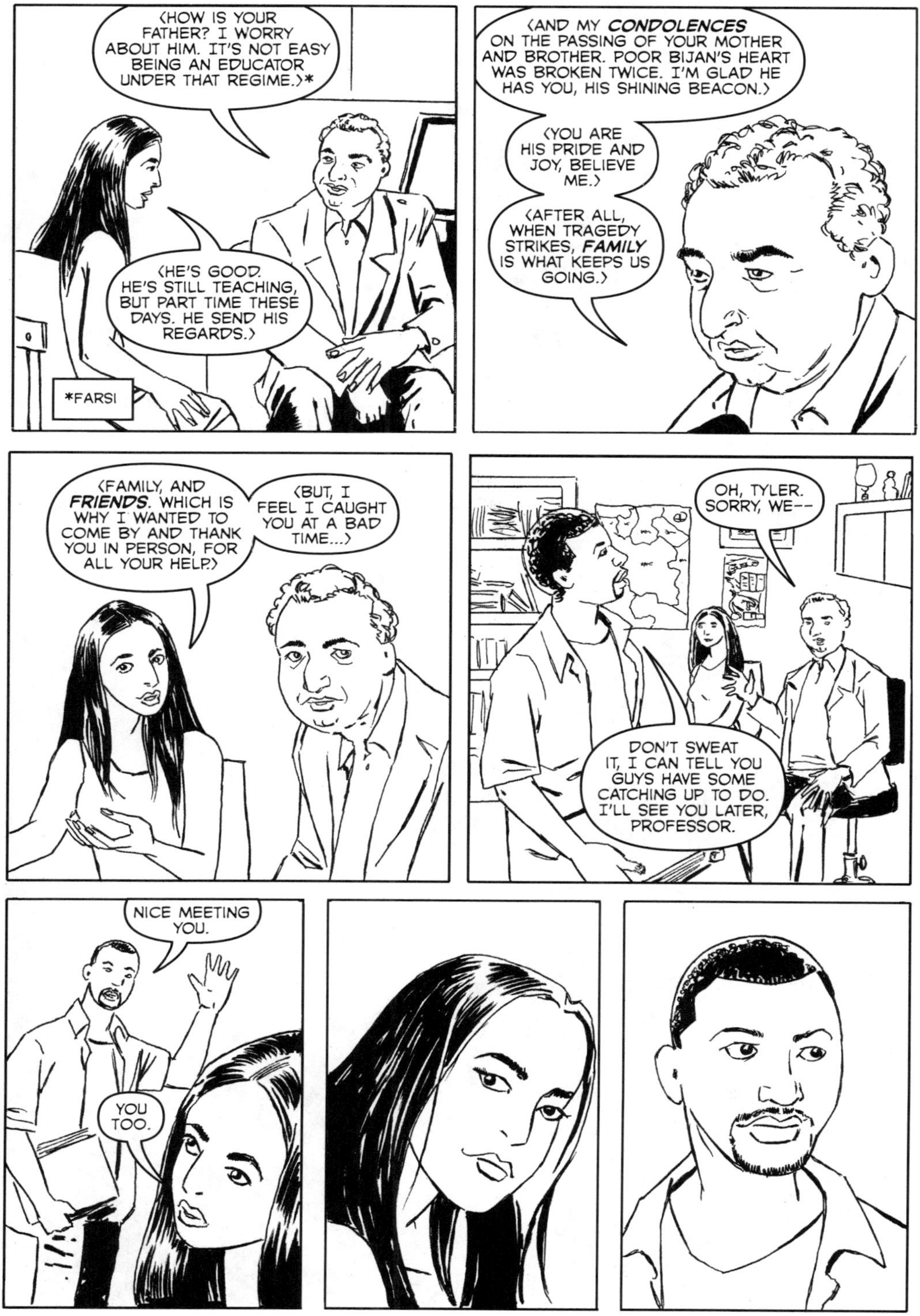

<HOW IS YOUR FATHER? I WORRY ABOUT HIM. IT'S NOT EASY BEING AN EDUCATOR UNDER THAT REGIME.>*
<HE'S GOOD. HE'S STILL TEACHING, BUT PART TIME THESE DAYS. HE SEND HIS REGARDS.>
*FARSI
<AND MY CONDOLENCES ON THE PASSING OF YOUR MOTHER AND BROTHER. POOR BIJAN'S HEART WAS BROKEN TWICE. I'M GLAD HE HAS YOU, HIS SHINING BEACON.>
<YOU ARE HIS PRIDE AND JOY, BELIEVE ME.>
<AFTER ALL, WHEN TRAGEDY STRIKES, FAMILY IS WHAT KEEPS US GOING.>
<FAMILY, AND FRIENDS. WHICH IS WHY I WANTED TO COME BY AND THANK YOU IN PERSON, FOR ALL YOUR HELP.>
<BUT, I FEEL I CAUGHT YOU AT A BAD TIME...>
OH, TYLER. SORRY, WE--
DON'T SWEAT IT, I CAN TELL YOU GUYS HAVE SOME CATCHING UP TO DO. I'LL SEE YOU LATER, PROFESSOR.
NICE MEETING YOU.
YOU TOO.

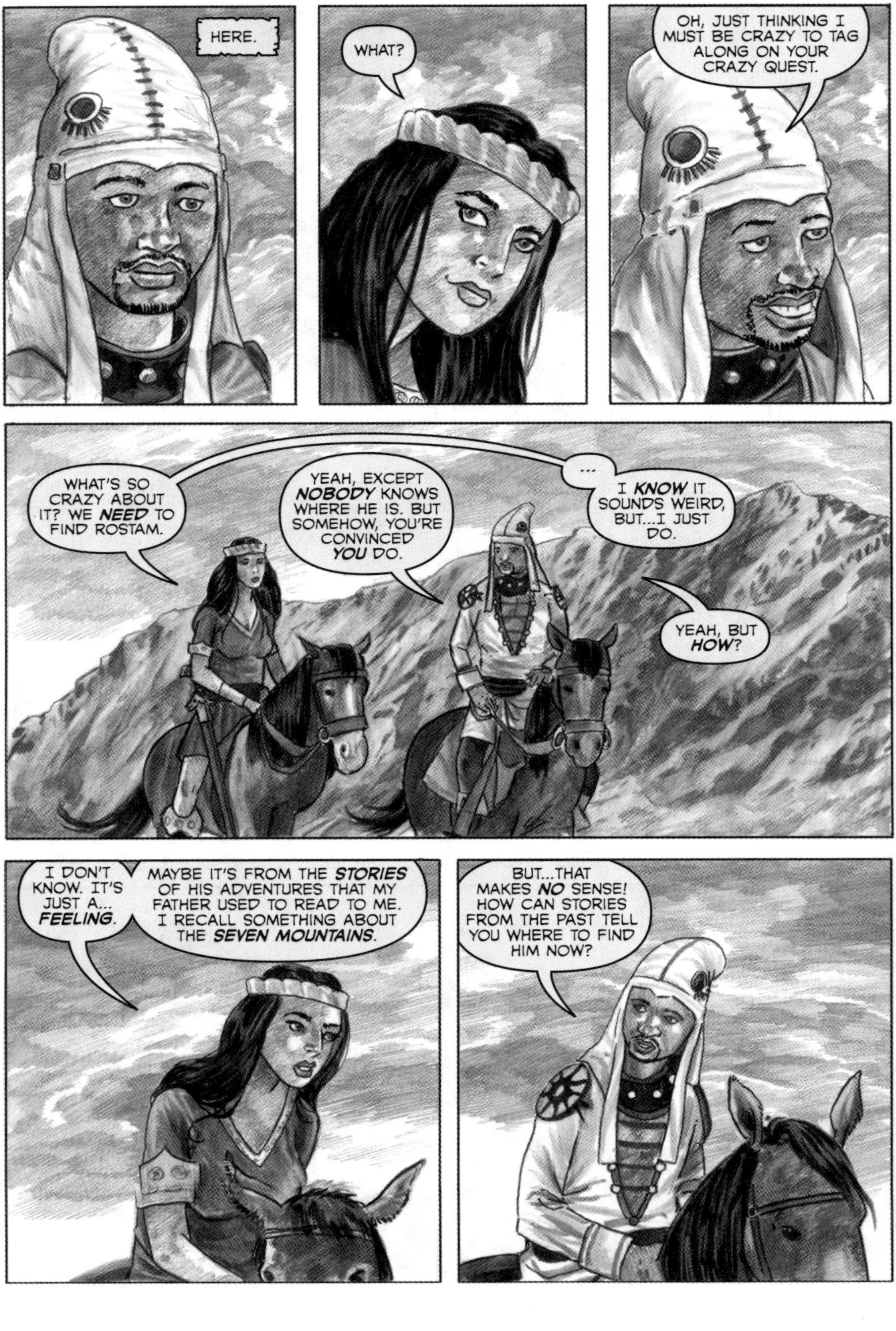
HERE.
WHAT?
OH, JUST THINKING I MUST BE CRAZY TO TAG ALONG ON YOUR CRAZY QUEST.
WHAT'S SO CRAZY ABOUT IT? WE NEED TO FIND ROSTAM.
YEAH, EXCEPT NOBODY KNOWS WHERE HE IS. BUT SOMEHOW, YOU'RE CONVINCED YOU DO.
...
I KNOW IT SOUNDS WEIRD, BUT...I JUST DO.
YEAH, BUT HOW?
I DON'T KNOW. IT'S JUST A... FEELING.
MAYBE IT'S FROM THE STORIES OF HIS ADVENTURES THAT MY FATHER USED TO READ TO ME. I RECALL SOMETHING ABOUT THE SEVEN MOUNTAINS.
BUT...THAT MAKES NO SENSE! HOW CAN STORIES FROM THE PAST TELL YOU WHERE TO FIND HIM NOW?

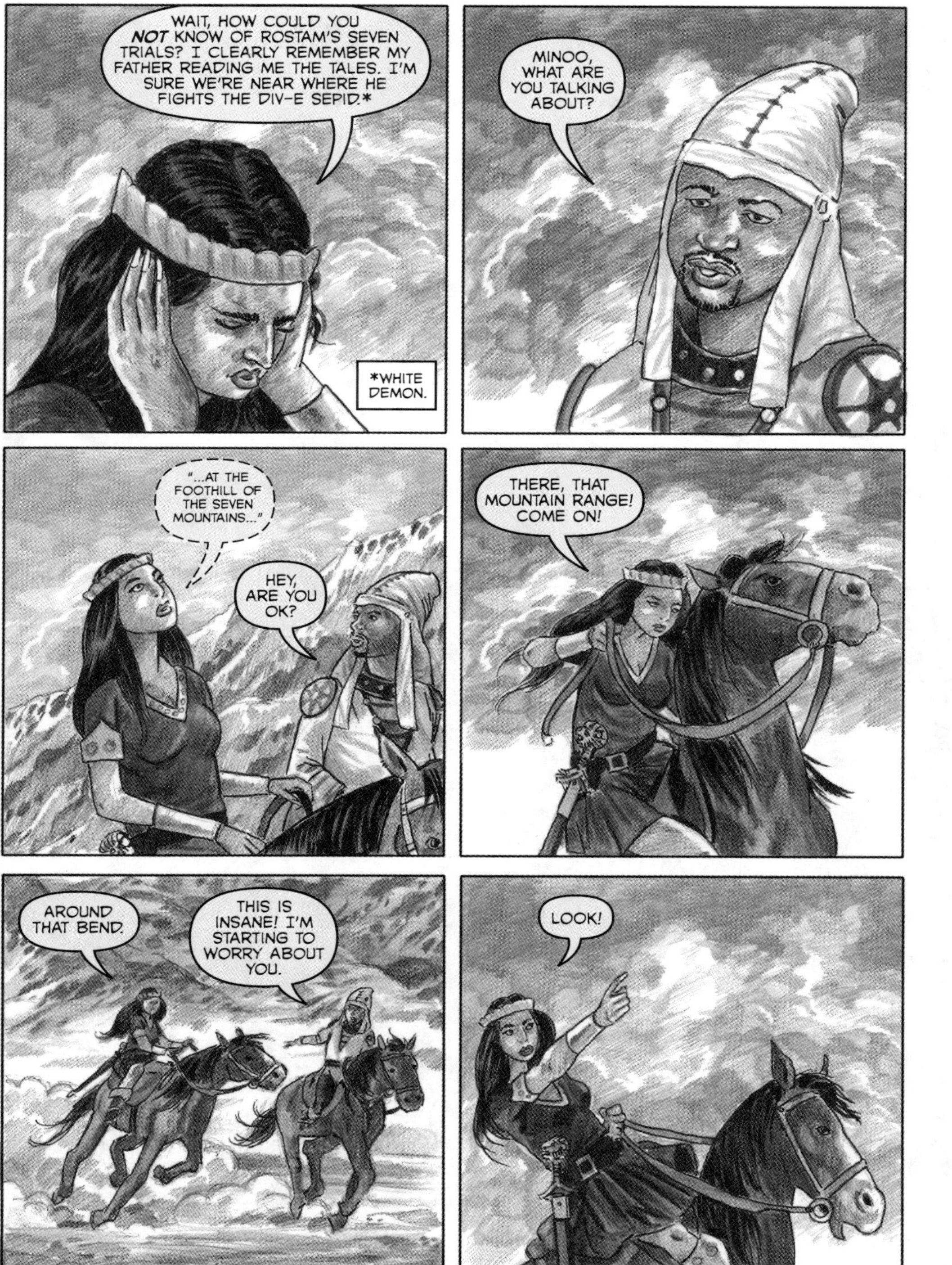
WAIT, HOW COULD YOU NOT KNOW OF ROSTAM'S SEVEN TRIALS? I CLEARLY REMEMBER MY FATHER READING ME THE TALES. I'M SURE WE'RE NEAR WHERE HE FIGHTS THE DIV-E SEPID.*
*WHITE DEMON.
MINOO, WHAT ARE YOU TALKING ABOUT?
"...AT THE FOOTHILL OF THE SEVEN MOUNTAINS..."
HEY, ARE YOU OK?
THERE, THAT MOUNTAIN RANGE! COME ON!
AROUND THAT BEND.
THIS IS INSANE! I'M STARTING TO WORRY ABOUT YOU.
LOOK!

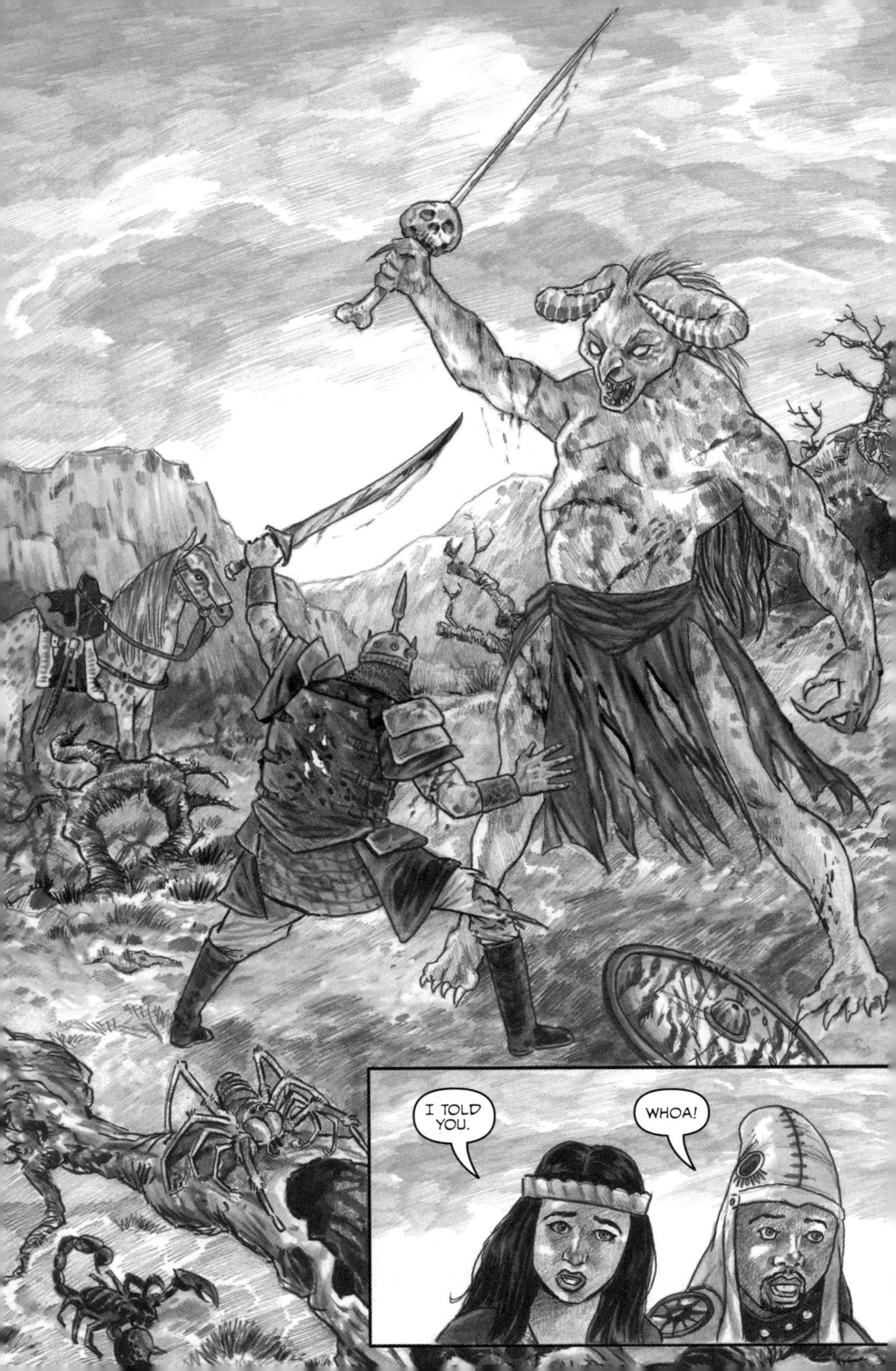
I TOLD YOU.
WHOA!

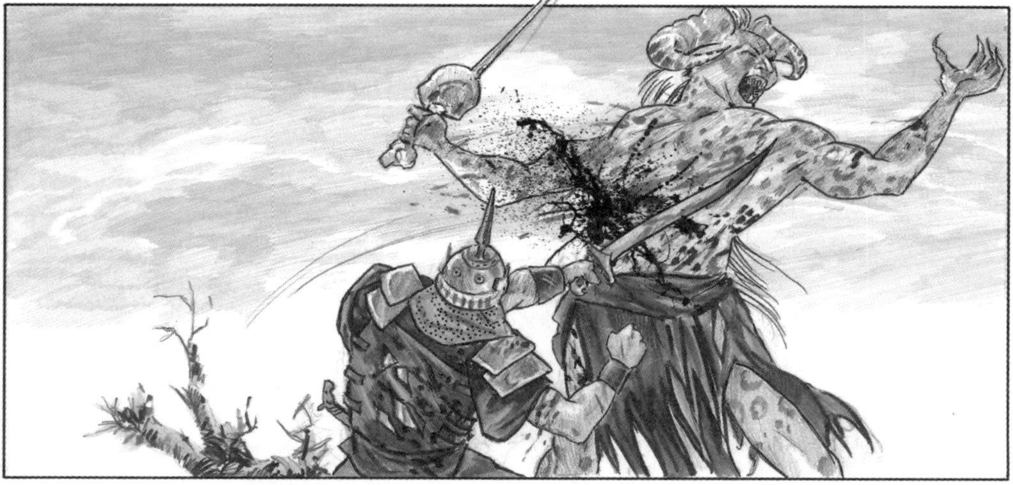

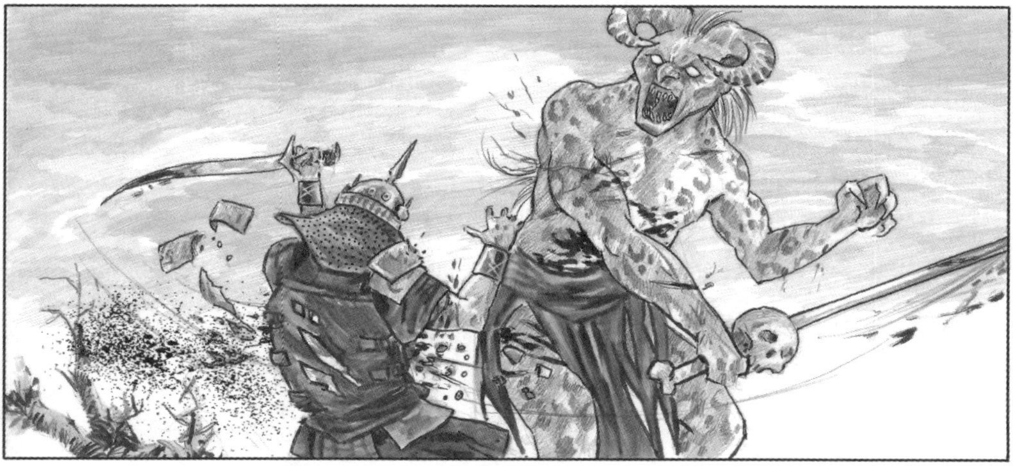

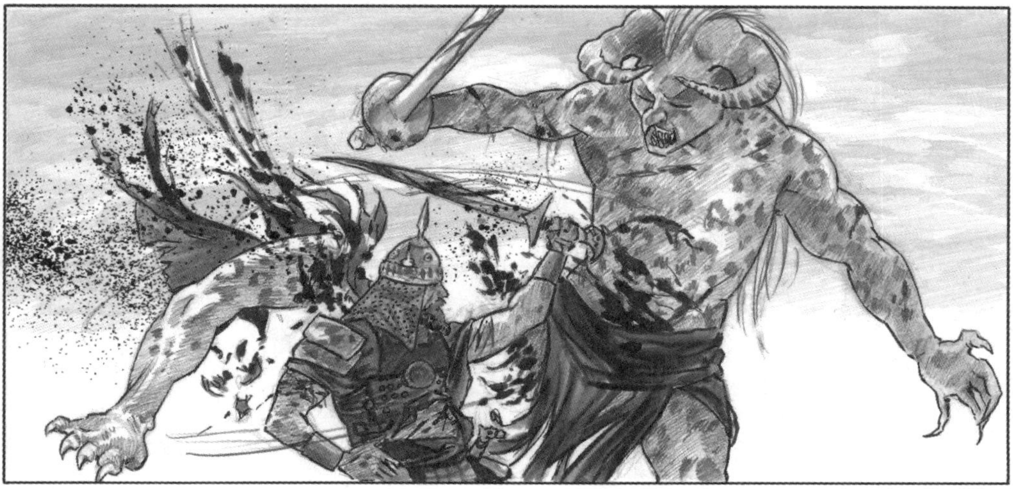

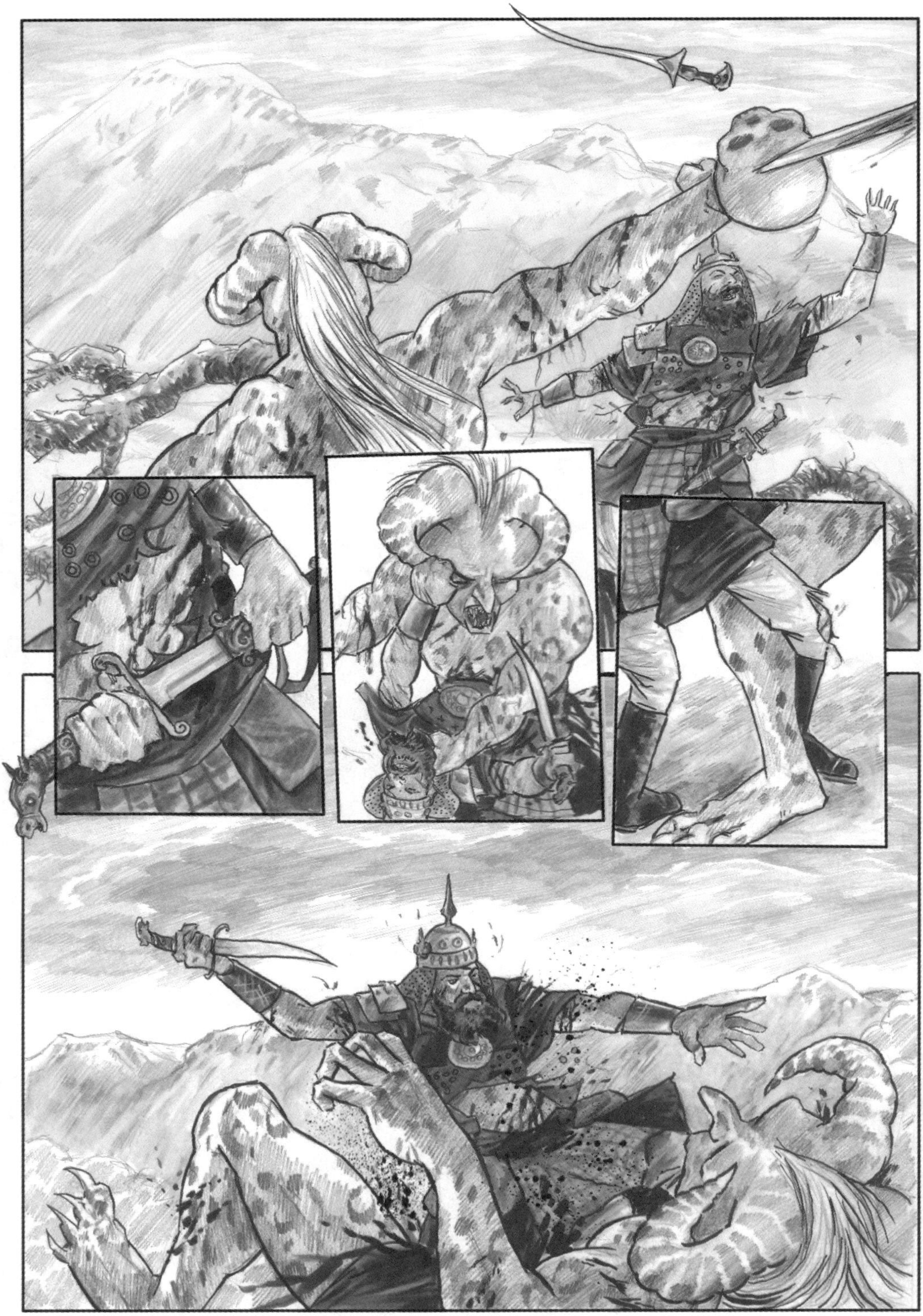

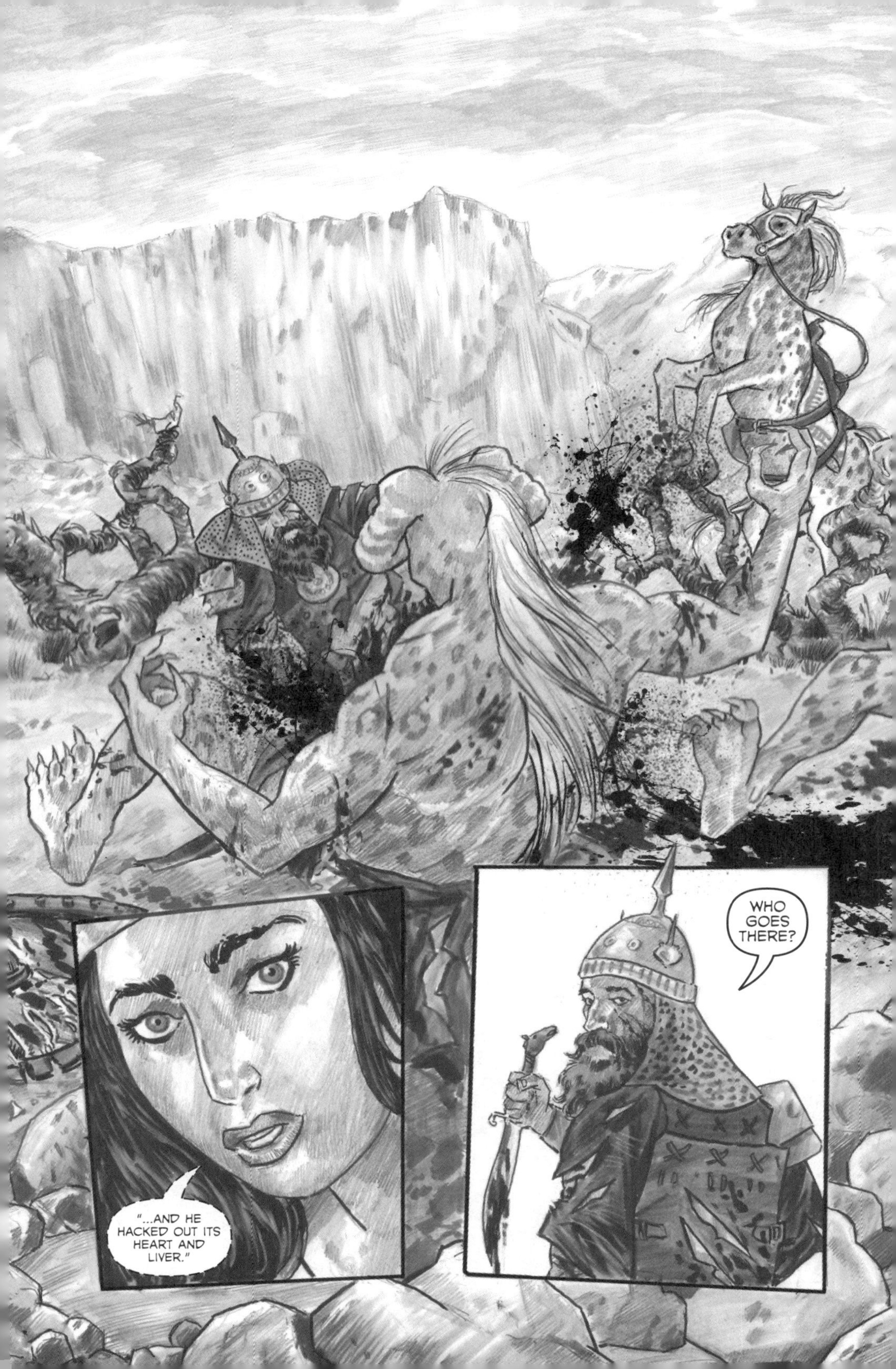
"...AND HE HACKED OUT ITS HEART AND LIVER."
WHO GOES THERE?

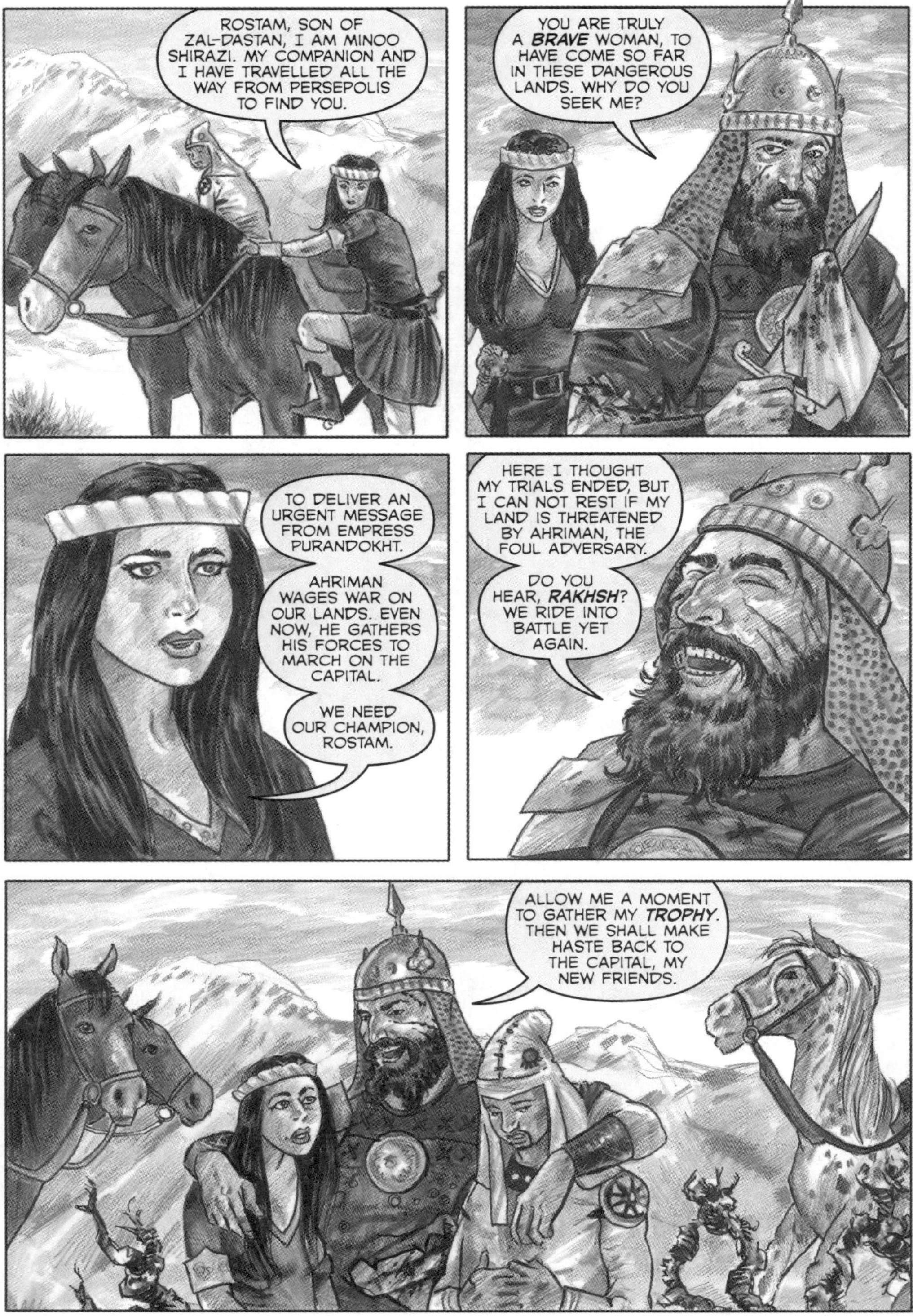
ROSTAM, SON OF ZAL-DASTAN, I AM MINOO SHIRAZI. MY COMPANION AND I HAVE TRAVELLED ALL THE WAY FROM PERSEPOLIS TO FIND YOU.
YOU ARE TRULY A *BRAVE* WOMAN, TO HAVE COME SO FAR IN THESE DANGEROUS LANDS. WHY DO YOU SEEK ME?
TO DELIVER AN URGENT MESSAGE FROM EMPRESS PURANDOKHT.
AHRIMAN WAGES WAR ON OUR LANDS. EVEN NOW, HE GATHERS HIS FORCES TO MARCH ON THE CAPITAL.
WE NEED OUR CHAMPION, ROSTAM.
HERE I THOUGHT MY TRIALS ENDED, BUT I CAN NOT REST IF MY LAND IS THREATENED BY AHRIMAN, THE FOUL ADVERSARY.
DO YOU HEAR, *RAKHSH*? WE RIDE INTO BATTLE YET AGAIN.
ALLOW ME A MOMENT TO GATHER MY *TROPHY*. THEN WE SHALL MAKE HASTE BACK TO THE CAPITAL, MY NEW FRIENDS.

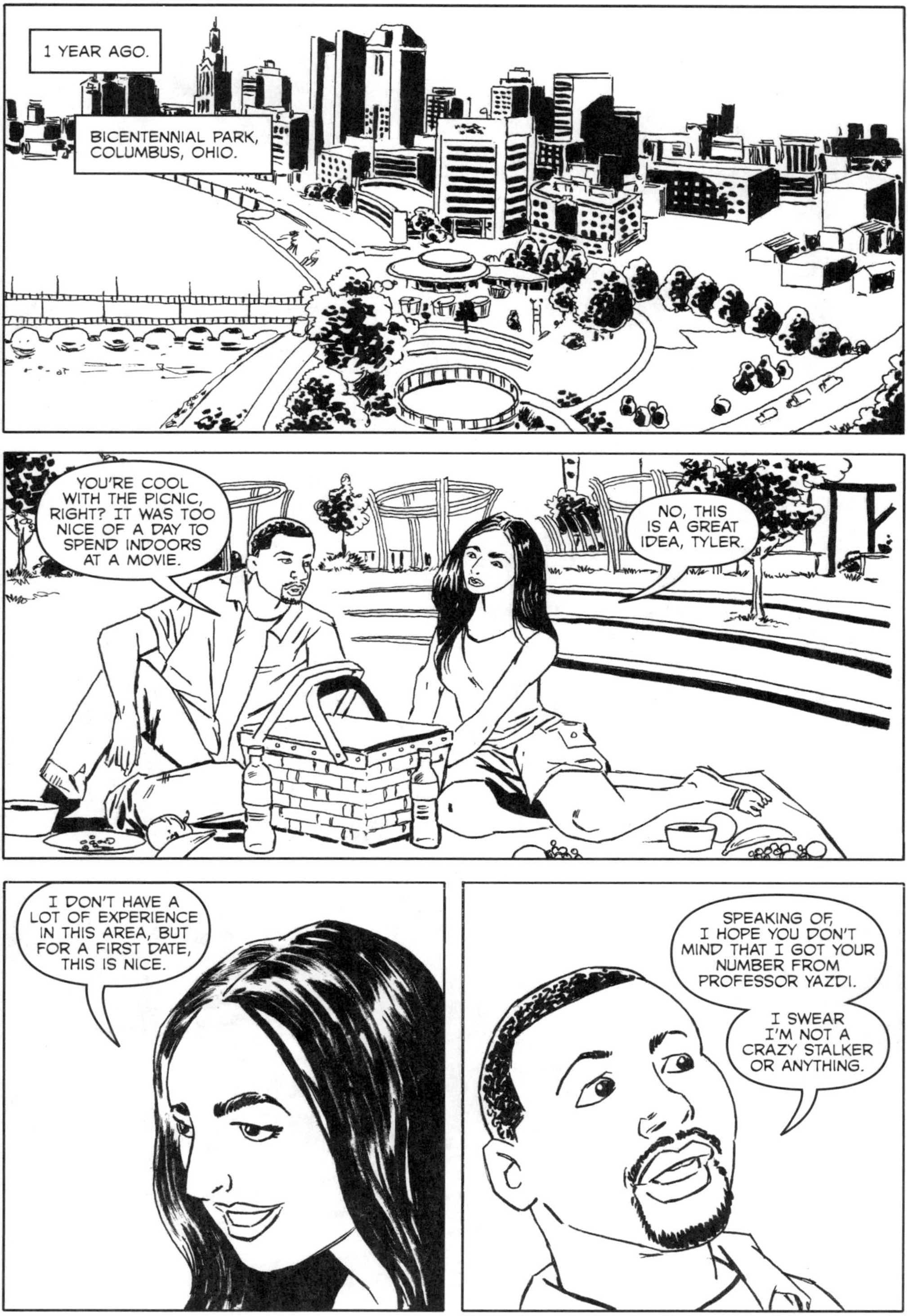
1 YEAR AGO.
BICENTENNIAL PARK, COLUMBUS, OHIO.
YOU'RE COOL WITH THE PICNIC, RIGHT? IT WAS TOO NICE OF A DAY TO SPEND INDOORS AT A MOVIE.
NO, THIS IS A GREAT IDEA, TYLER.
I DON'T HAVE A LOT OF EXPERIENCE IN THIS AREA, BUT FOR A FIRST DATE, THIS IS NICE.
SPEAKING OF, I HOPE YOU DON'T MIND THAT I GOT YOUR NUMBER FROM PROFESSOR YAZDI.
I SWEAR I'M NOT A CRAZY STALKER OR ANYTHING.

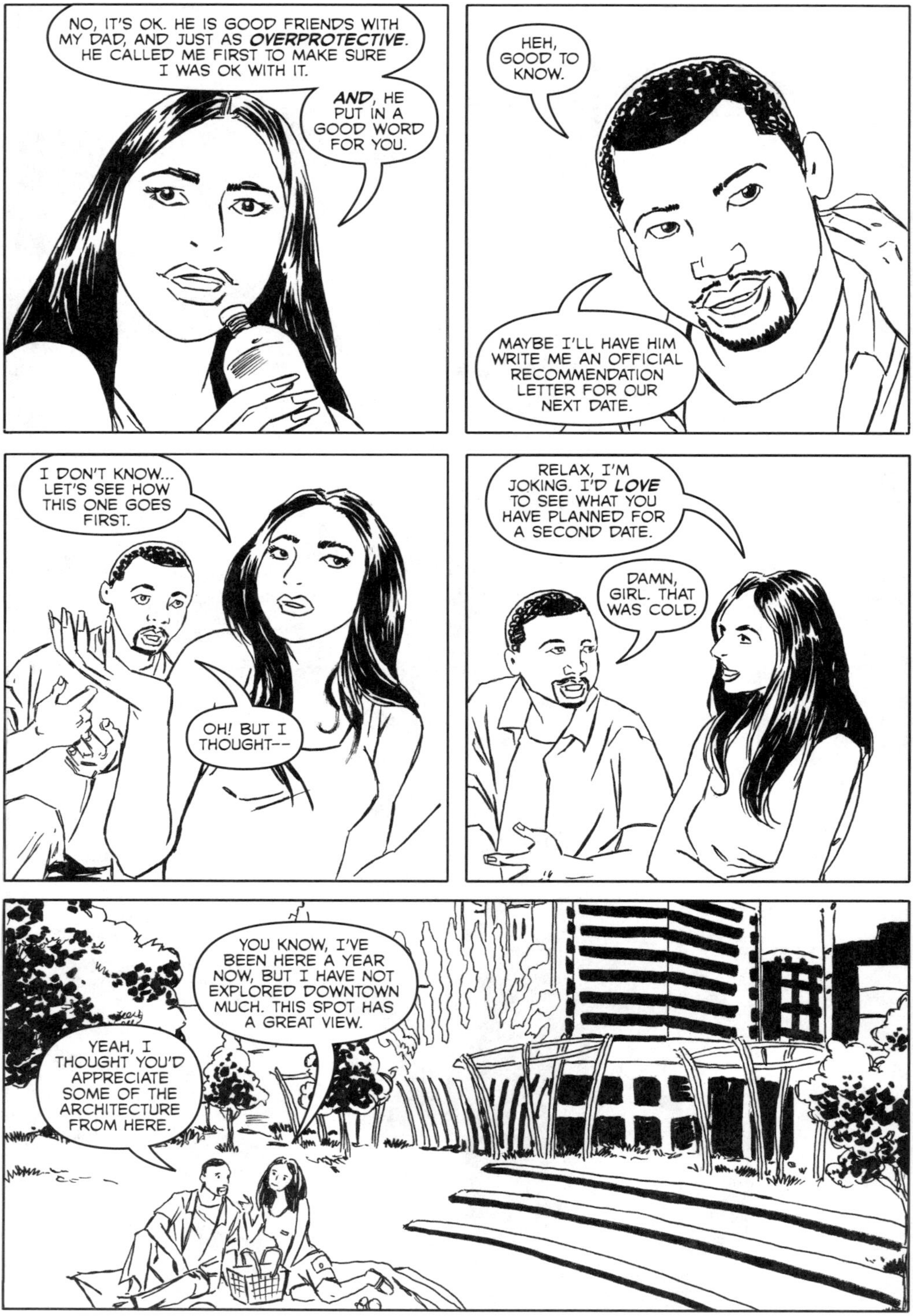
NO, IT'S OK. HE IS GOOD FRIENDS WITH MY DAD, AND JUST AS *OVERPROTECTIVE*. HE CALLED ME FIRST TO MAKE SURE I WAS OK WITH IT.
AND, HE PUT IN A GOOD WORD FOR YOU.
HEH, GOOD TO KNOW.
MAYBE I'LL HAVE HIM WRITE ME AN OFFICIAL RECOMMENDATION LETTER FOR OUR NEXT DATE.
I DON'T KNOW... LET'S SEE HOW THIS ONE GOES FIRST.
OH! BUT I THOUGHT--
RELAX, I'M JOKING. I'D *LOVE* TO SEE WHAT YOU HAVE PLANNED FOR A SECOND DATE.
DAMN, GIRL. THAT WAS COLD.
YOU KNOW, I'VE BEEN HERE A YEAR NOW, BUT I HAVE NOT EXPLORED DOWNTOWN MUCH. THIS SPOT HAS A GREAT VIEW.
YEAH, I THOUGHT YOU'D APPRECIATE SOME OF THE ARCHITECTURE FROM HERE.

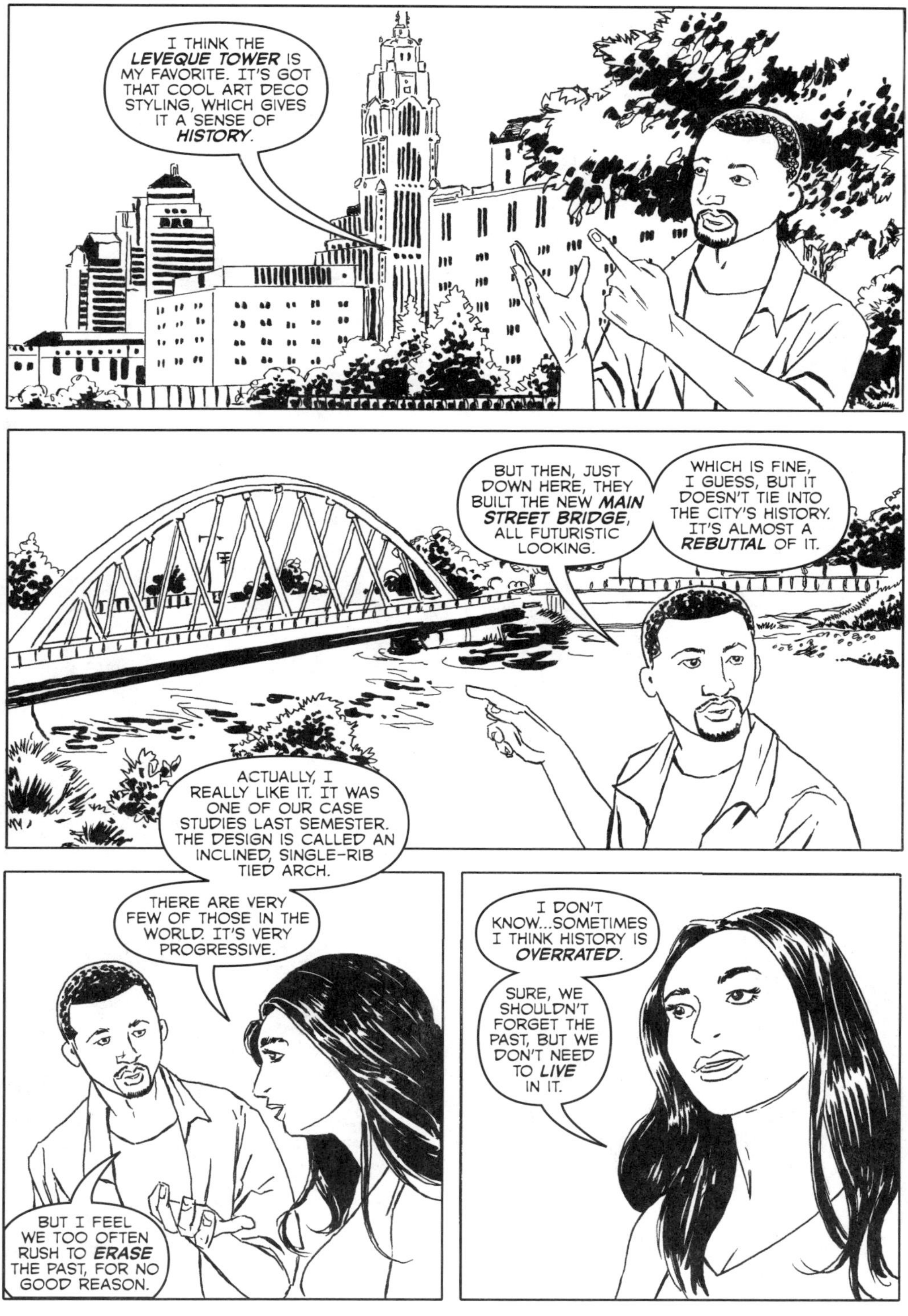

I THINK THE LEVEQUE TOWER IS MY FAVORITE. IT'S GOT THAT COOL ART DECO STYLING, WHICH GIVES IT A SENSE OF HISTORY.
BUT THEN, JUST DOWN HERE, THEY BUILT THE NEW MAIN STREET BRIDGE, ALL FUTURISTIC LOOKING.
WHICH IS FINE, I GUESS, BUT IT DOESN'T TIE INTO THE CITY'S HISTORY. IT'S ALMOST A REBUTTAL OF IT.
ACTUALLY, I REALLY LIKE IT. IT WAS ONE OF OUR CASE STUDIES LAST SEMESTER. THE DESIGN IS CALLED AN INCLINED, SINGLE-RIB TIED ARCH.
THERE ARE VERY FEW OF THOSE IN THE WORLD. IT'S VERY PROGRESSIVE.
BUT I FEEL WE TOO OFTEN RUSH TO ERASE THE PAST, FOR NO GOOD REASON.
I DON'T KNOW...SOMETIMES I THINK HISTORY IS OVERRATED.
SURE, WE SHOULDN'T FORGET THE PAST, BUT WE DON'T NEED TO LIVE IN IT.

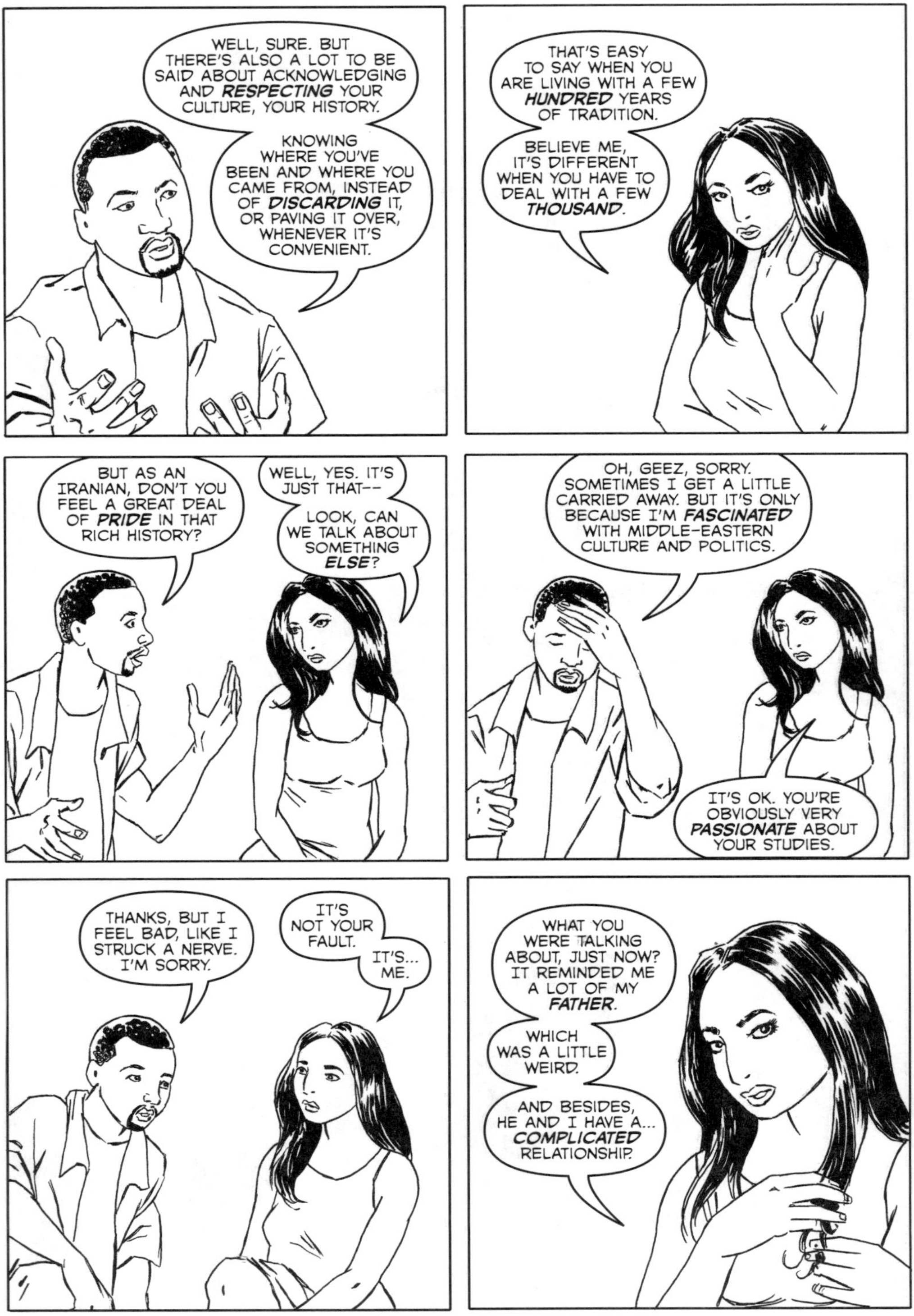
WELL, SURE. BUT THERE'S ALSO A LOT TO BE SAID ABOUT ACKNOWLEDGING AND RESPECTING YOUR CULTURE, YOUR HISTORY.
KNOWING WHERE YOU'VE BEEN AND WHERE YOU CAME FROM, INSTEAD OF DISCARDING IT, OR PAVING IT OVER, WHENEVER IT'S CONVENIENT.
THAT'S EASY TO SAY WHEN YOU ARE LIVING WITH A FEW HUNDRED YEARS OF TRADITION.
BELIEVE ME, IT'S DIFFERENT WHEN YOU HAVE TO DEAL WITH A FEW THOUSAND.
BUT AS AN IRANIAN, DON'T YOU FEEL A GREAT DEAL OF PRIDE IN THAT RICH HISTORY?
WELL, YES. IT'S JUST THAT--
LOOK, CAN WE TALK ABOUT SOMETHING ELSE?
OH, GEEZ, SORRY. SOMETIMES I GET A LITTLE CARRIED AWAY. BUT IT'S ONLY BECAUSE I'M FASCINATED WITH MIDDLE-EASTERN CULTURE AND POLITICS.
IT'S OK. YOU'RE OBVIOUSLY VERY PASSIONATE ABOUT YOUR STUDIES.
THANKS, BUT I FEEL BAD, LIKE I STRUCK A NERVE. I'M SORRY.
IT'S NOT YOUR FAULT.
IT'S... ME.
WHAT YOU WERE TALKING ABOUT, JUST NOW? IT REMINDED ME A LOT OF MY FATHER.
WHICH WAS A LITTLE WEIRD.
AND BESIDES, HE AND I HAVE A... COMPLICATED RELATIONSHIP.

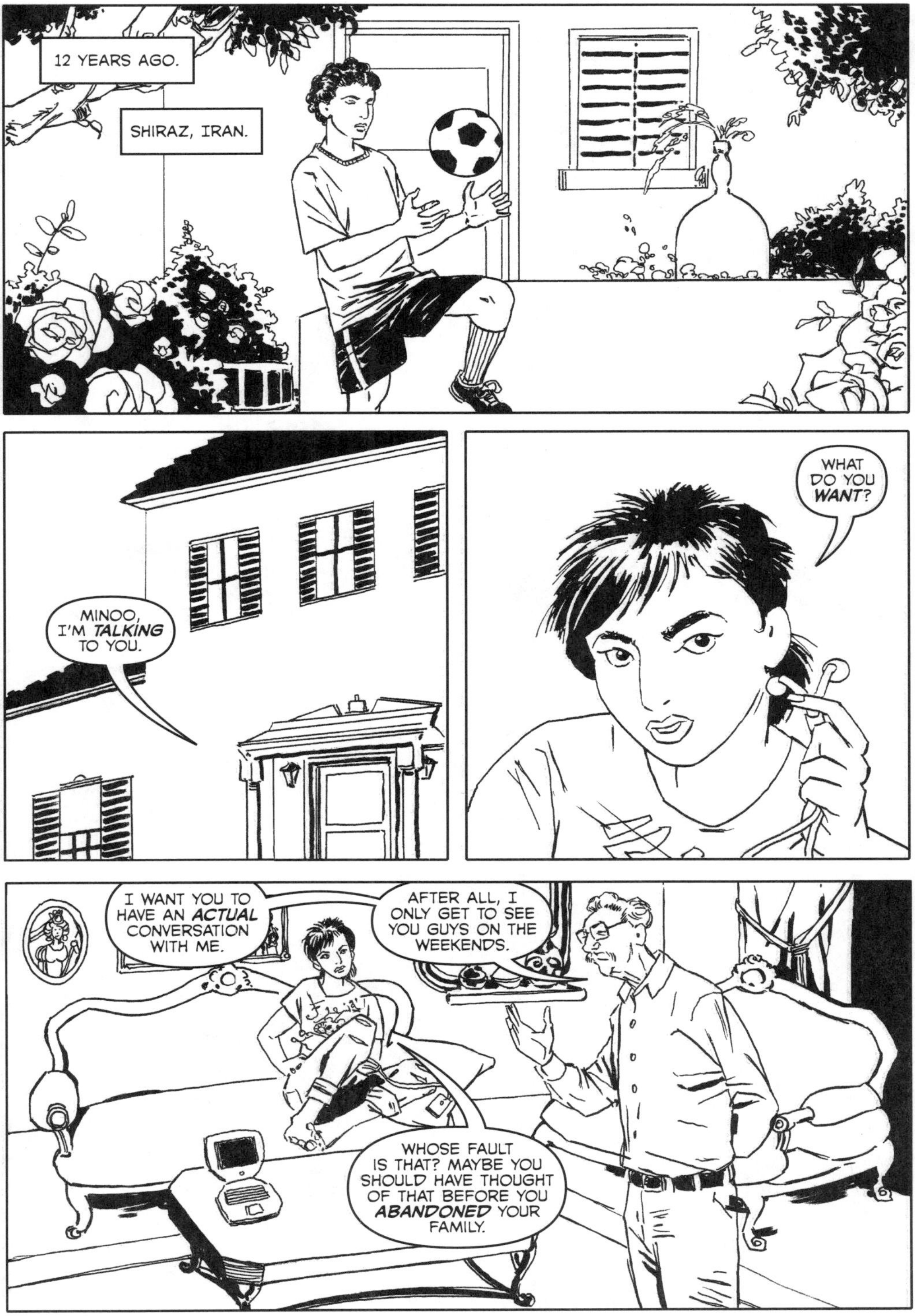
12 YEARS AGO.
SHIRAZ, IRAN.
MINOO, I'M *TALKING* TO YOU.
WHAT DO YOU *WANT*?
I WANT YOU TO HAVE AN *ACTUAL* CONVERSATION WITH ME.
AFTER ALL, I ONLY GET TO SEE YOU GUYS ON THE WEEKENDS.
WHOSE FAULT IS THAT? MAYBE YOU SHOULD HAVE THOUGHT OF THAT BEFORE YOU *ABANDONED* YOUR FAMILY.

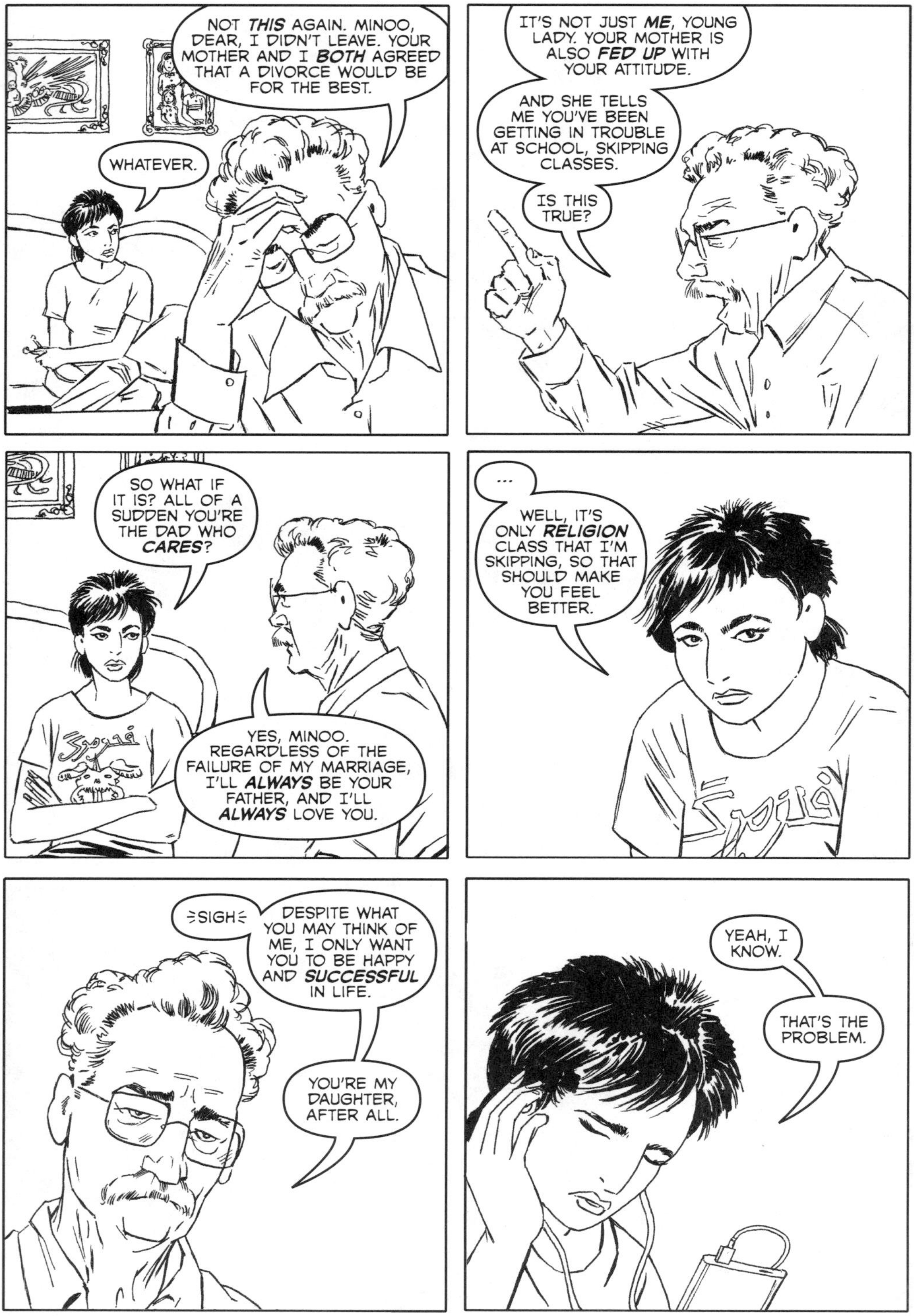
NOT *THIS* AGAIN. MINOO, DEAR, I DIDN'T LEAVE. YOUR MOTHER AND I *BOTH* AGREED THAT A DIVORCE WOULD BE FOR THE BEST.
WHATEVER.
IT'S NOT JUST *ME*, YOUNG LADY. YOUR MOTHER IS ALSO *FED UP* WITH YOUR ATTITUDE.
AND SHE TELLS ME YOU'VE BEEN GETTING IN TROUBLE AT SCHOOL, SKIPPING CLASSES.
IS THIS TRUE?
SO WHAT IF IT IS? ALL OF A SUDDEN YOU'RE THE DAD WHO *CARES*?
YES, MINOO. REGARDLESS OF THE FAILURE OF MY MARRIAGE, I'LL *ALWAYS* BE YOUR FATHER, AND I'LL *ALWAYS* LOVE YOU.
...
WELL, IT'S ONLY *RELIGION* CLASS THAT I'M SKIPPING, SO THAT SHOULD MAKE YOU FEEL BETTER.
⩵SIGH⩵
DESPITE WHAT YOU MAY THINK OF ME, I ONLY WANT YOU TO BE HAPPY AND *SUCCESSFUL* IN LIFE.
YOU'RE MY DAUGHTER, AFTER ALL.
YEAH, I KNOW.
THAT'S THE PROBLEM.

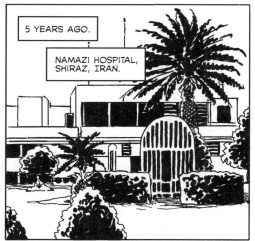

5 YEARS AGO.

NAMAZI HOSPITAL, SHIRAZ, IRAN.

≋GROAAAN≋

I DON'T THINK THOSE PAIN KILLERS ARE DOING ANYTHING.

JUST TAKE IT EASY, DAD. THE DOCTOR SAYS YOU'RE *LUCKY* NOT TO HAVE ANY BROKEN BONES.

FEH. I GET ASSAULTED AND HE CALLS ME LUCKY.

SPEAKING OF WHICH, I'M STILL CONFUSED.

THE GUY WHO WITNESSED IT TOLD THE POLICE THAT YOU GOT INTO AN ARGUMENT WITH THE MUGGERS FIRST?

THEY WEREN'T MUGGERS. THEY WERE FORMER STUDENTS OF MINE.

A COUPLE OF *PUNKS* I HAD EXPELLED FROM THE UNIVERSITY FOR CHEATING.

HEH. I GOT IN A FEW GOOD JABS ON ONE.

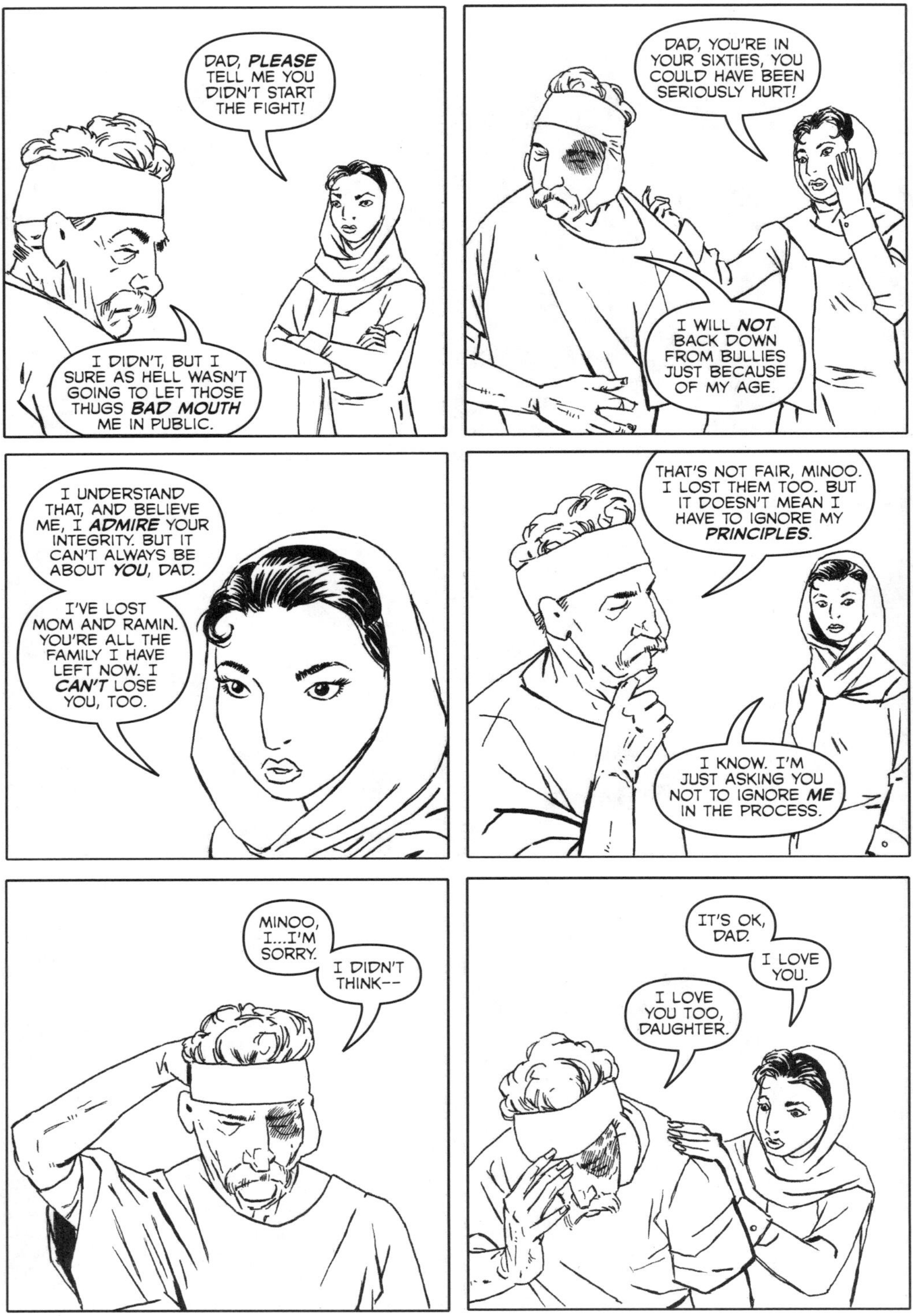
DAD, PLEASE TELL ME YOU DIDN'T START THE FIGHT!
I DIDN'T, BUT I SURE AS HELL WASN'T GOING TO LET THOSE THUGS BAD MOUTH ME IN PUBLIC.
DAD, YOU'RE IN YOUR SIXTIES, YOU COULD HAVE BEEN SERIOUSLY HURT!
I WILL NOT BACK DOWN FROM BULLIES JUST BECAUSE OF MY AGE.
I UNDERSTAND THAT, AND BELIEVE ME, I ADMIRE YOUR INTEGRITY. BUT IT CAN'T ALWAYS BE ABOUT YOU, DAD.
I'VE LOST MOM AND RAMIN. YOU'RE ALL THE FAMILY I HAVE LEFT NOW. I CAN'T LOSE YOU, TOO.
THAT'S NOT FAIR, MINOO. I LOST THEM TOO. BUT IT DOESN'T MEAN I HAVE TO IGNORE MY PRINCIPLES.
I KNOW. I'M JUST ASKING YOU NOT TO IGNORE ME IN THE PROCESS.
MINOO, I...I'M SORRY.
I DIDN'T THINK--
IT'S OK, DAD.
I LOVE YOU.
I LOVE YOU TOO, DAUGHTER.

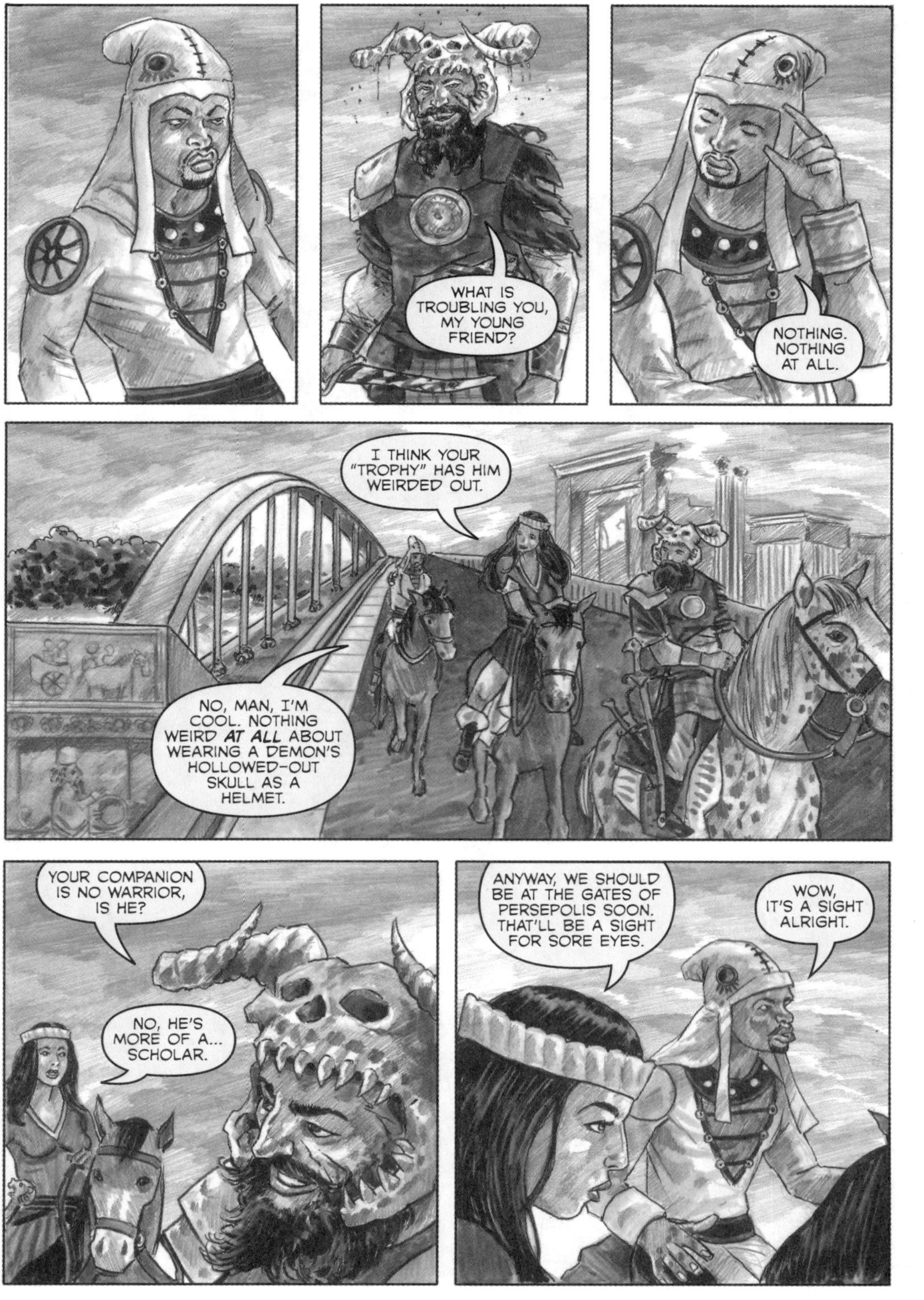
WHAT IS TROUBLING YOU, MY YOUNG FRIEND?
NOTHING. NOTHING AT ALL.
I THINK YOUR "TROPHY" HAS HIM WEIRDED OUT.
NO, MAN, I'M COOL. NOTHING WEIRD AT ALL ABOUT WEARING A DEMON'S HOLLOWED-OUT SKULL AS A HELMET.
YOUR COMPANION IS NO WARRIOR, IS HE?
NO, HE'S MORE OF A... SCHOLAR.
ANYWAY, WE SHOULD BE AT THE GATES OF PERSEPOLIS SOON. THAT'LL BE A SIGHT FOR SORE EYES.
WOW, IT'S A SIGHT ALRIGHT.

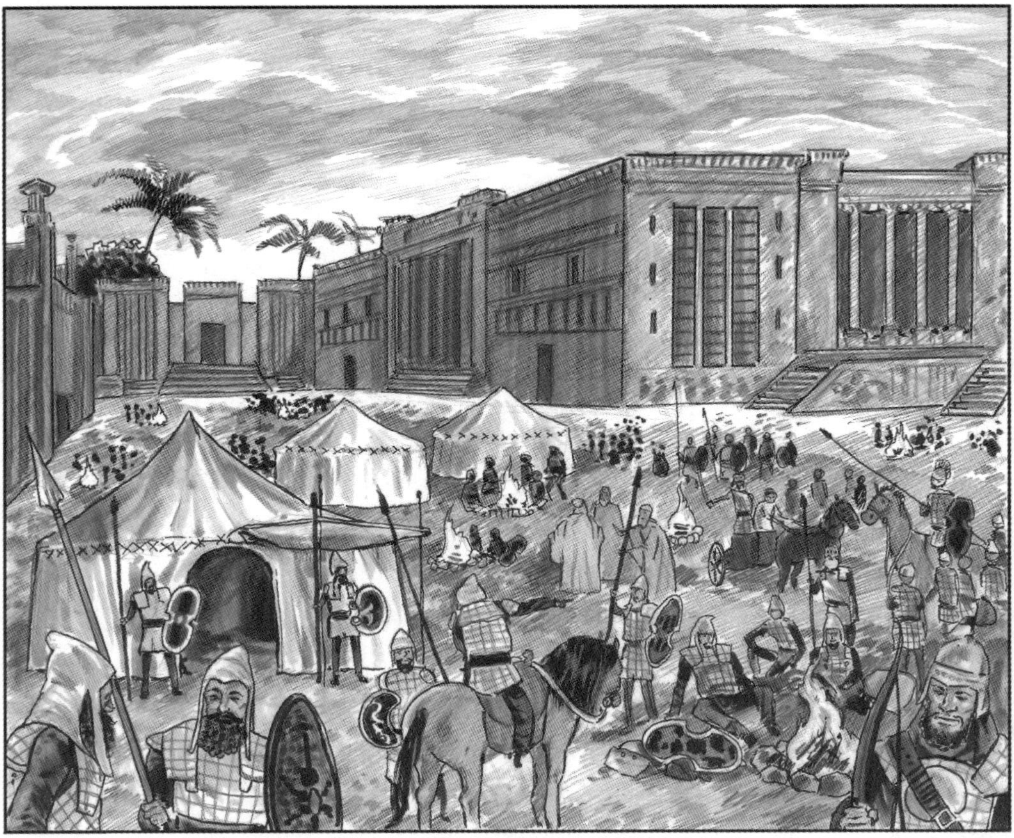

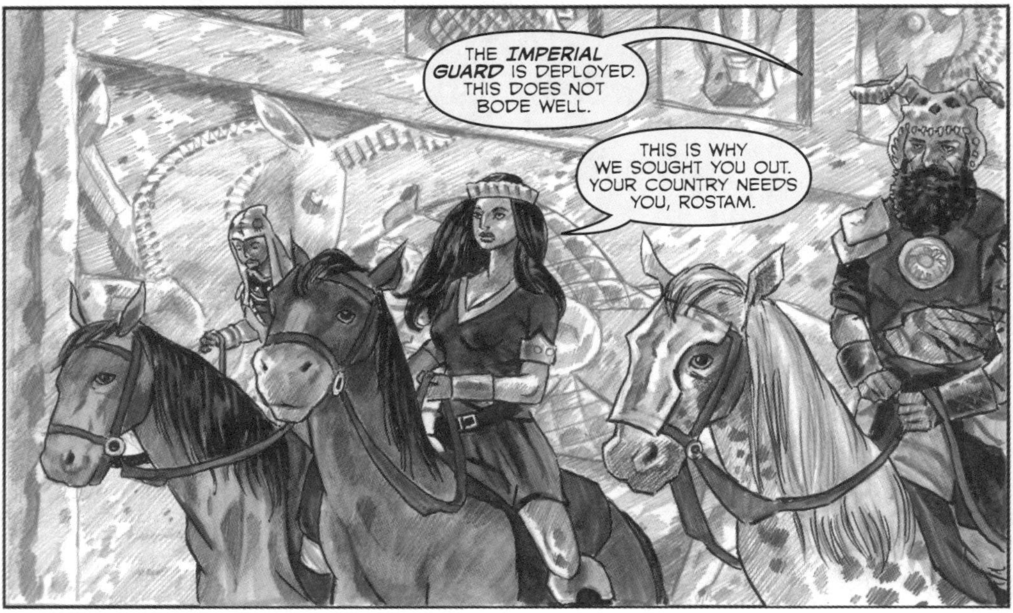
THE IMPERIAL GUARD IS DEPLOYED. THIS DOES NOT BODE WELL.
THIS IS WHY WE SOUGHT YOU OUT. YOUR COUNTRY NEEDS YOU, ROSTAM.

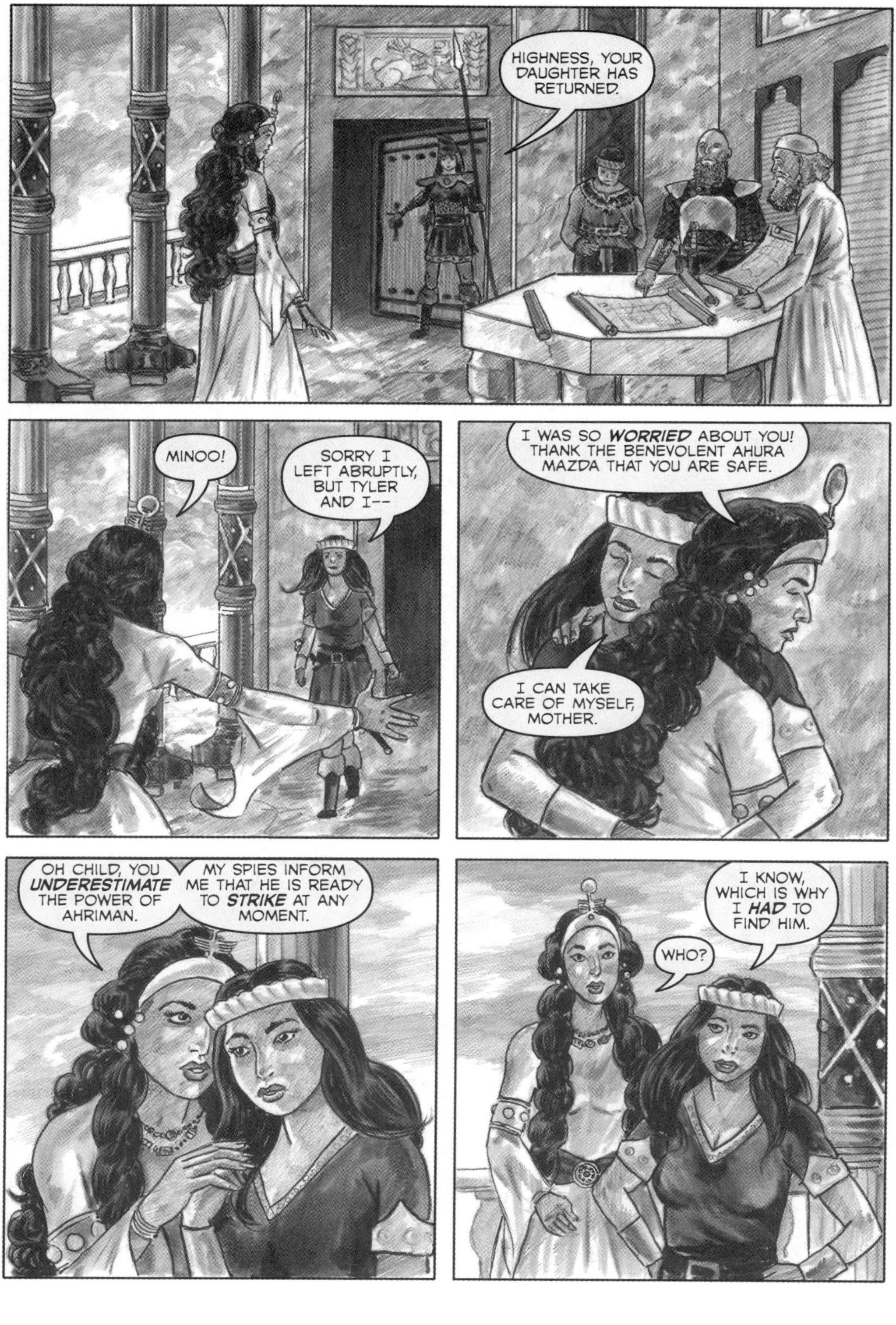
HIGHNESS, YOUR DAUGHTER HAS RETURNED.
MINOO!
SORRY I LEFT ABRUPTLY, BUT TYLER AND I--
I WAS SO **WORRIED** ABOUT YOU! THANK THE BENEVOLENT AHURA MAZDA THAT YOU ARE SAFE.
I CAN TAKE CARE OF MYSELF, MOTHER.
OH CHILD, YOU **UNDERESTIMATE** THE POWER OF AHRIMAN.
MY SPIES INFORM ME THAT HE IS READY TO **STRIKE** AT ANY MOMENT.
I KNOW, WHICH IS WHY I **HAD** TO FIND HIM.
WHO?

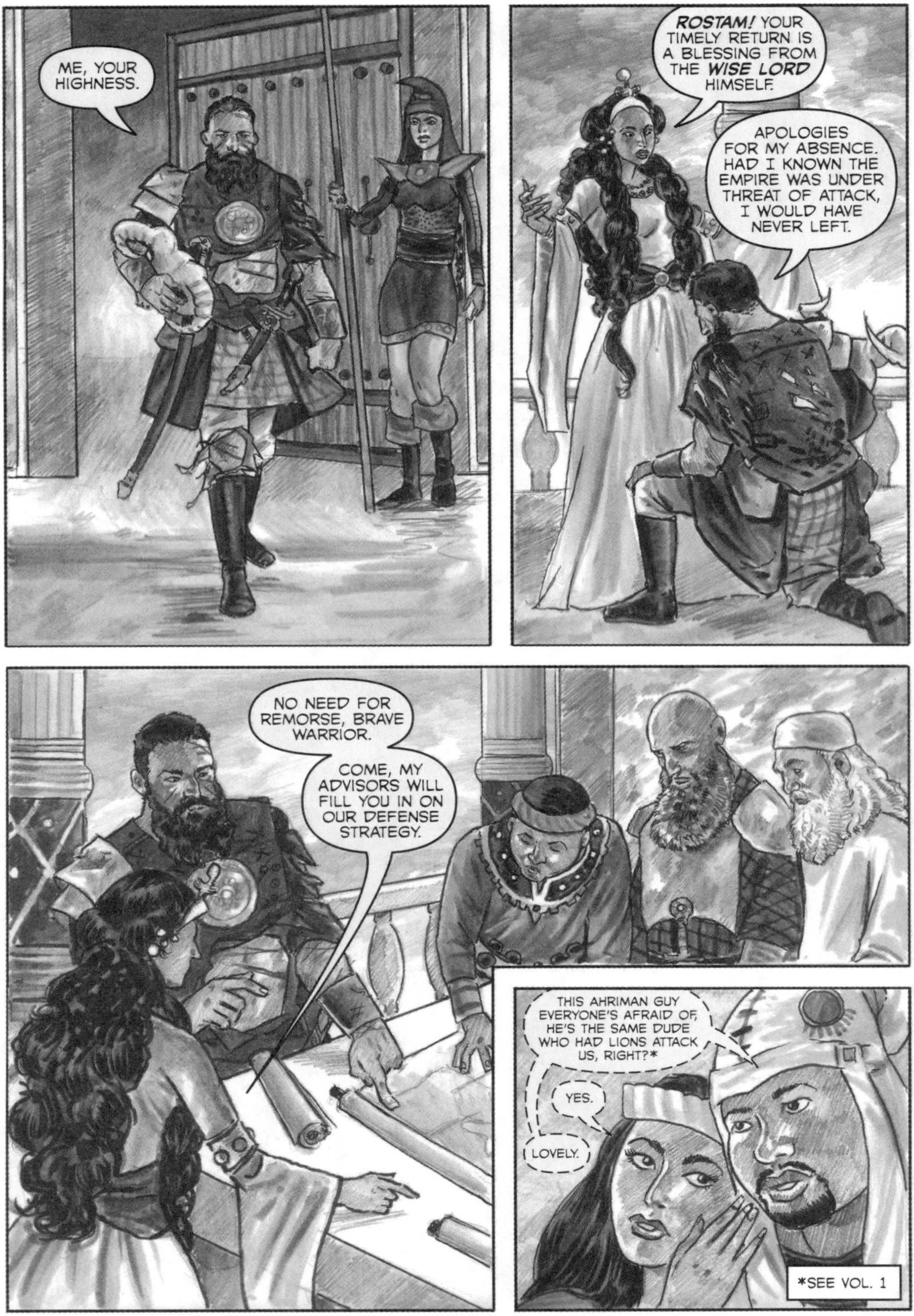
ME, YOUR HIGHNESS.
ROSTAM! YOUR TIMELY RETURN IS A BLESSING FROM THE WISE LORD HIMSELF.
APOLOGIES FOR MY ABSENCE. HAD I KNOWN THE EMPIRE WAS UNDER THREAT OF ATTACK, I WOULD HAVE NEVER LEFT.
NO NEED FOR REMORSE, BRAVE WARRIOR.
COME, MY ADVISORS WILL FILL YOU IN ON OUR DEFENSE STRATEGY.
THIS AHRIMAN GUY EVERYONE'S AFRAID OF, HE'S THE SAME DUDE WHO HAD LIONS ATTACK US, RIGHT?*
YES.
LOVELY.
*SEE VOL. 1

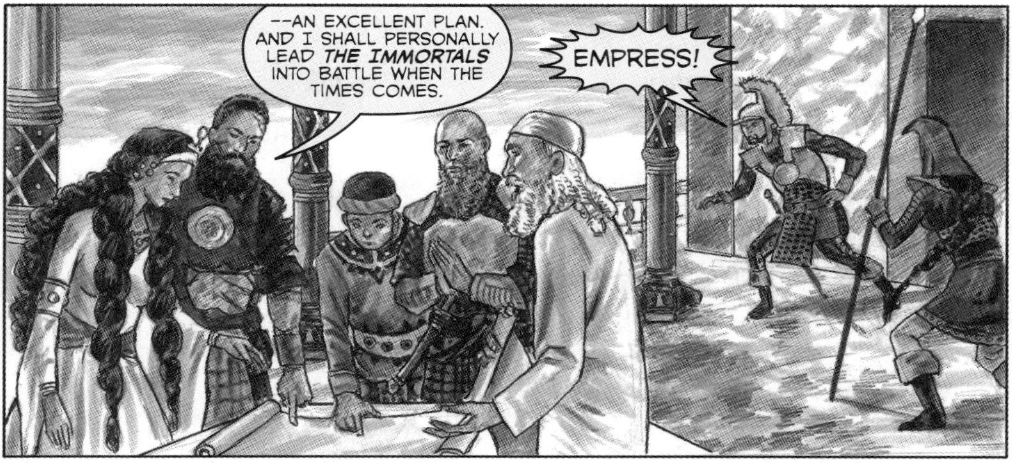
--AN EXCELLENT PLAN. AND I SHALL PERSONALLY LEAD ***THE IMMORTALS*** INTO BATTLE WHEN THE TIMES COMES.
EMPRESS!

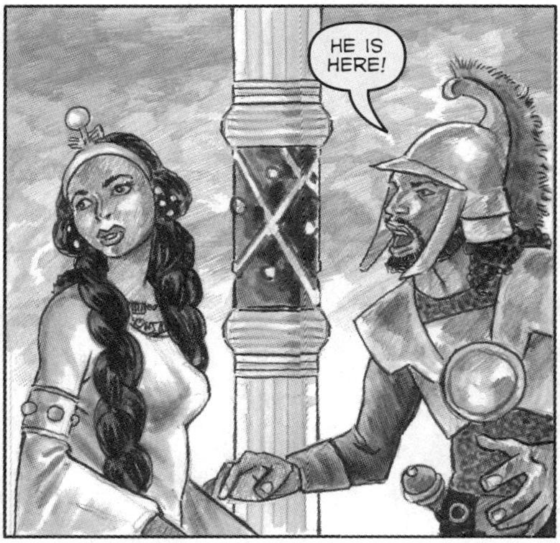
HE IS HERE!

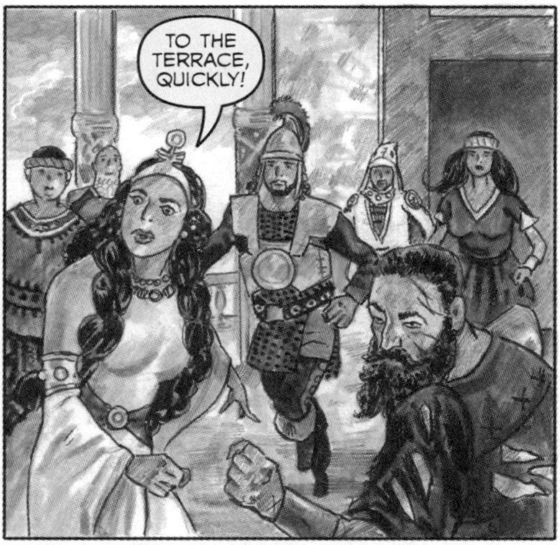
TO THE TERRACE, QUICKLY!

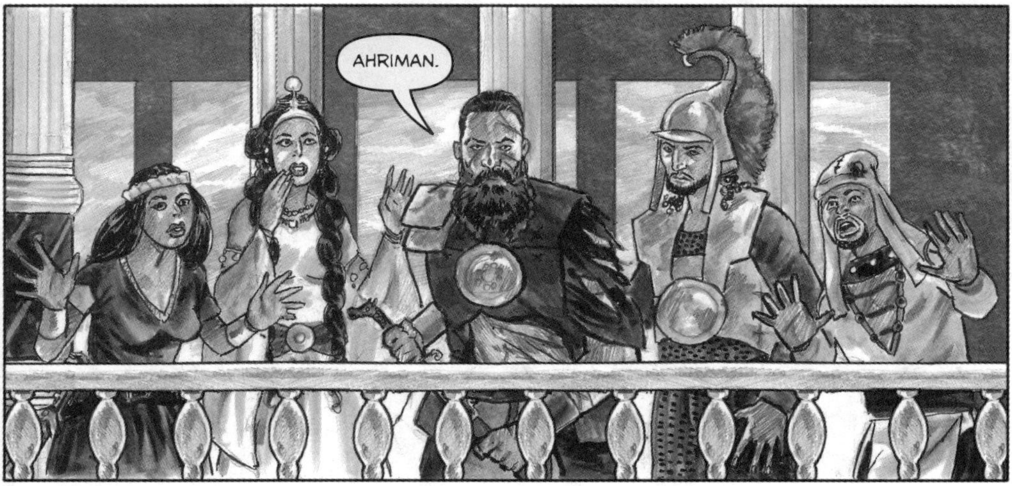
AHRIMAN.

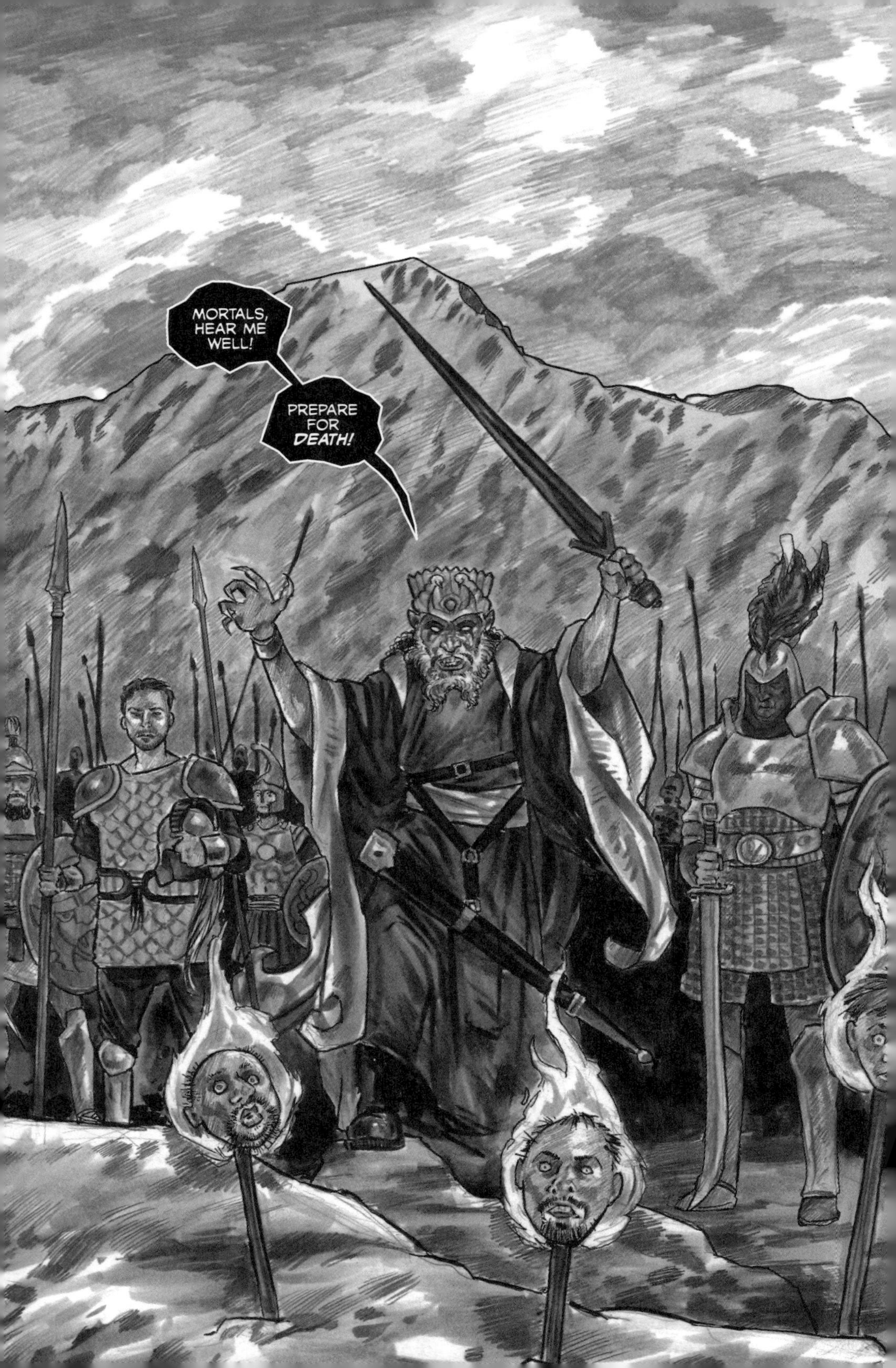
MORTALS, HEAR ME WELL!
PREPARE FOR *DEATH!*

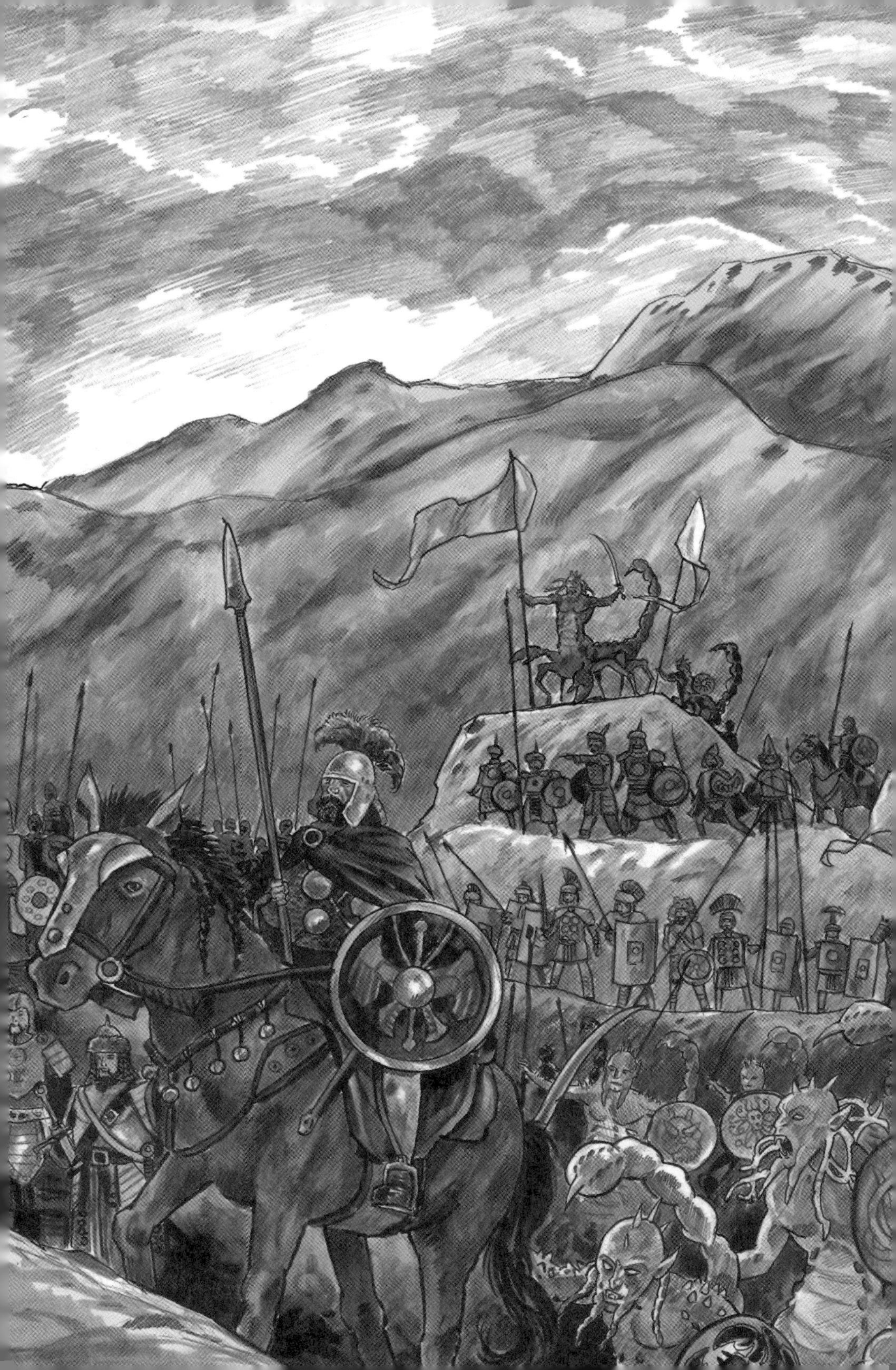

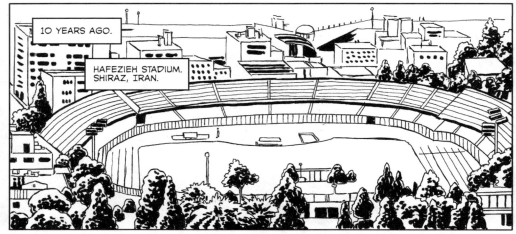

10 YEARS AGO.

HAFEZIEH STADIUM. SHIRAZ, IRAN.

SISTER, I'M *WARNING* YOU. MOVE ALONG.

WHY? WE'RE NOT CAUSING ANY HARM.

WE'RE JUST SILENTLY PROTESTING THE FACT THAT WE CAN'T WATCH A SOCCER MATCH SIMPLY BECAUSE WE'RE *WOMEN*.

THAT RULE IS IN PLACE TO PROTECT OUR *DELICATE FLOWERS* FROM THE CRASS LANGUAGE AND RUDE BEHAVIOR THAT MEN OFTEN DISPLAY AT SUCH EVENTS.

THAT'S SUCH *HYPOCRISY*.

WHY NOT ENFORCE A "NO CUSSING" RULE ON THE *MEN* INSTEAD?

ENOUGH! LEAVE *NOW*, OR I'LL ARREST *ALL* OF YOU.

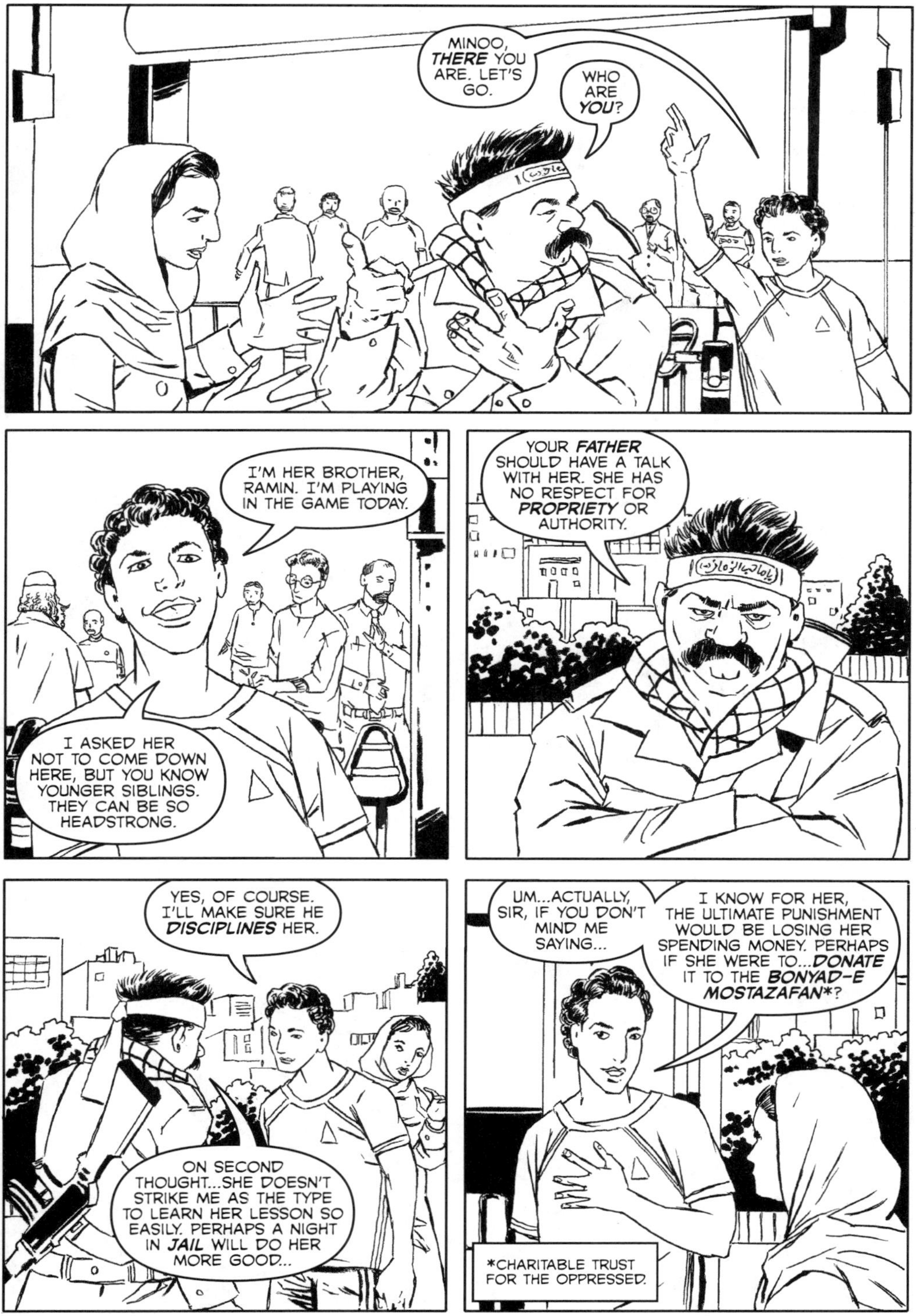
MINOO, THERE YOU ARE. LET'S GO.
WHO ARE YOU?
I'M HER BROTHER, RAMIN. I'M PLAYING IN THE GAME TODAY.
I ASKED HER NOT TO COME DOWN HERE, BUT YOU KNOW YOUNGER SIBLINGS. THEY CAN BE SO HEADSTRONG.
YOUR FATHER SHOULD HAVE A TALK WITH HER. SHE HAS NO RESPECT FOR PROPRIETY OR AUTHORITY.
YES, OF COURSE. I'LL MAKE SURE HE DISCIPLINES HER.
ON SECOND THOUGHT...SHE DOESN'T STRIKE ME AS THE TYPE TO LEARN HER LESSON SO EASILY. PERHAPS A NIGHT IN JAIL WILL DO HER MORE GOOD...
UM...ACTUALLY, SIR, IF YOU DON'T MIND ME SAYING...
I KNOW FOR HER, THE ULTIMATE PUNISHMENT WOULD BE LOSING HER SPENDING MONEY. PERHAPS IF SHE WERE TO...DONATE IT TO THE BONYAD-E MOSTAZAFAN*?
*CHARITABLE TRUST FOR THE OPPRESSED.

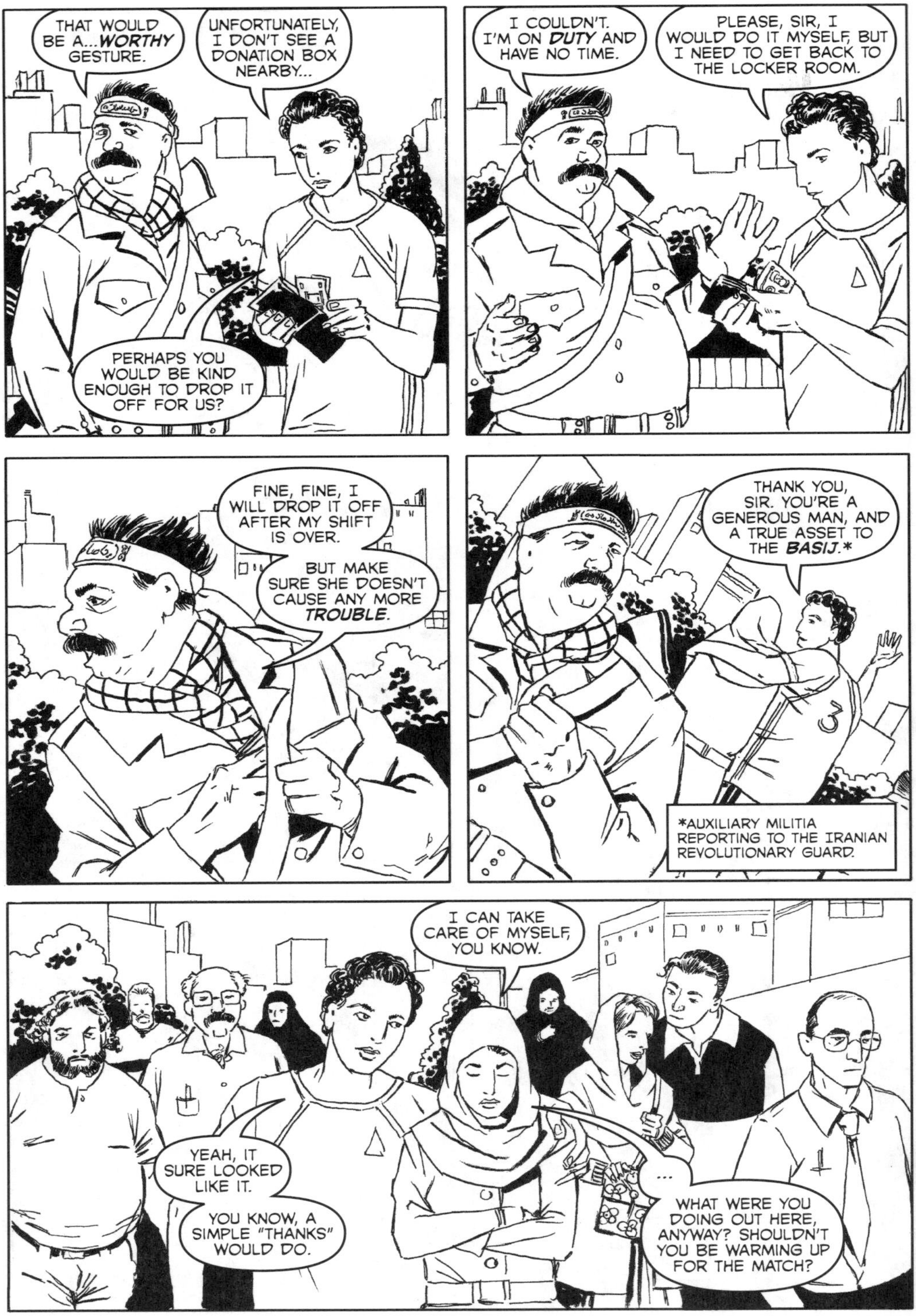
THAT WOULD BE A...WORTHY GESTURE.
UNFORTUNATELY, I DON'T SEE A DONATION BOX NEARBY...
PERHAPS YOU WOULD BE KIND ENOUGH TO DROP IT OFF FOR US?
I COULDN'T. I'M ON DUTY AND HAVE NO TIME.
PLEASE, SIR, I WOULD DO IT MYSELF, BUT I NEED TO GET BACK TO THE LOCKER ROOM.
FINE, FINE, I WILL DROP IT OFF AFTER MY SHIFT IS OVER.
BUT MAKE SURE SHE DOESN'T CAUSE ANY MORE TROUBLE.
THANK YOU, SIR. YOU'RE A GENEROUS MAN, AND A TRUE ASSET TO THE BASIJ.*
*AUXILIARY MILITIA REPORTING TO THE IRANIAN REVOLUTIONARY GUARD.
I CAN TAKE CARE OF MYSELF, YOU KNOW.
YEAH, IT SURE LOOKED LIKE IT.
YOU KNOW, A SIMPLE "THANKS" WOULD DO.
...
WHAT WERE YOU DOING OUT HERE, ANYWAY? SHOULDN'T YOU BE WARMING UP FOR THE MATCH?

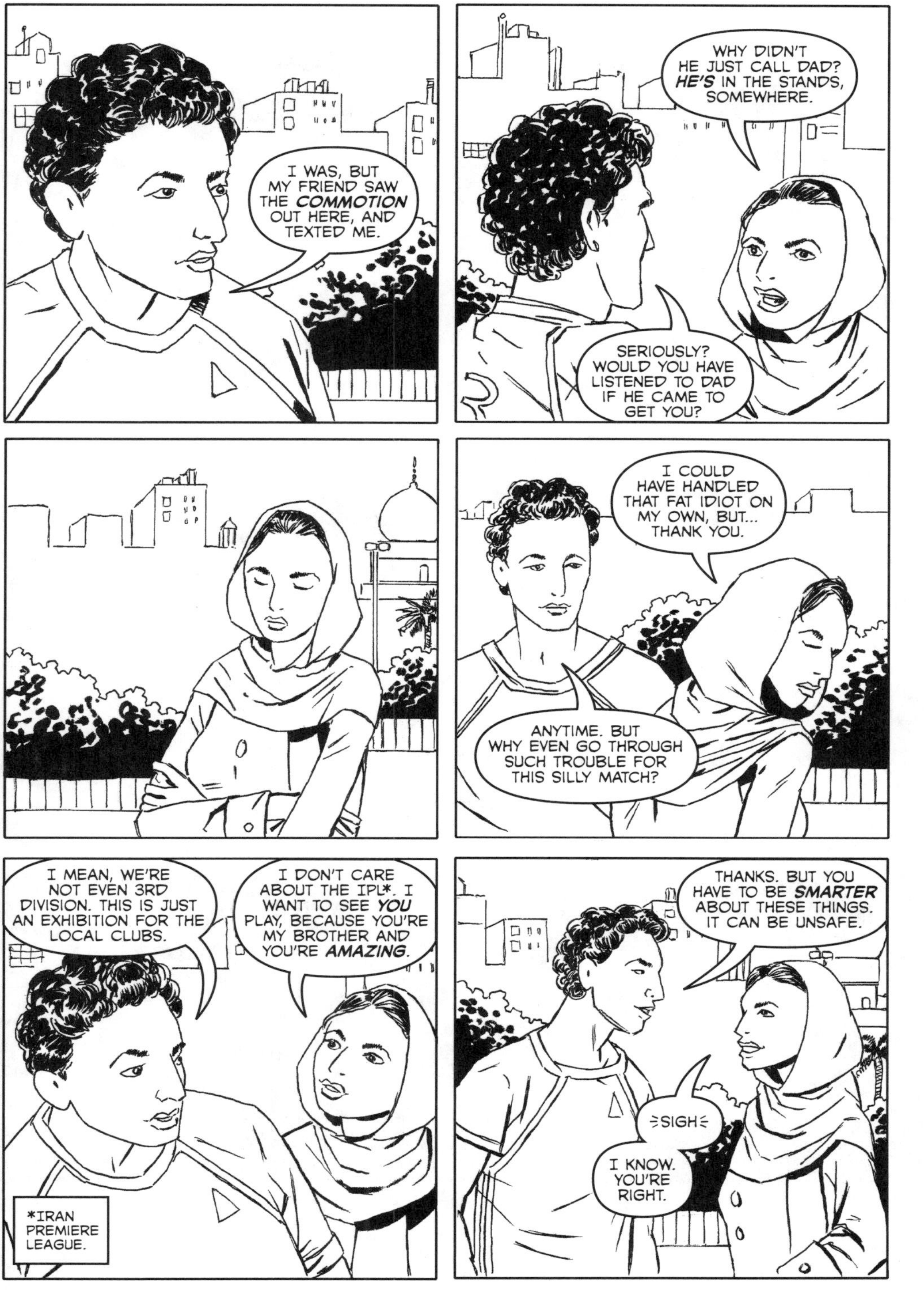
I WAS, BUT MY FRIEND SAW THE ***COMMOTION*** OUT HERE, AND TEXTED ME.
WHY DIDN'T HE JUST CALL DAD? ***HE'S*** IN THE STANDS, SOMEWHERE.
SERIOUSLY? WOULD YOU HAVE LISTENED TO DAD IF HE CAME TO GET YOU?
I COULD HAVE HANDLED THAT FAT IDIOT ON MY OWN, BUT... THANK YOU.
ANYTIME. BUT WHY EVEN GO THROUGH SUCH TROUBLE FOR THIS SILLY MATCH?
I MEAN, WE'RE NOT EVEN 3RD DIVISION. THIS IS JUST AN EXHIBITION FOR THE LOCAL CLUBS.
I DON'T CARE ABOUT THE IPL*. I WANT TO SEE ***YOU*** PLAY, BECAUSE YOU'RE MY BROTHER AND YOU'RE ***AMAZING***.
*IRAN PREMIERE LEAGUE.
THANKS. BUT YOU HAVE TO BE ***SMARTER*** ABOUT THESE THINGS. IT CAN BE UNSAFE.
SIGH
I KNOW. YOU'RE RIGHT.

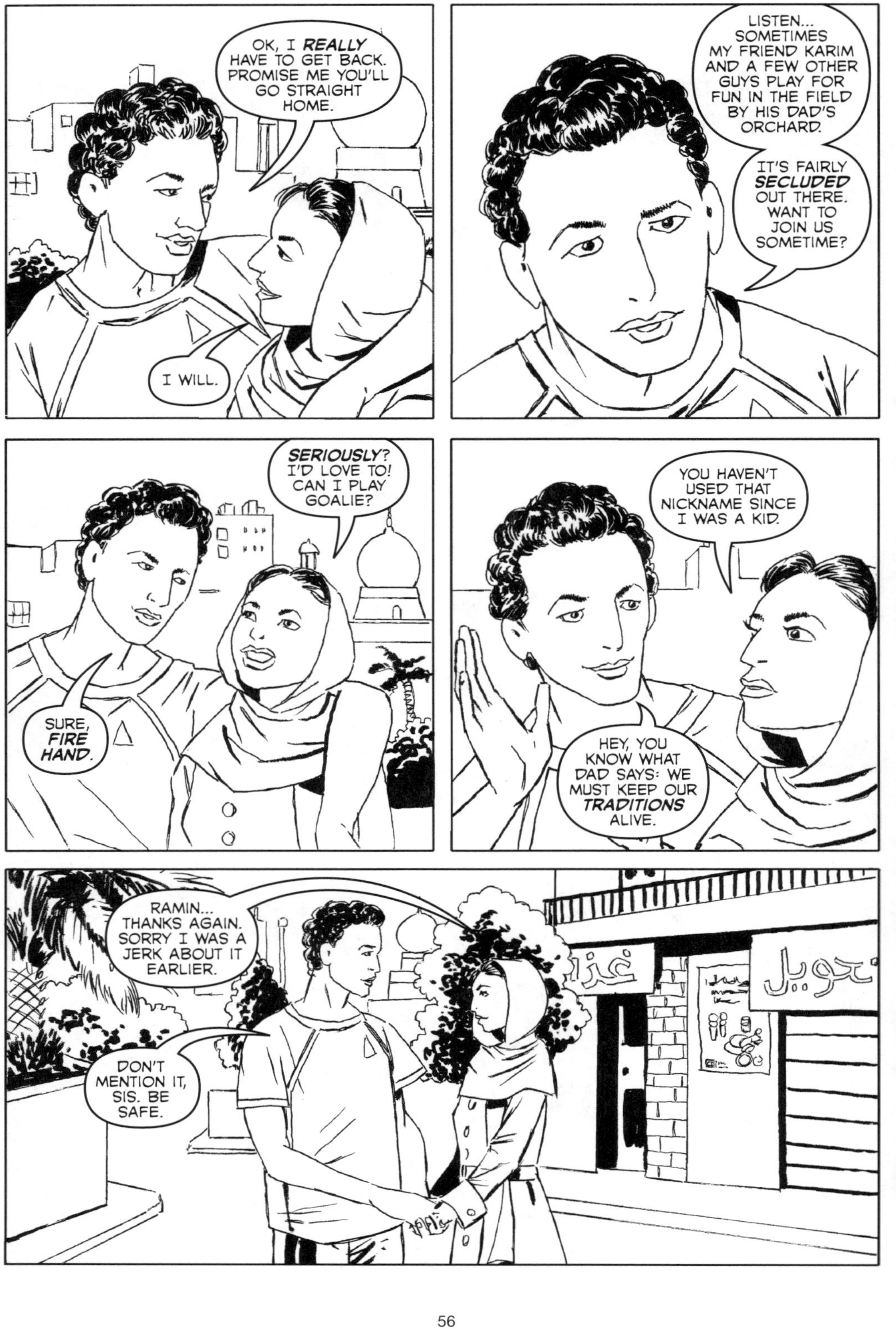
OK, I **REALLY** HAVE TO GET BACK. PROMISE ME YOU'LL GO STRAIGHT HOME.
I WILL.
LISTEN... SOMETIMES MY FRIEND KARIM AND A FEW OTHER GUYS PLAY FOR FUN IN THE FIELD BY HIS DAD'S ORCHARD.
IT'S FAIRLY **SECLUDED** OUT THERE. WANT TO JOIN US SOMETIME?
SERIOUSLY? I'D LOVE TO! CAN I PLAY GOALIE?
SURE, **FIRE HAND**.
YOU HAVEN'T USED THAT NICKNAME SINCE I WAS A KID.
HEY, YOU KNOW WHAT DAD SAYS: WE MUST KEEP OUR **TRADITIONS** ALIVE.
RAMIN... THANKS AGAIN. SORRY I WAS A JERK ABOUT IT EARLIER.
DON'T MENTION IT, SIS. BE SAFE.

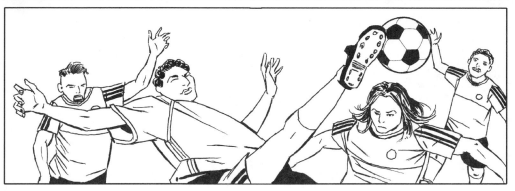

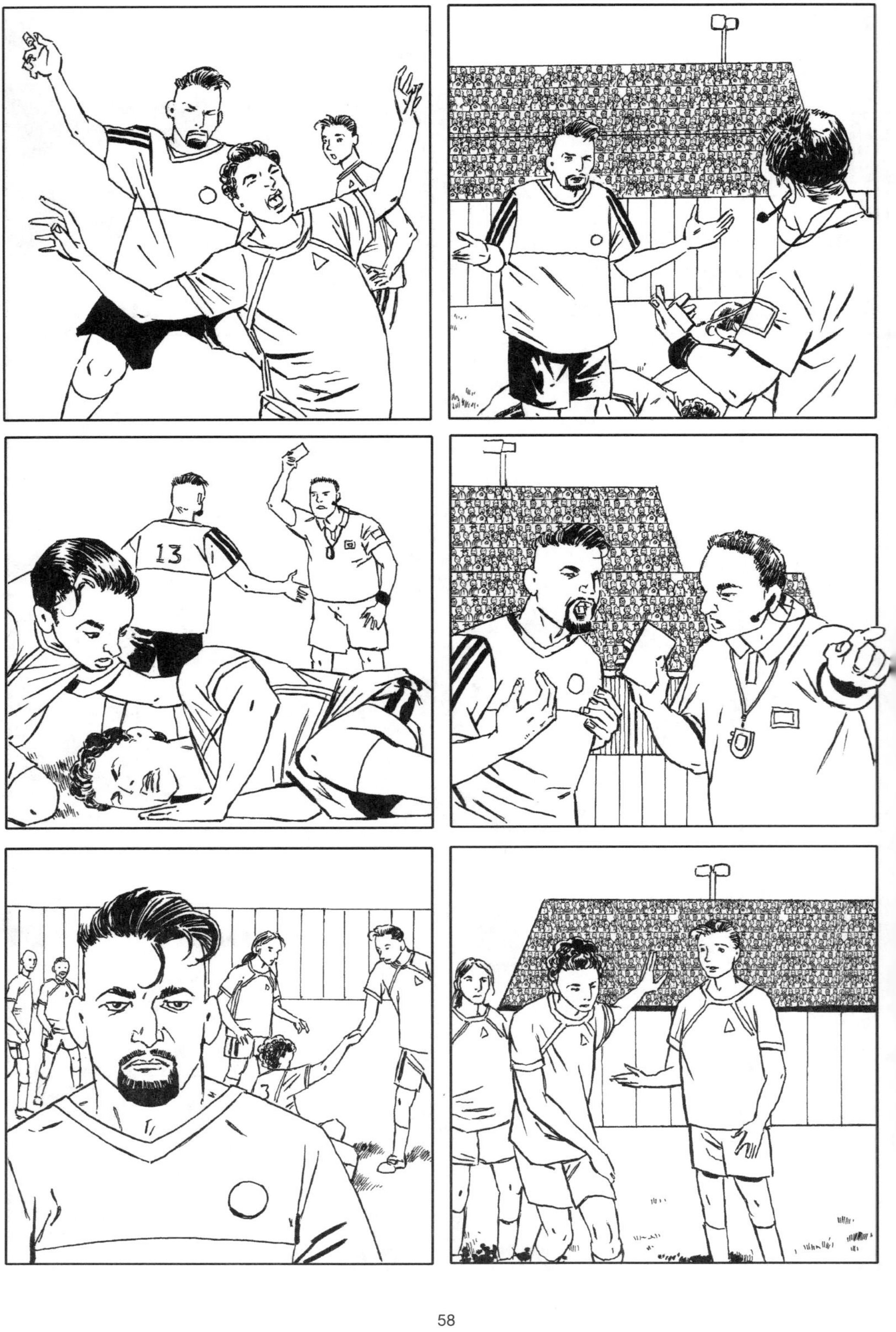
13

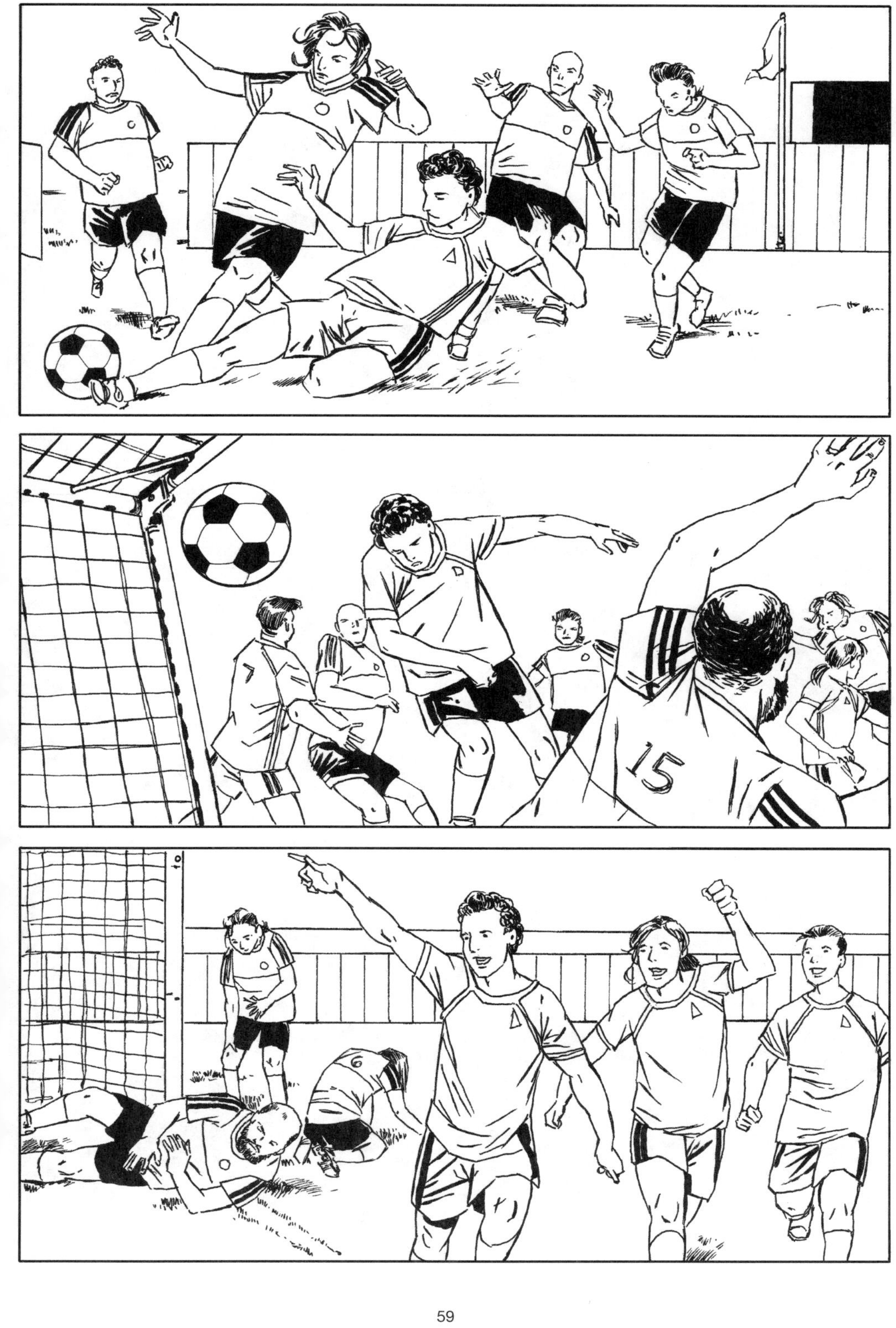

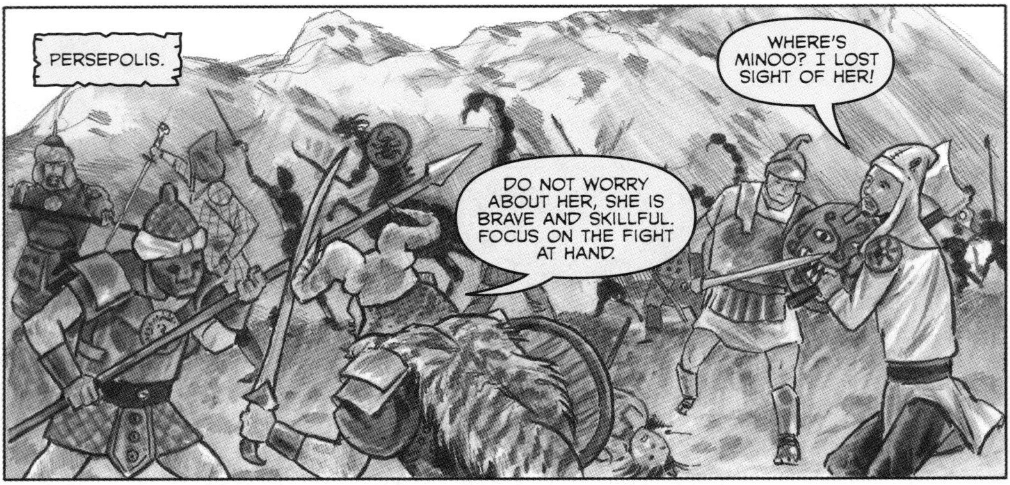
PERSEPOLIS.
WHERE'S MINOO? I LOST SIGHT OF HER!
DO NOT WORRY ABOUT HER, SHE IS BRAVE AND SKILLFUL. FOCUS ON THE FIGHT AT HAND.

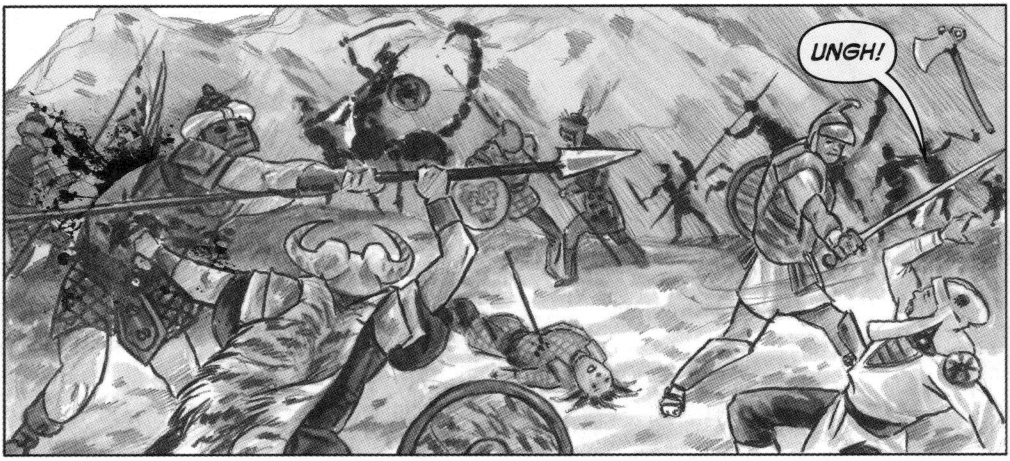
UNGH!

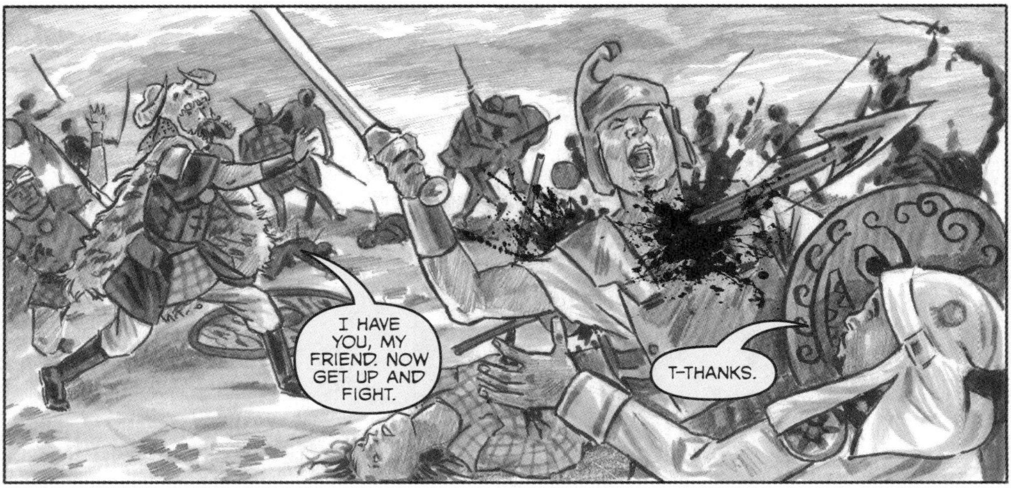
I HAVE YOU, MY FRIEND. NOW GET UP AND FIGHT.
T-THANKS.

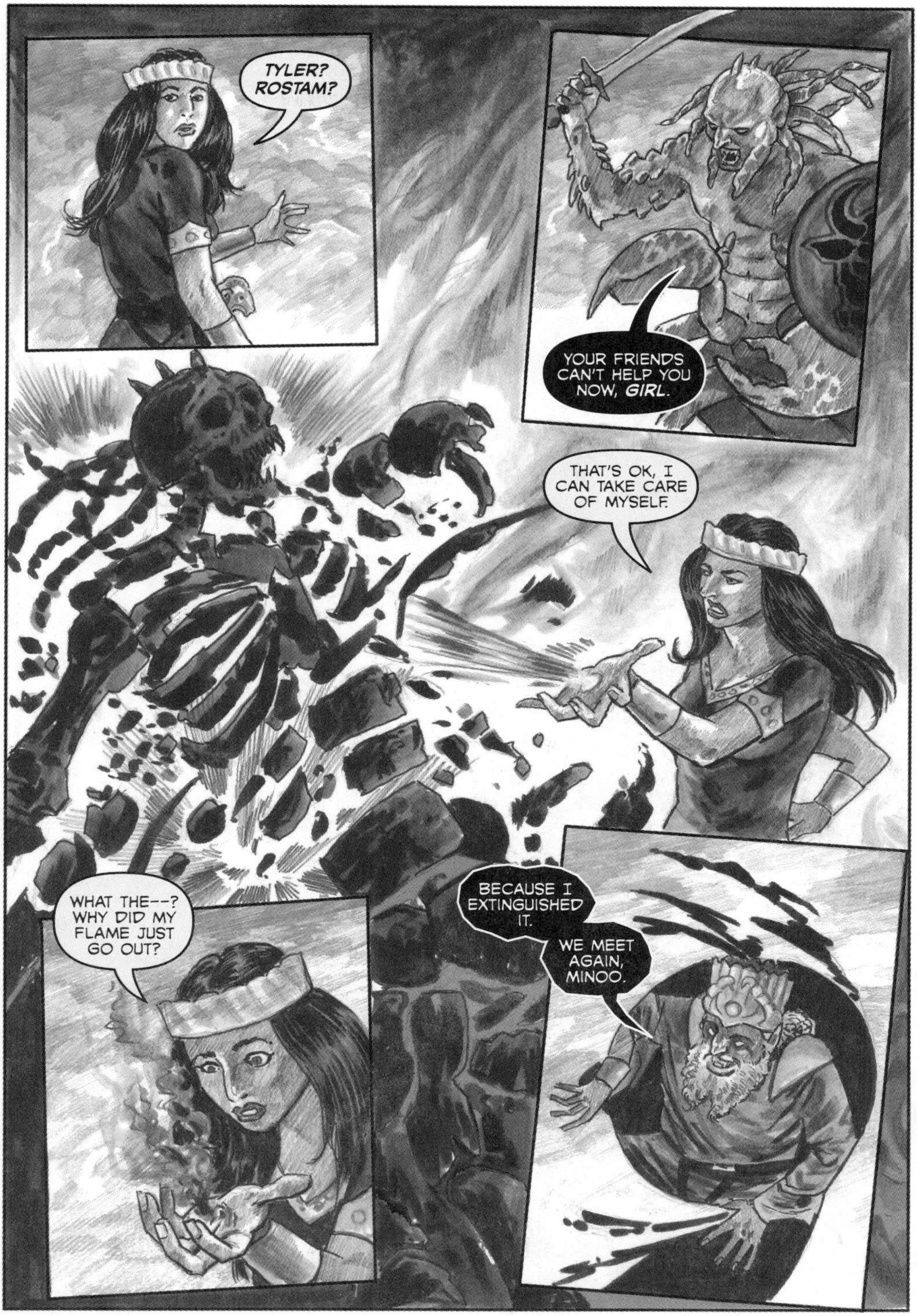
TYLER? ROSTAM?
YOUR FRIENDS CAN'T HELP YOU NOW, GIRL.
THAT'S OK, I CAN TAKE CARE OF MYSELF.
WHAT THE--? WHY DID MY FLAME JUST GO OUT?
BECAUSE I EXTINGUISHED IT.
WE MEET AGAIN, MINOO.

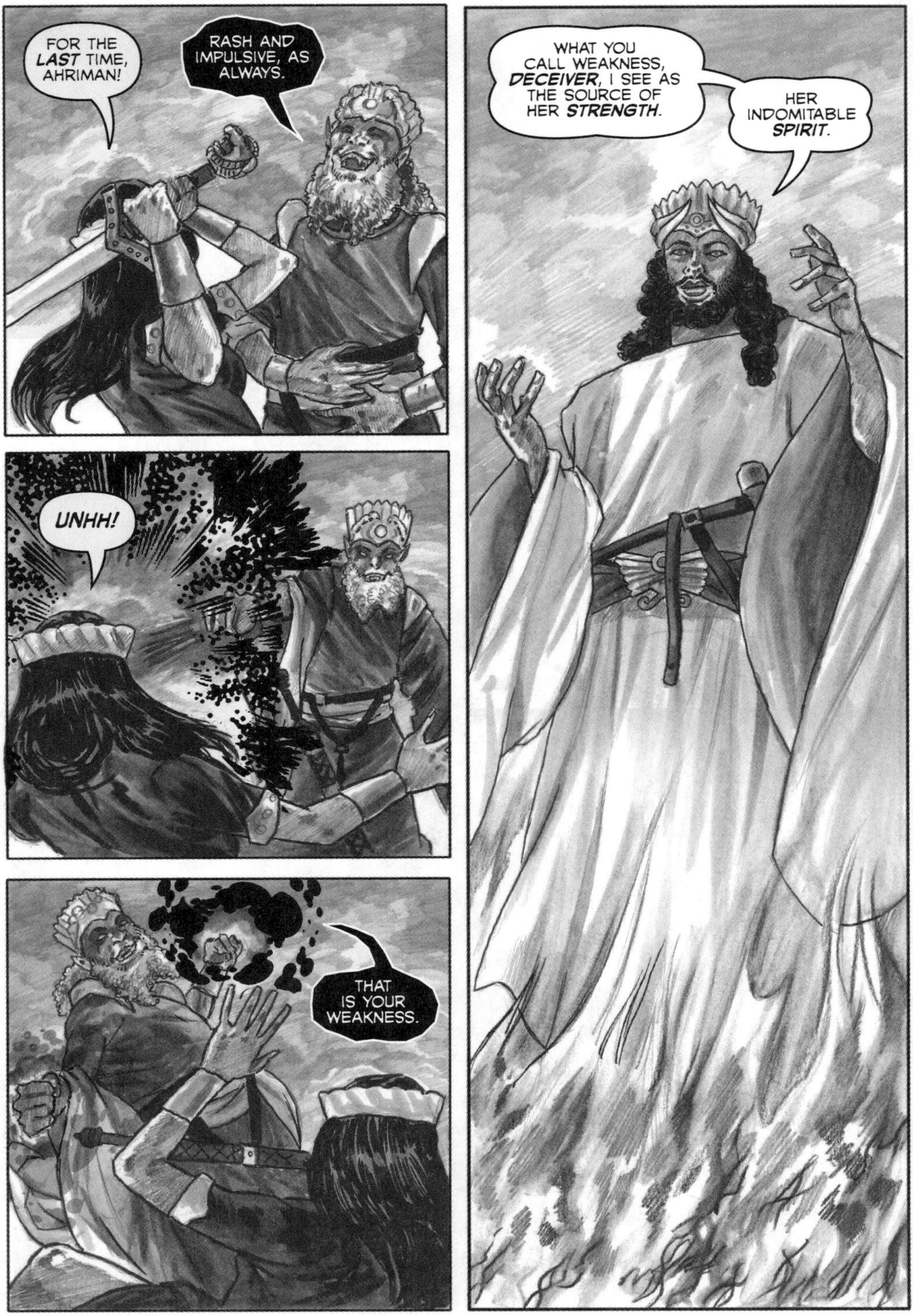
FOR THE LAST TIME, AHRIMAN!
RASH AND IMPULSIVE, AS ALWAYS.
UNHH!
THAT IS YOUR WEAKNESS.
WHAT YOU CALL WEAKNESS, DECEIVER, I SEE AS THE SOURCE OF HER STRENGTH.
HER INDOMITABLE SPIRIT.

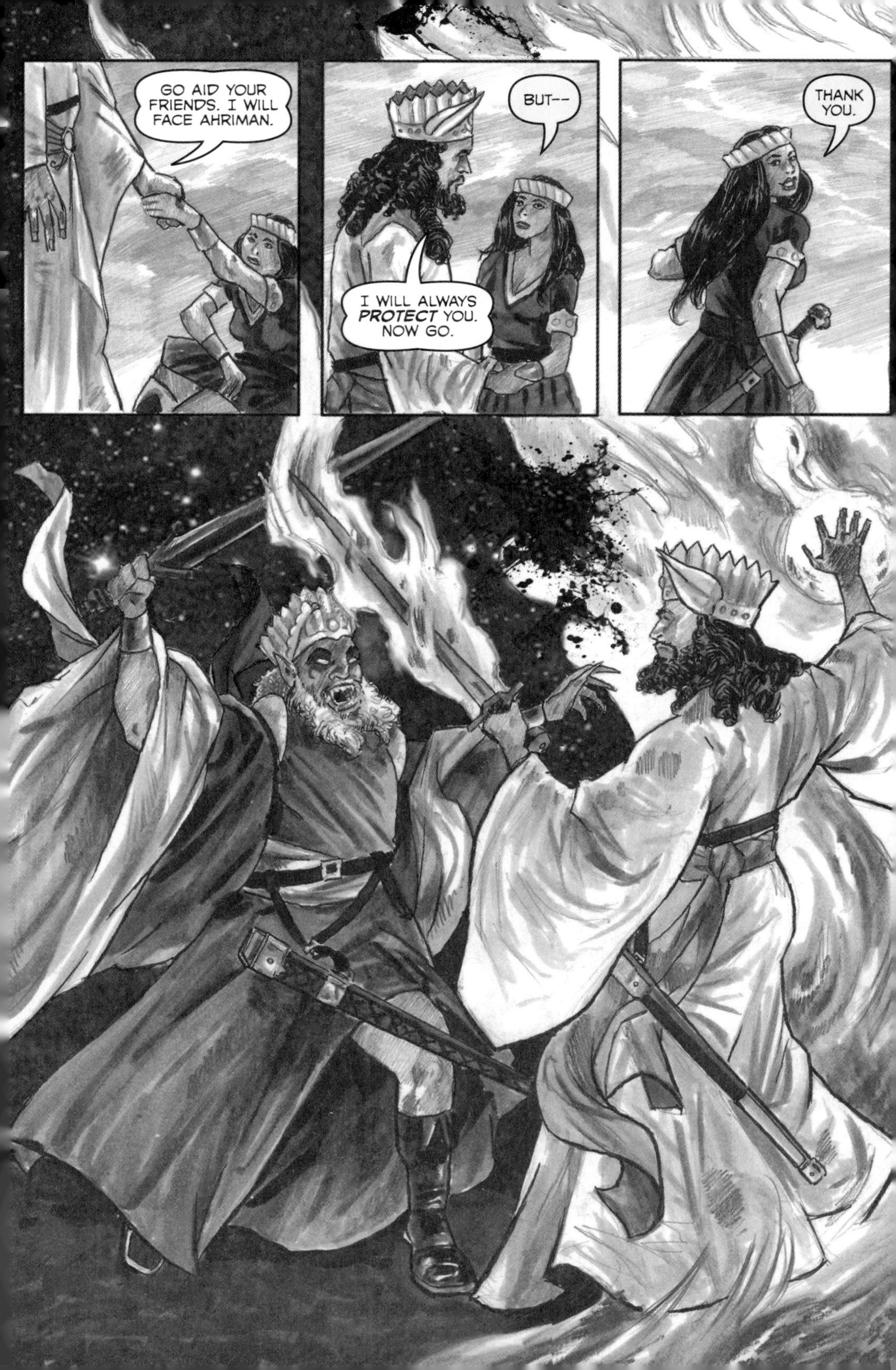

GO AID YOUR FRIENDS. I WILL FACE AHRIMAN.
BUT--
I WILL ALWAYS *PROTECT* YOU. NOW GO.
THANK YOU.

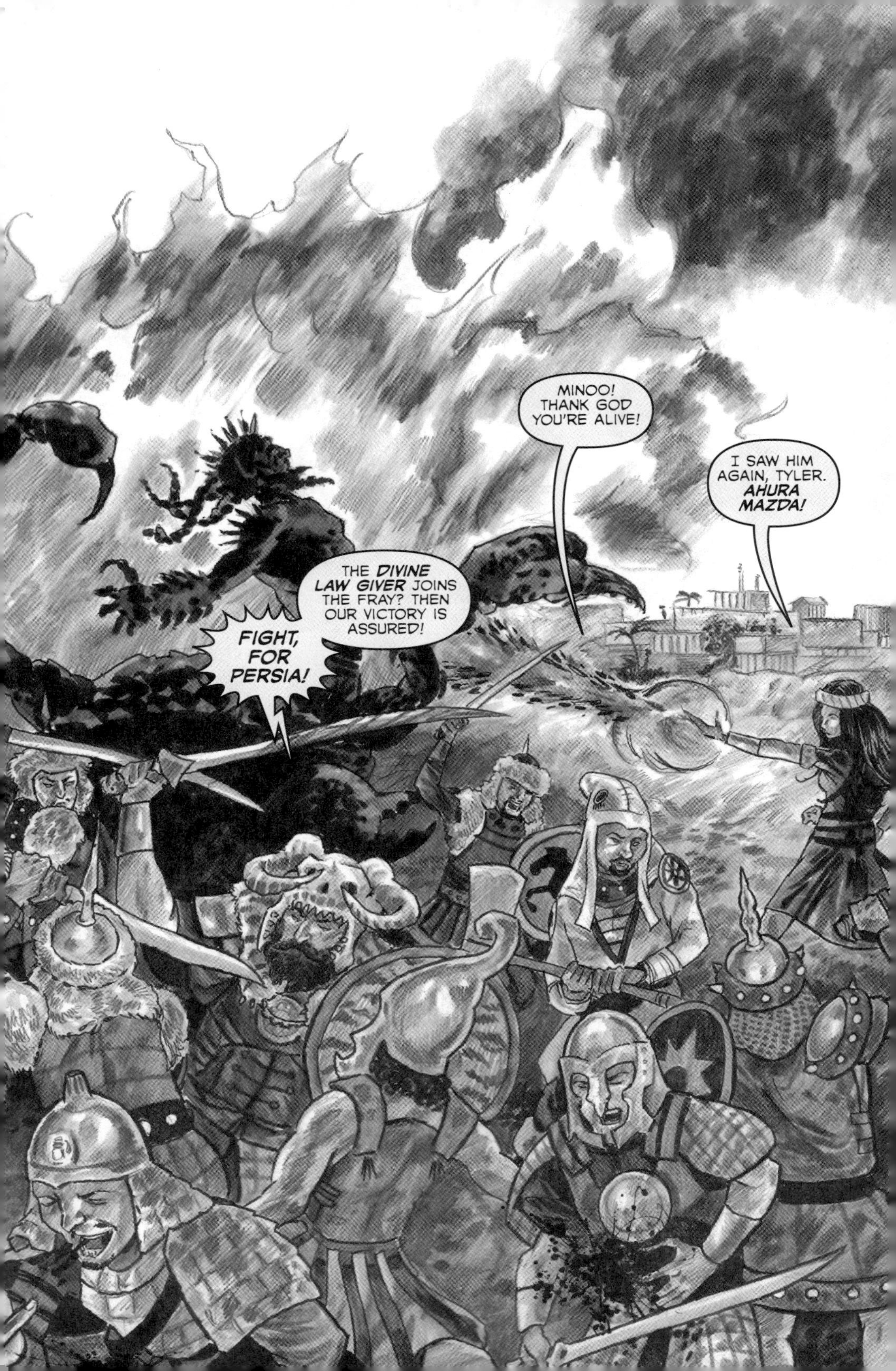
FIGHT, FOR PERSIA!
THE *DIVINE LAW GIVER* JOINS THE FRAY? THEN OUR VICTORY IS ASSURED!
MINOO! THANK GOD YOU'RE ALIVE!
I SAW HIM AGAIN, TYLER. *AHURA MAZDA!*

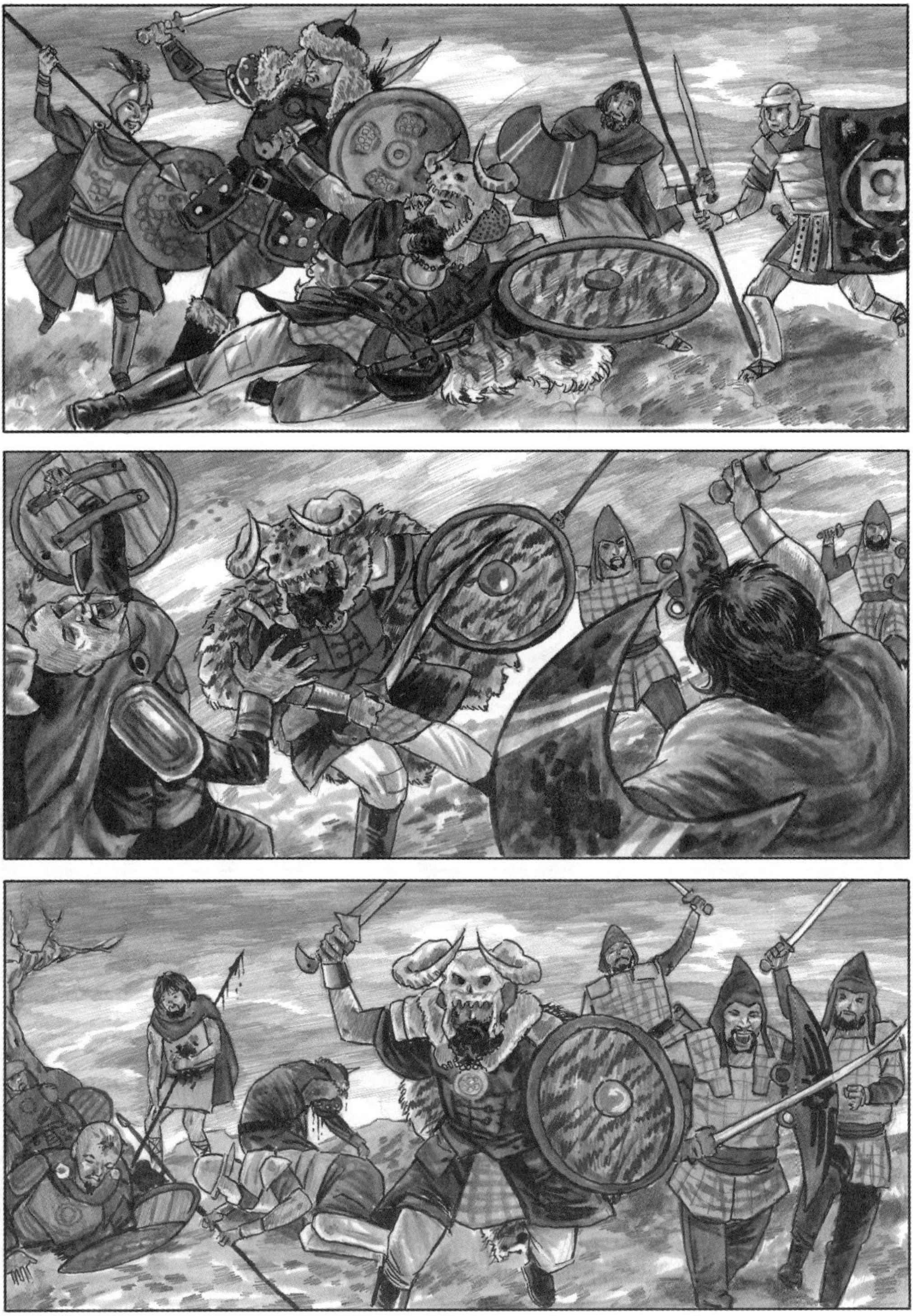

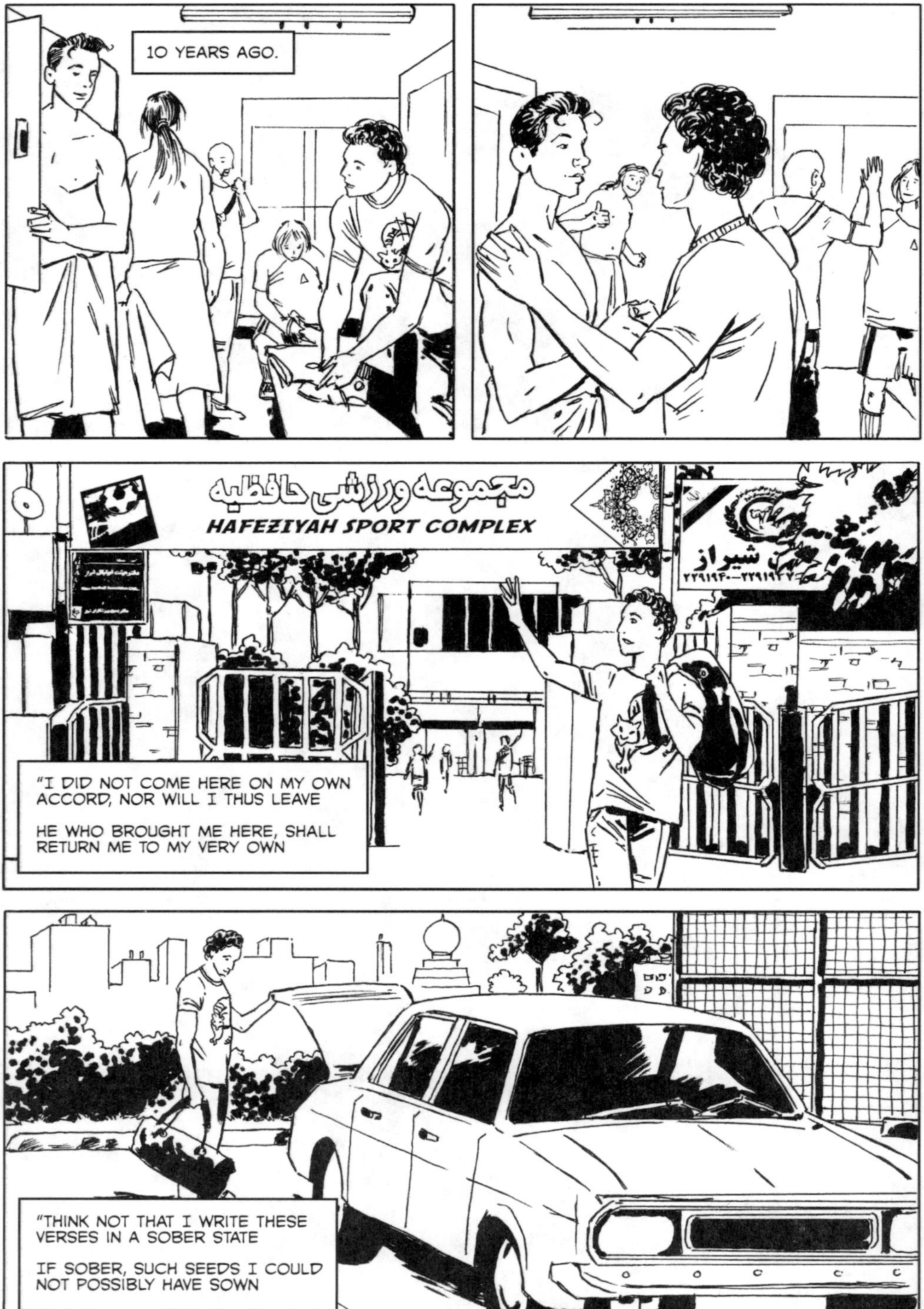
10 YEARS AGO.
مجموعه ورزشی حافظیه
HAFEZIYAH SPORT COMPLEX
شیراز
"I DID NOT COME HERE ON MY OWN ACCORD, NOR WILL I THUS LEAVE
HE WHO BROUGHT ME HERE, SHALL RETURN ME TO MY VERY OWN
"THINK NOT THAT I WRITE THESE VERSES IN A SOBER STATE
IF SOBER, SUCH SEEDS I COULD NOT POSSIBLY HAVE SOWN

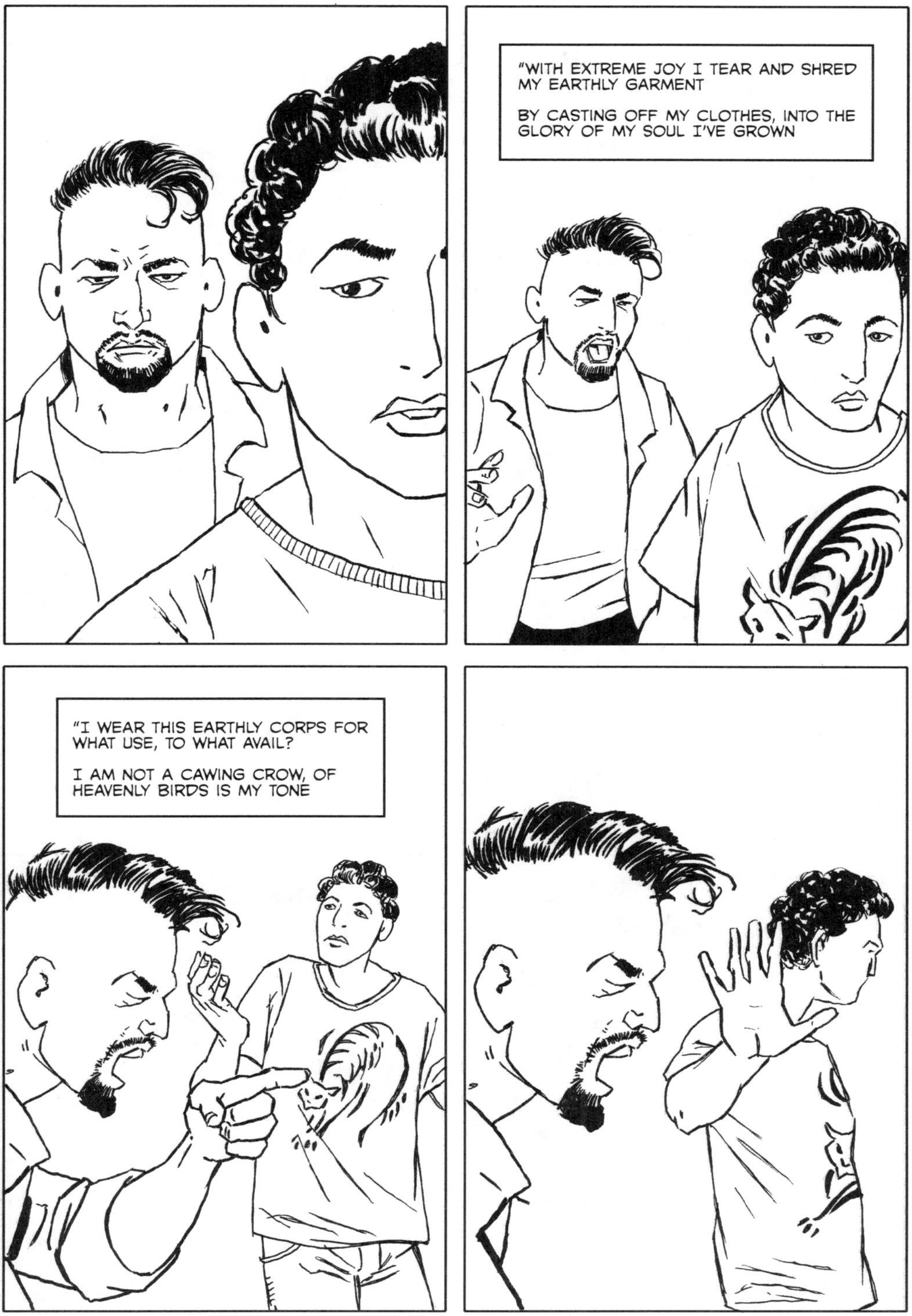
"WITH EXTREME JOY I TEAR AND SHRED MY EARTHLY GARMENT
BY CASTING OFF MY CLOTHES, INTO THE GLORY OF MY SOUL I'VE GROWN
"I WEAR THIS EARTHLY CORPS FOR WHAT USE, TO WHAT AVAIL?
I AM NOT A CAWING CROW, OF HEAVENLY BIRDS IS MY TONE

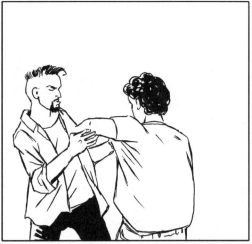

"I AM A BIRD OF PARADISE, I AM NOT OF THE EARTHLY REALM

"FOR A FEW DAYS IMPRISONED IN MY CAGE OF FLESH AND BONE

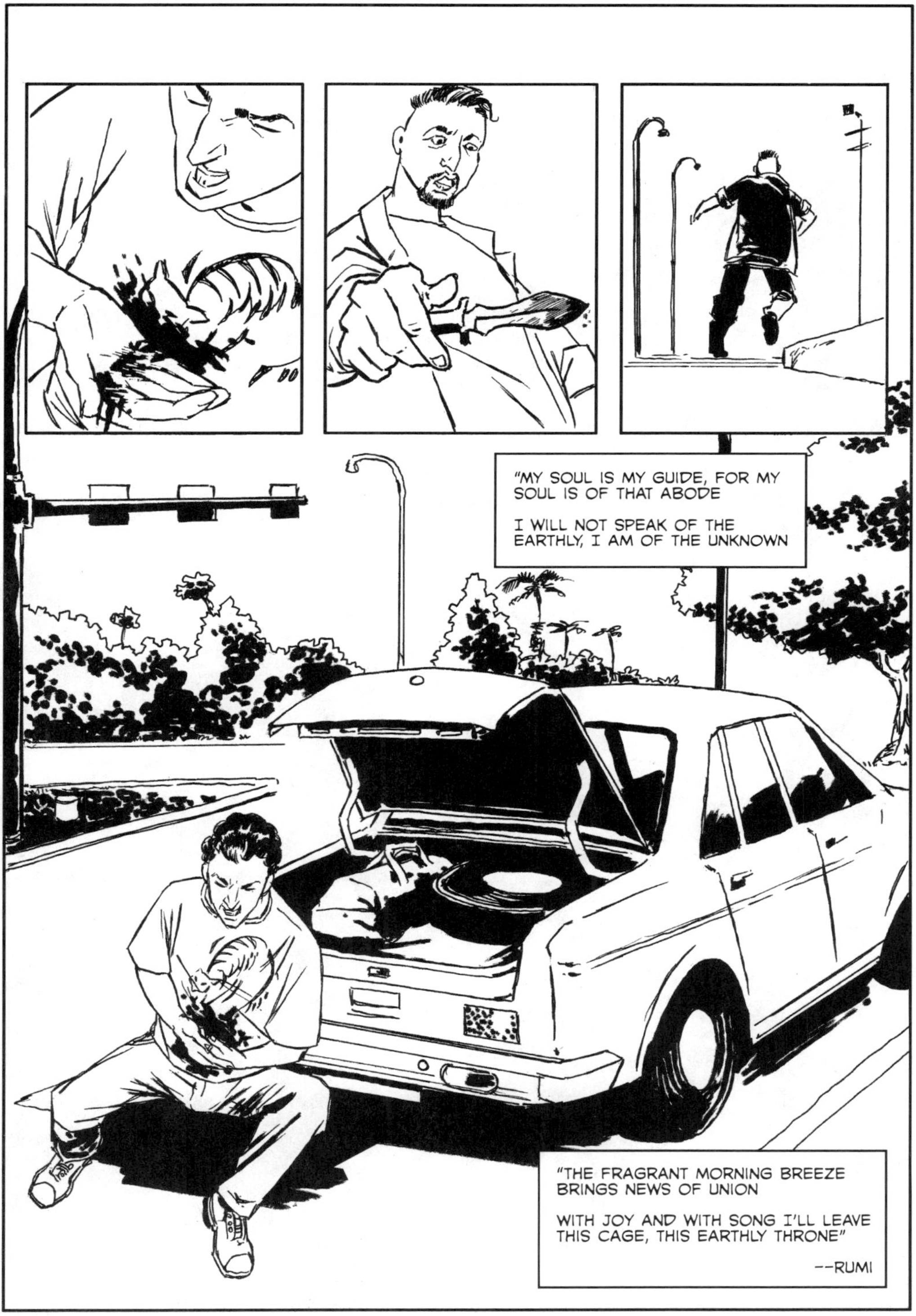
"MY SOUL IS MY GUIDE, FOR MY SOUL IS OF THAT ABODE
I WILL NOT SPEAK OF THE EARTHLY, I AM OF THE UNKNOWN
"THE FRAGRANT MORNING BREEZE BRINGS NEWS OF UNION
WITH JOY AND WITH SONG I'LL LEAVE THIS CAGE, THIS EARTHLY THRONE"
--RUMI

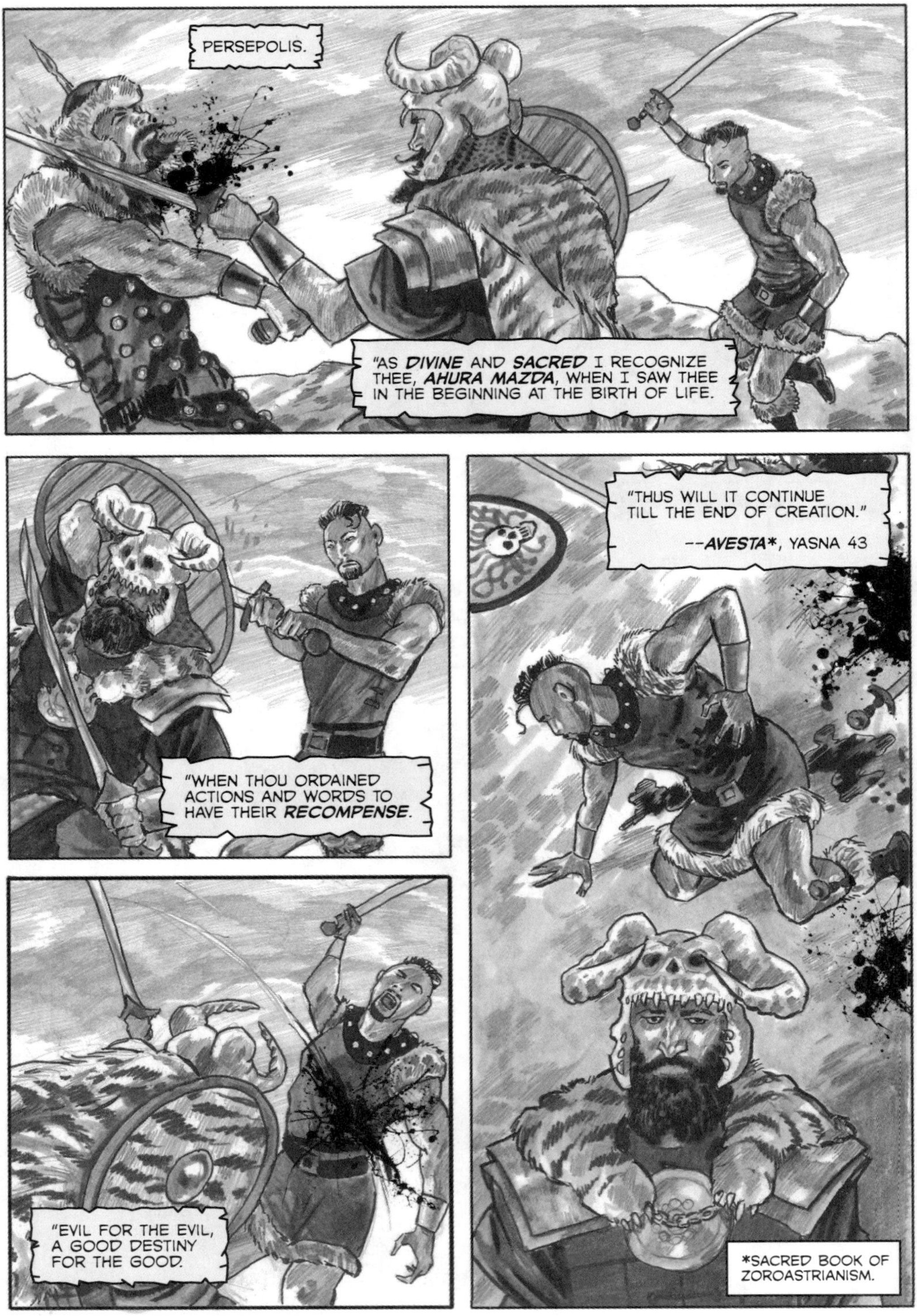
PERSEPOLIS.
"AS DIVINE AND SACRED I RECOGNIZE THEE, AHURA MAZDA, WHEN I SAW THEE IN THE BEGINNING AT THE BIRTH OF LIFE.
"WHEN THOU ORDAINED ACTIONS AND WORDS TO HAVE THEIR RECOMPENSE.
"EVIL FOR THE EVIL, A GOOD DESTINY FOR THE GOOD.
"THUS WILL IT CONTINUE TILL THE END OF CREATION."
--AVESTA*, YASNA 43
*SACRED BOOK OF ZOROASTRIANISM.

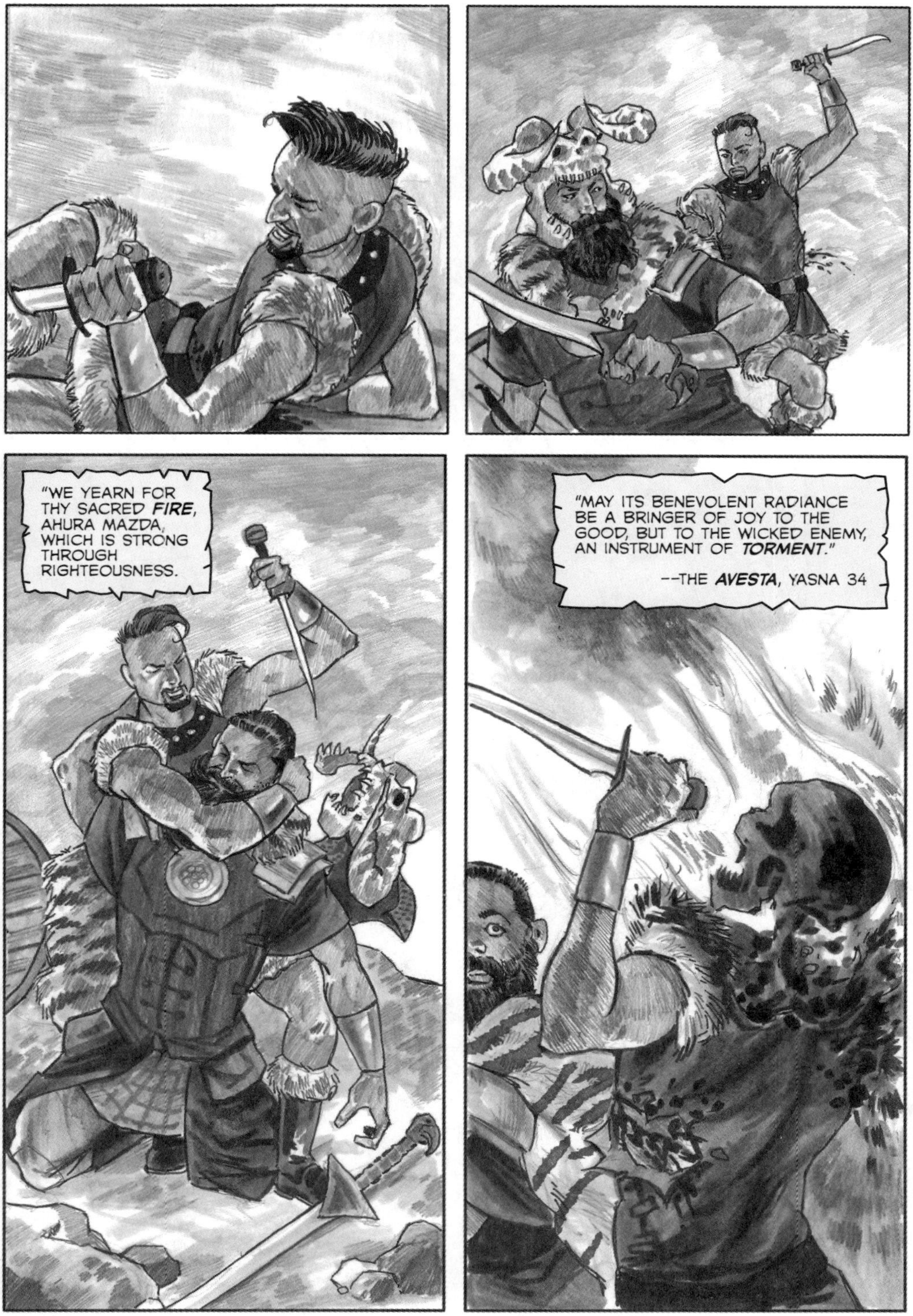
"WE YEARN FOR THY SACRED **FIRE**, AHURA MAZDA, WHICH IS STRONG THROUGH RIGHTEOUSNESS.
"MAY ITS BENEVOLENT RADIANCE BE A BRINGER OF JOY TO THE GOOD, BUT TO THE WICKED ENEMY, AN INSTRUMENT OF **TORMENT**."
--THE **AVESTA**, YASNA 34

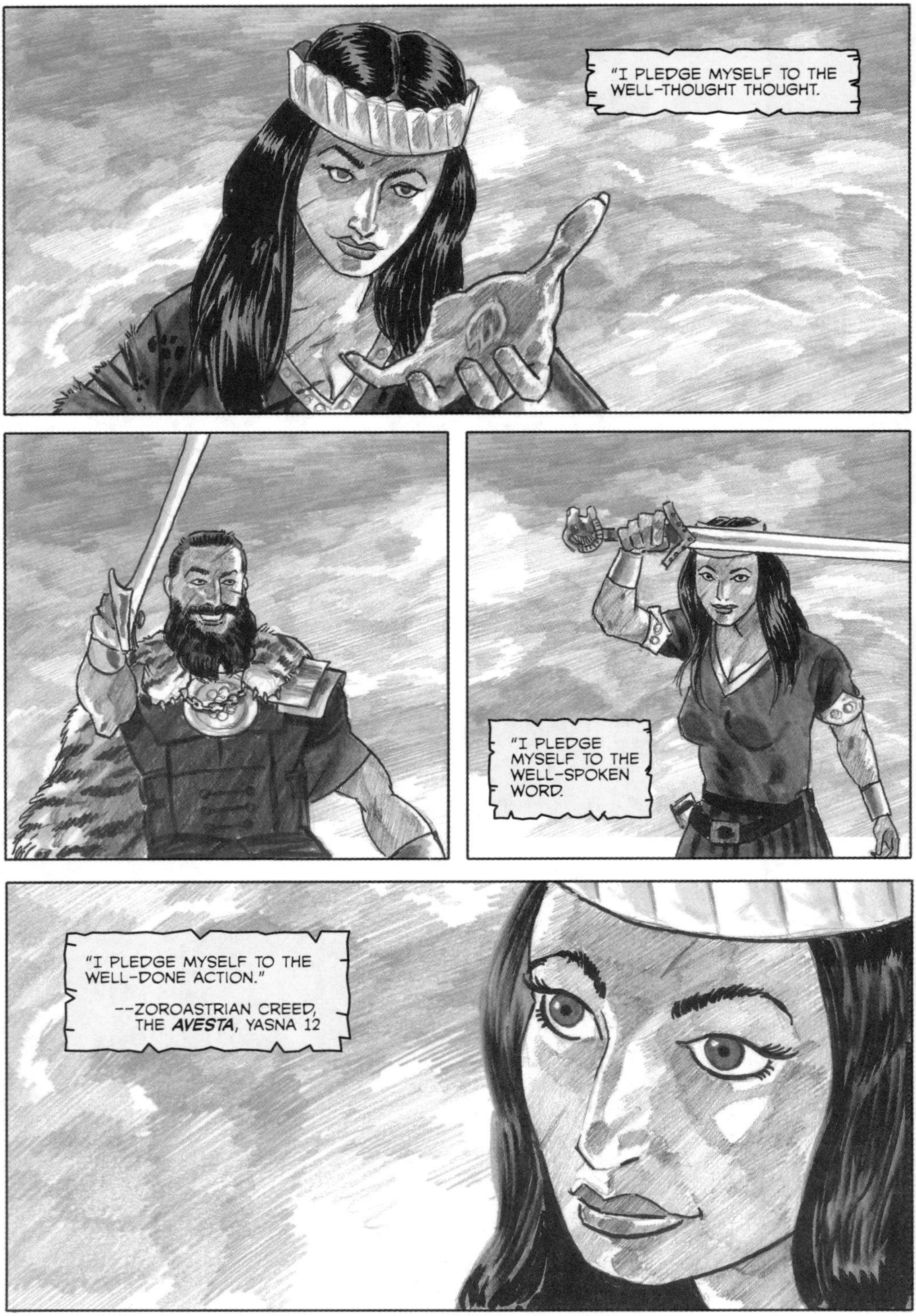
"I PLEDGE MYSELF TO THE WELL-THOUGHT THOUGHT.
"I PLEDGE MYSELF TO THE WELL-SPOKEN WORD.
"I PLEDGE MYSELF TO THE WELL-DONE ACTION."
--ZOROASTRIAN CREED, THE *AVESTA*, YASNA 12

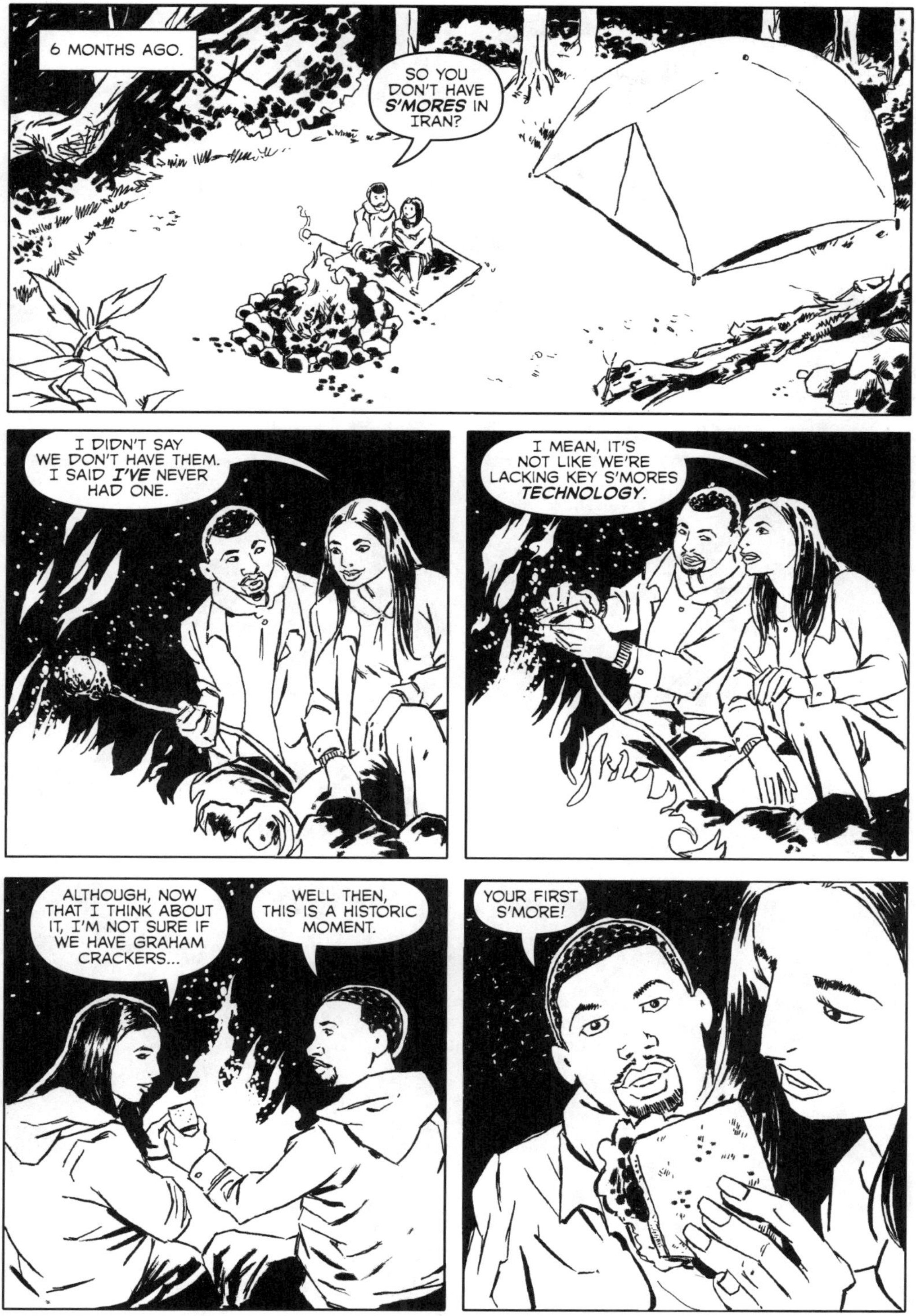
6 MONTHS AGO.
SO YOU DON'T HAVE S'MORES IN IRAN?
I DIDN'T SAY WE DON'T HAVE THEM. I SAID I'VE NEVER HAD ONE.
I MEAN, IT'S NOT LIKE WE'RE LACKING KEY S'MORES TECHNOLOGY.
ALTHOUGH, NOW THAT I THINK ABOUT IT, I'M NOT SURE IF WE HAVE GRAHAM CRACKERS...
WELL THEN, THIS IS A HISTORIC MOMENT.
YOUR FIRST S'MORE!

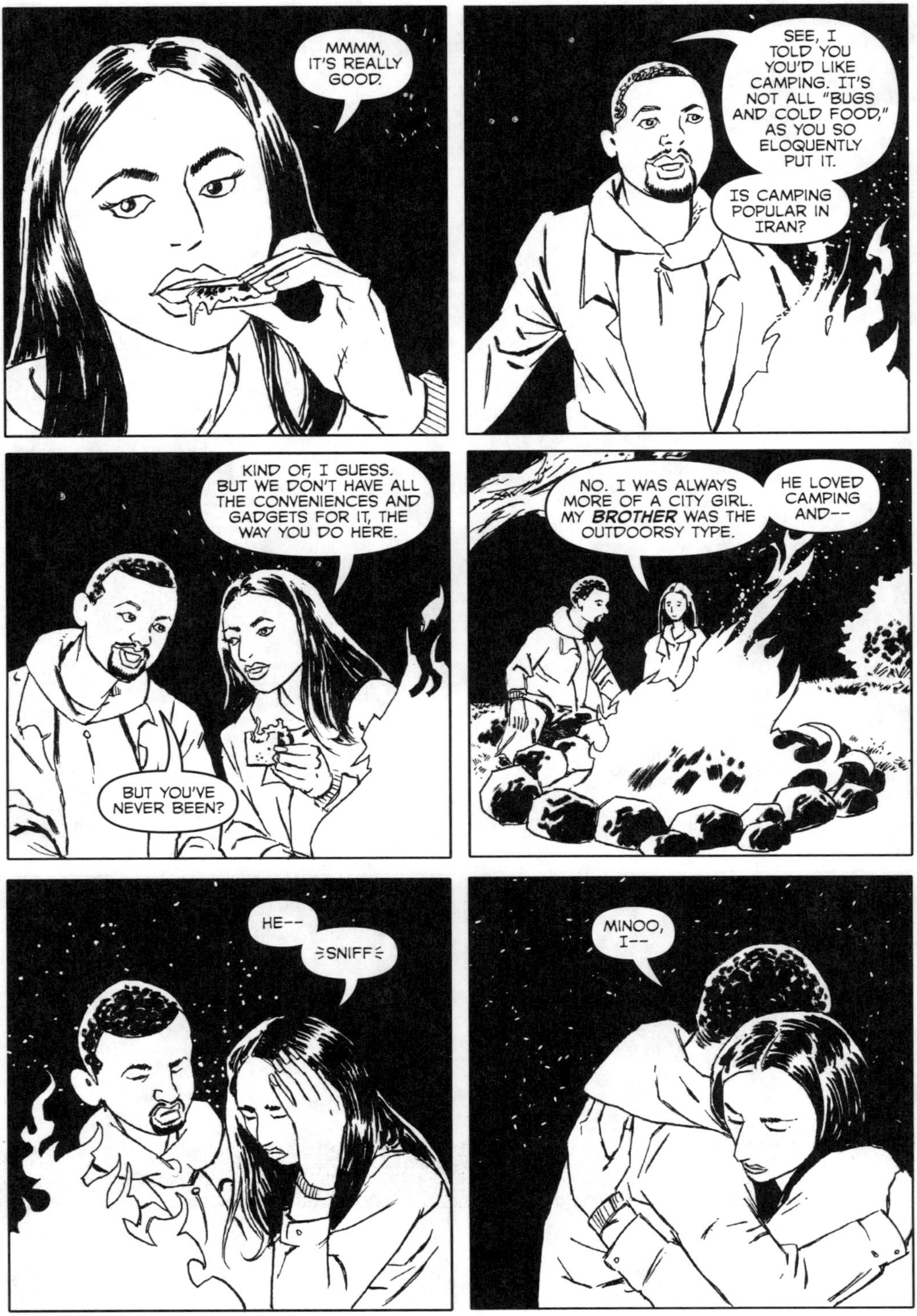
MMMM, IT'S REALLY GOOD.
SEE, I TOLD YOU YOU'D LIKE CAMPING. IT'S NOT ALL "BUGS AND COLD FOOD," AS YOU SO ELOQUENTLY PUT IT.
IS CAMPING POPULAR IN IRAN?
KIND OF, I GUESS. BUT WE DON'T HAVE ALL THE CONVENIENCES AND GADGETS FOR IT, THE WAY YOU DO HERE.
BUT YOU'VE NEVER BEEN?
NO. I WAS ALWAYS MORE OF A CITY GIRL. MY ***BROTHER*** WAS THE OUTDOORSY TYPE.
HE LOVED CAMPING AND--
HE--
SNIFF
MINOO, I--

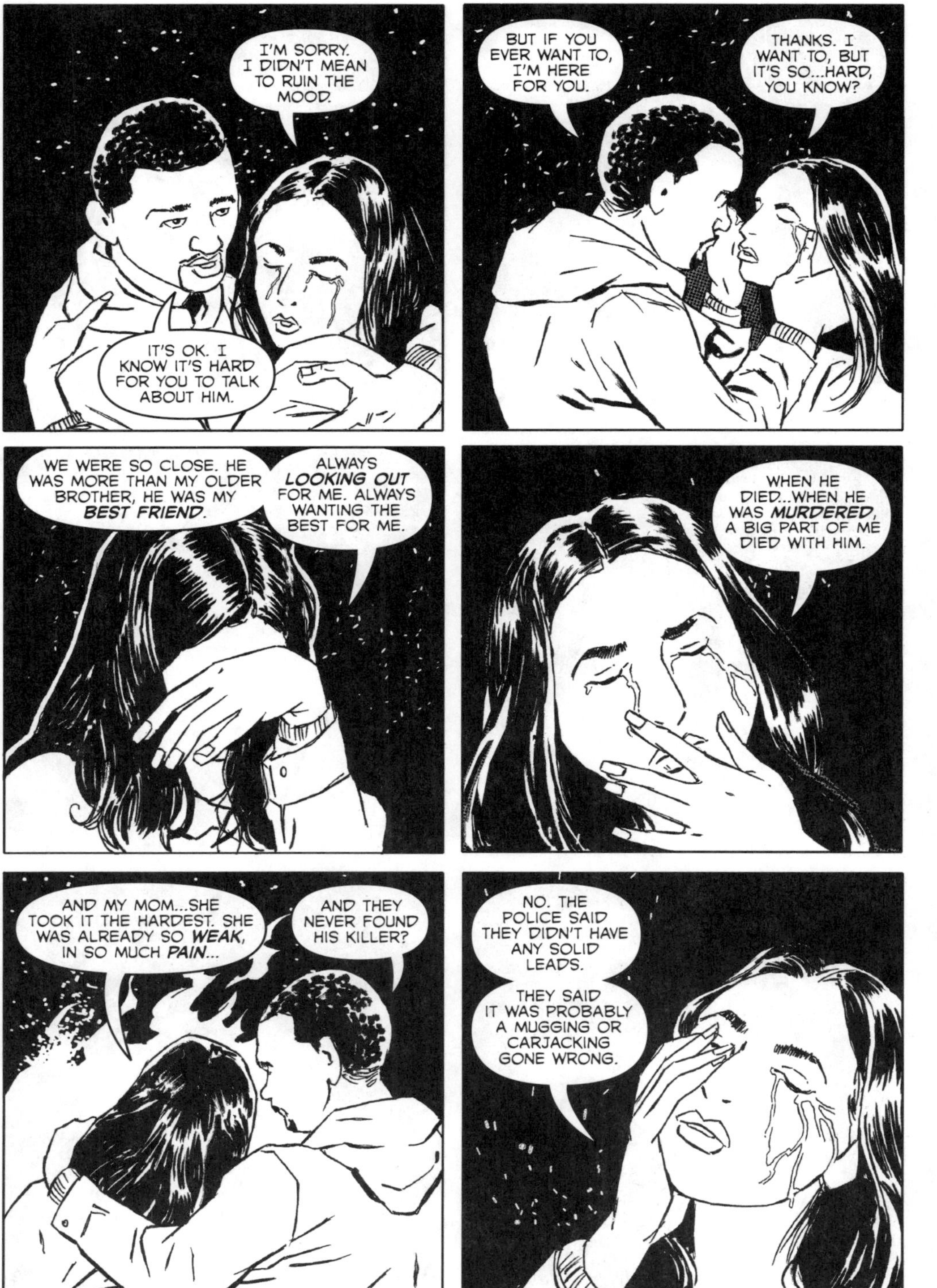
I'M SORRY. I DIDN'T MEAN TO RUIN THE MOOD.
IT'S OK. I KNOW IT'S HARD FOR YOU TO TALK ABOUT HIM.
BUT IF YOU EVER WANT TO, I'M HERE FOR YOU.
THANKS. I WANT TO, BUT IT'S SO...HARD, YOU KNOW?
WE WERE SO CLOSE. HE WAS MORE THAN MY OLDER BROTHER, HE WAS MY BEST FRIEND.
ALWAYS LOOKING OUT FOR ME. ALWAYS WANTING THE BEST FOR ME.
WHEN HE DIED...WHEN HE WAS MURDERED, A BIG PART OF ME DIED WITH HIM.
AND MY MOM...SHE TOOK IT THE HARDEST. SHE WAS ALREADY SO WEAK, IN SO MUCH PAIN...
AND THEY NEVER FOUND HIS KILLER?
NO. THE POLICE SAID THEY DIDN'T HAVE ANY SOLID LEADS.
THEY SAID IT WAS PROBABLY A MUGGING OR CARJACKING GONE WRONG.

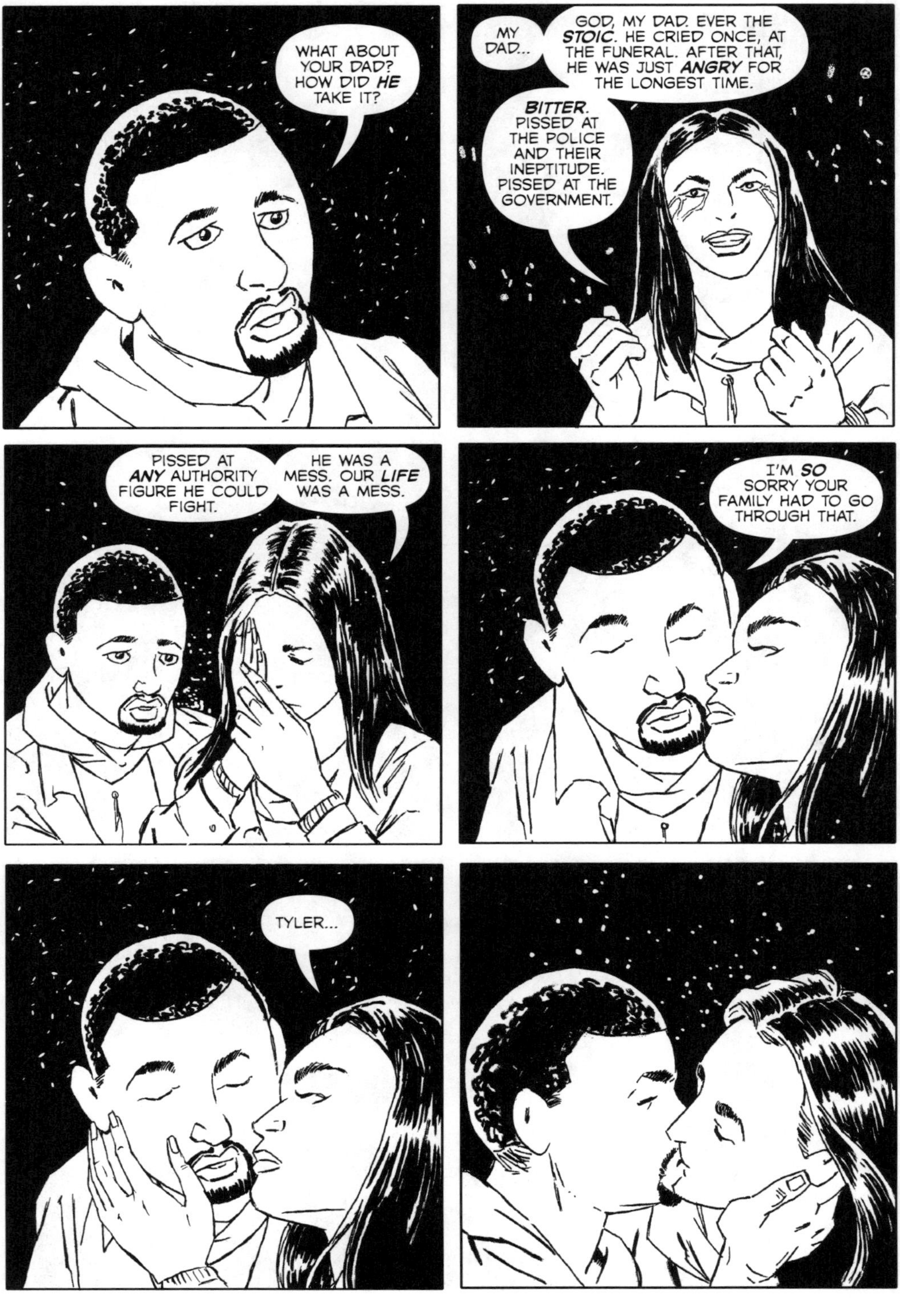
WHAT ABOUT YOUR DAD? HOW DID *HE* TAKE IT?
MY DAD...
GOD, MY DAD. EVER THE *STOIC*. HE CRIED ONCE, AT THE FUNERAL. AFTER THAT, HE WAS JUST *ANGRY* FOR THE LONGEST TIME.
BITTER. PISSED AT THE POLICE AND THEIR INEPTITUDE. PISSED AT THE GOVERNMENT.
PISSED AT *ANY* AUTHORITY FIGURE HE COULD FIGHT.
HE WAS A MESS. OUR *LIFE* WAS A MESS.
I'M *SO* SORRY YOUR FAMILY HAD TO GO THROUGH THAT.
TYLER...

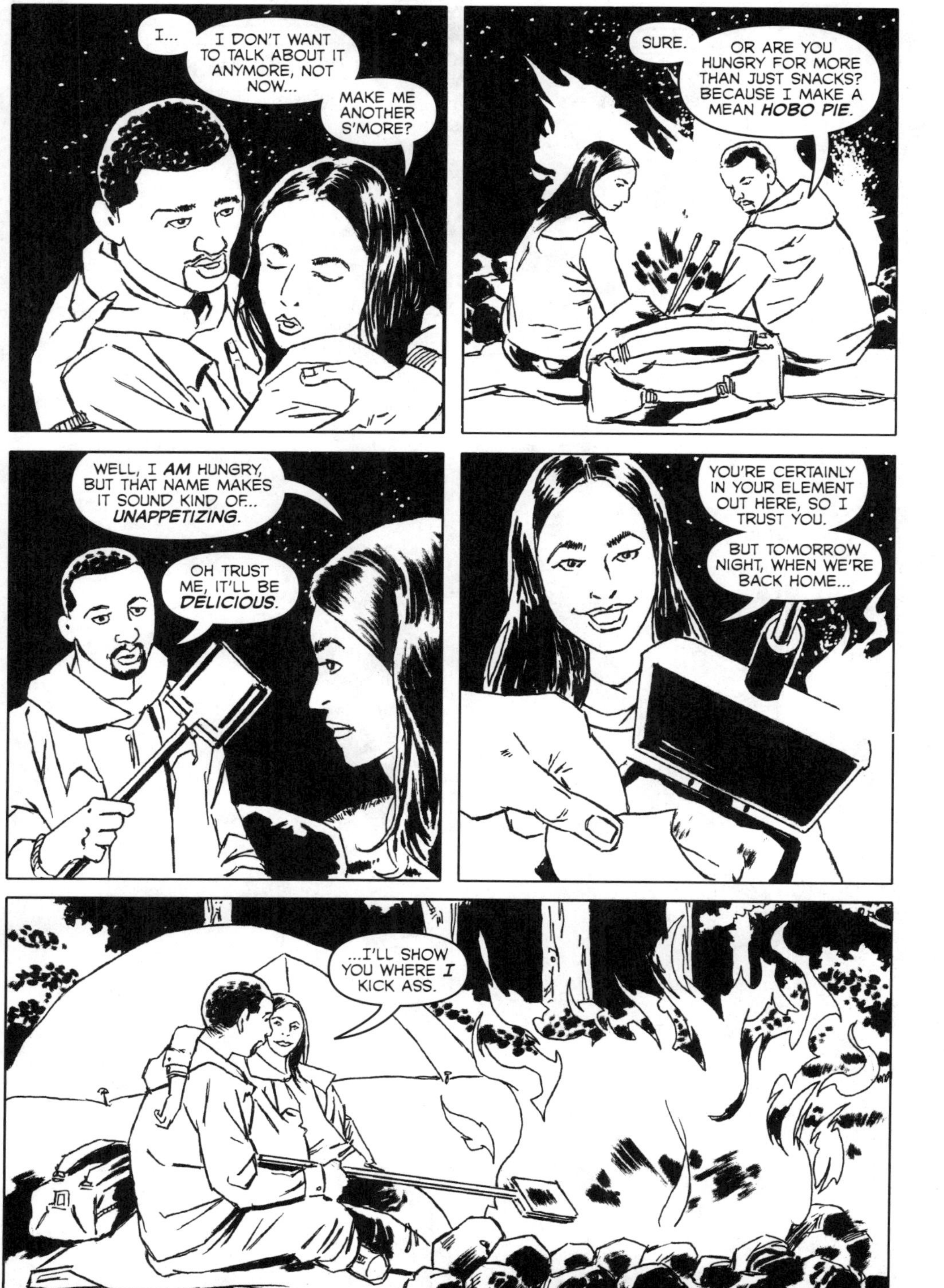
I...
I DON'T WANT TO TALK ABOUT IT ANYMORE, NOT NOW...
MAKE ME ANOTHER S'MORE?
SURE.
OR ARE YOU HUNGRY FOR MORE THAN JUST SNACKS? BECAUSE I MAKE A MEAN ***HOBO PIE***.
WELL, I ***AM*** HUNGRY, BUT THAT NAME MAKES IT SOUND KIND OF... ***UNAPPETIZING***.
OH TRUST ME, IT'LL BE ***DELICIOUS***.
YOU'RE CERTAINLY IN YOUR ELEMENT OUT HERE, SO I TRUST YOU.
BUT TOMORROW NIGHT, WHEN WE'RE BACK HOME...
...I'LL SHOW YOU WHERE ***I*** KICK ASS.

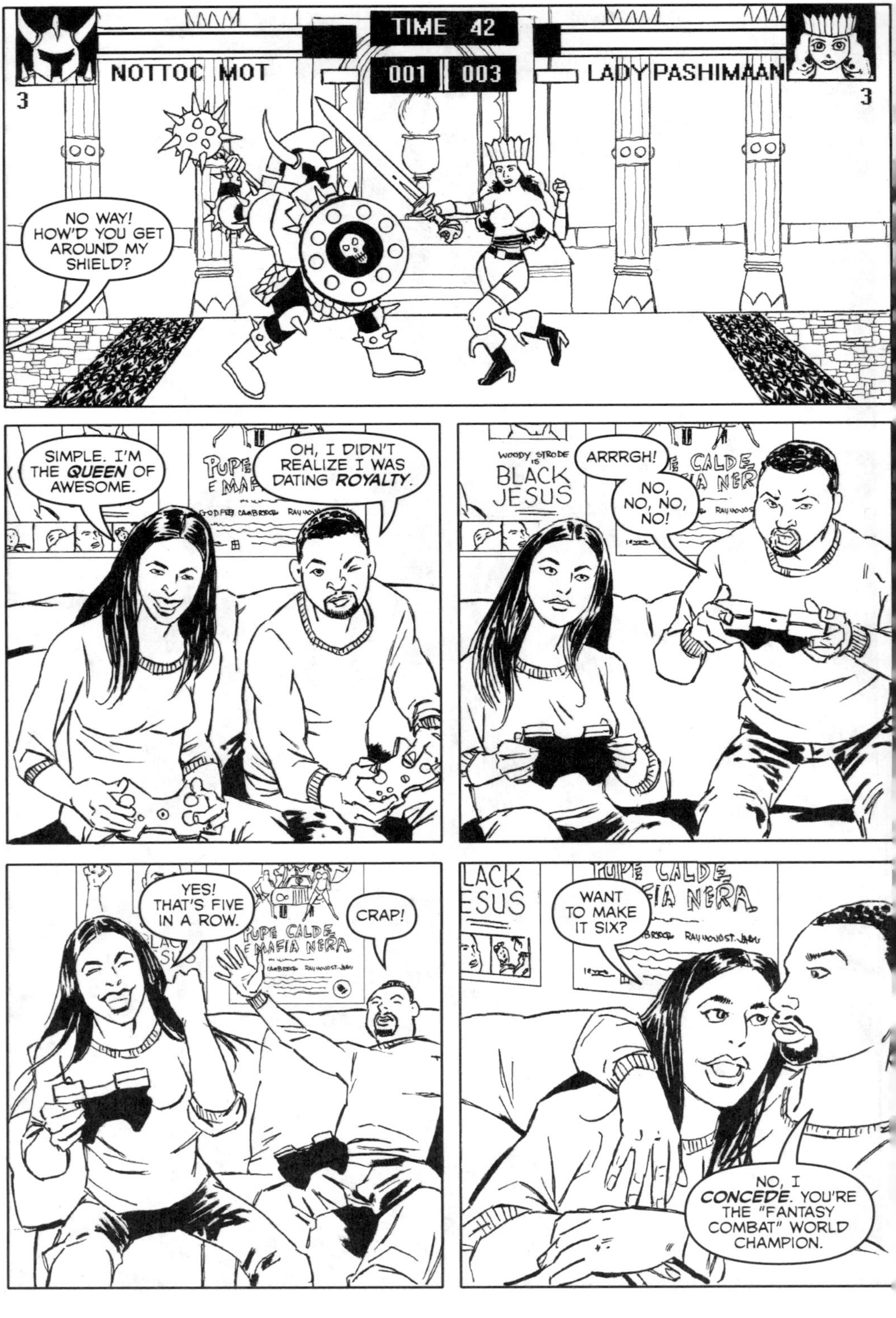
TIME 42
NOTTOC MOT
001 003
LADY PASHIMAAN
3
3
NO WAY! HOW'D YOU GET AROUND MY SHIELD?
SIMPLE. I'M THE QUEEN OF AWESOME.
OH, I DIDN'T REALIZE I WAS DATING ROYALTY.
WOODY STRODE IS BLACK JESUS
ARRRGH!
NO, NO, NO, NO!
YES! THAT'S FIVE IN A ROW.
CRAP!
PUPE CALDE E MAFIA NERA
WANT TO MAKE IT SIX?
NO, I CONCEDE. YOU'RE THE "FANTASY COMBAT" WORLD CHAMPION.

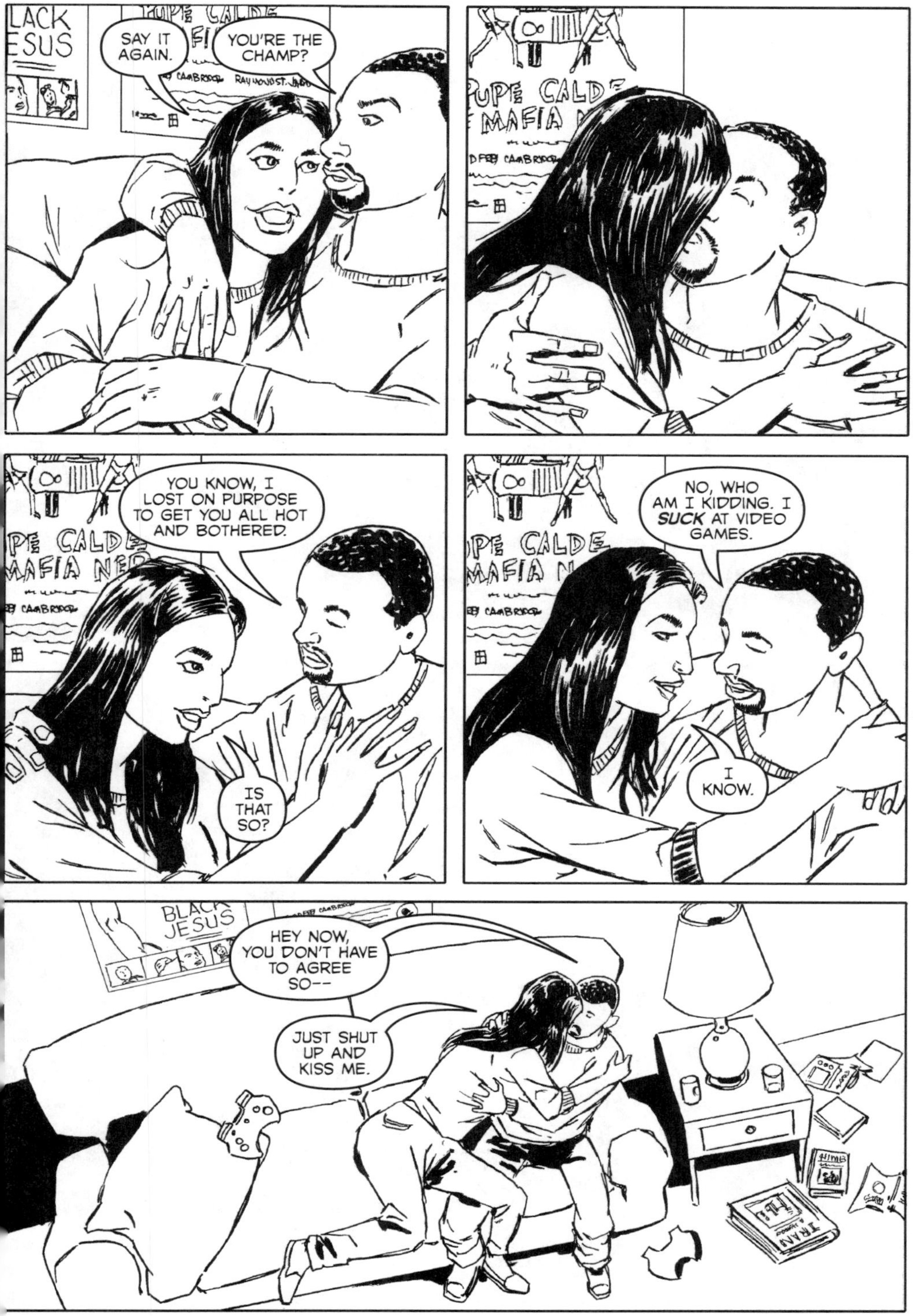
BLACK JESUS
SAY IT AGAIN.
YOU'RE THE CHAMP?
YOU KNOW, I LOST ON PURPOSE TO GET YOU ALL HOT AND BOTHERED.
IS THAT SO?
NO, WHO AM I KIDDING. I *SUCK* AT VIDEO GAMES.
I KNOW.
BLACK JESUS
HEY NOW, YOU DON'T HAVE TO AGREE SO--
JUST SHUT UP AND KISS ME.

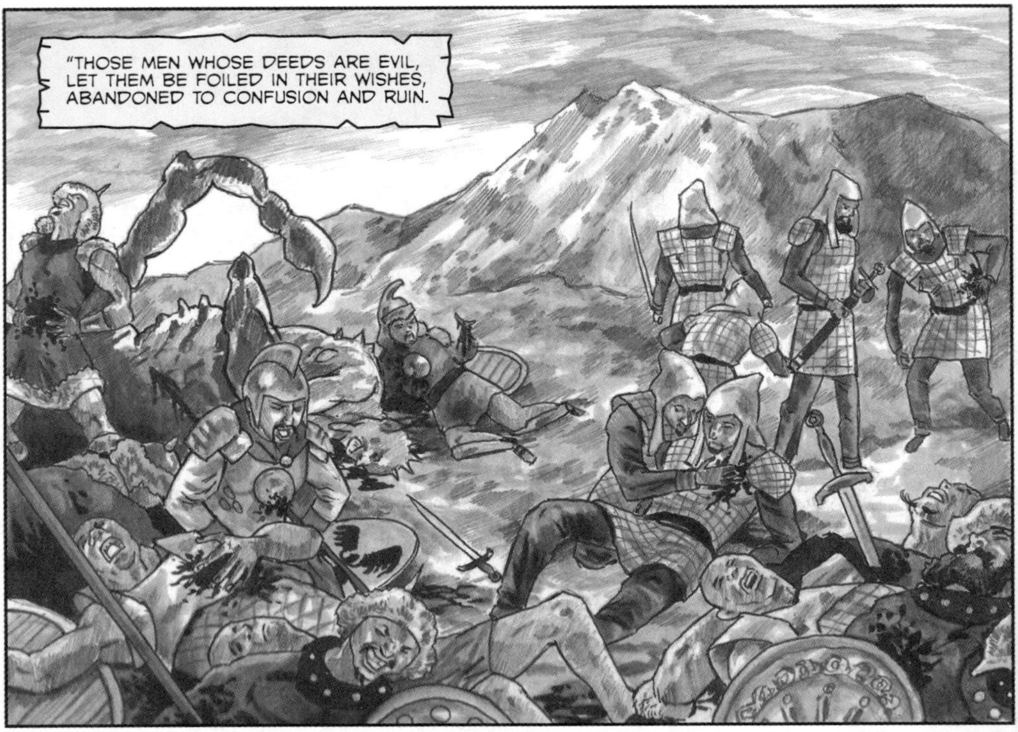
"THOSE MEN WHOSE DEEDS ARE EVIL, LET THEM BE FOILED IN THEIR WISHES, ABANDONED TO CONFUSION AND RUIN.

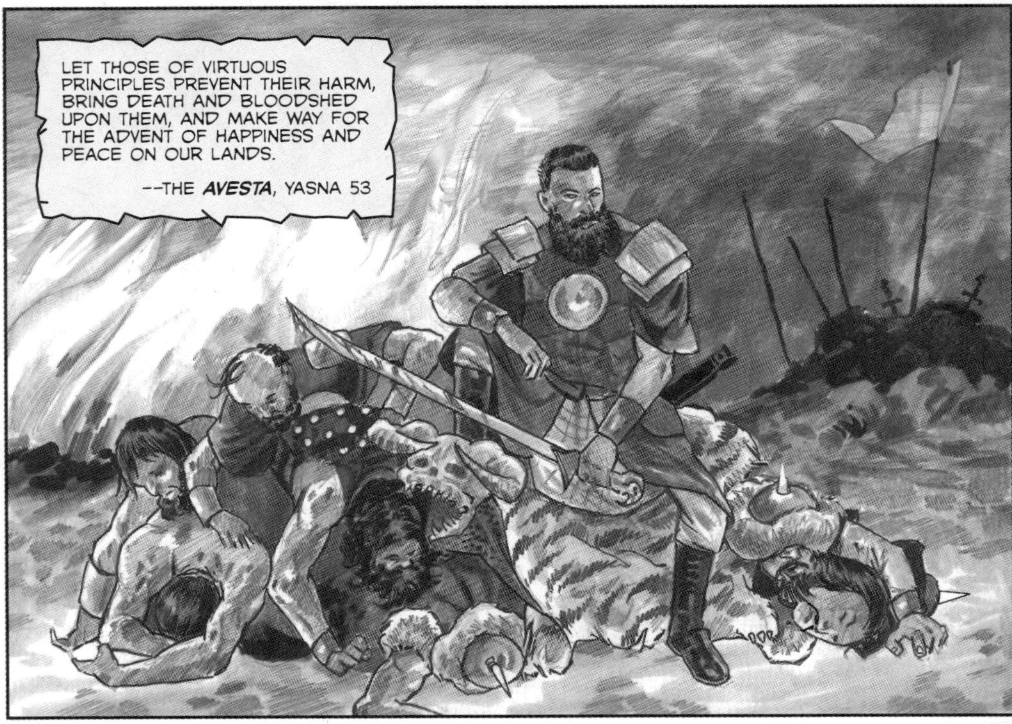
LET THOSE OF VIRTUOUS PRINCIPLES PREVENT THEIR HARM, BRING DEATH AND BLOODSHED UPON THEM, AND MAKE WAY FOR THE ADVENT OF HAPPINESS AND PEACE ON OUR LANDS.
--THE AVESTA, YASNA 53

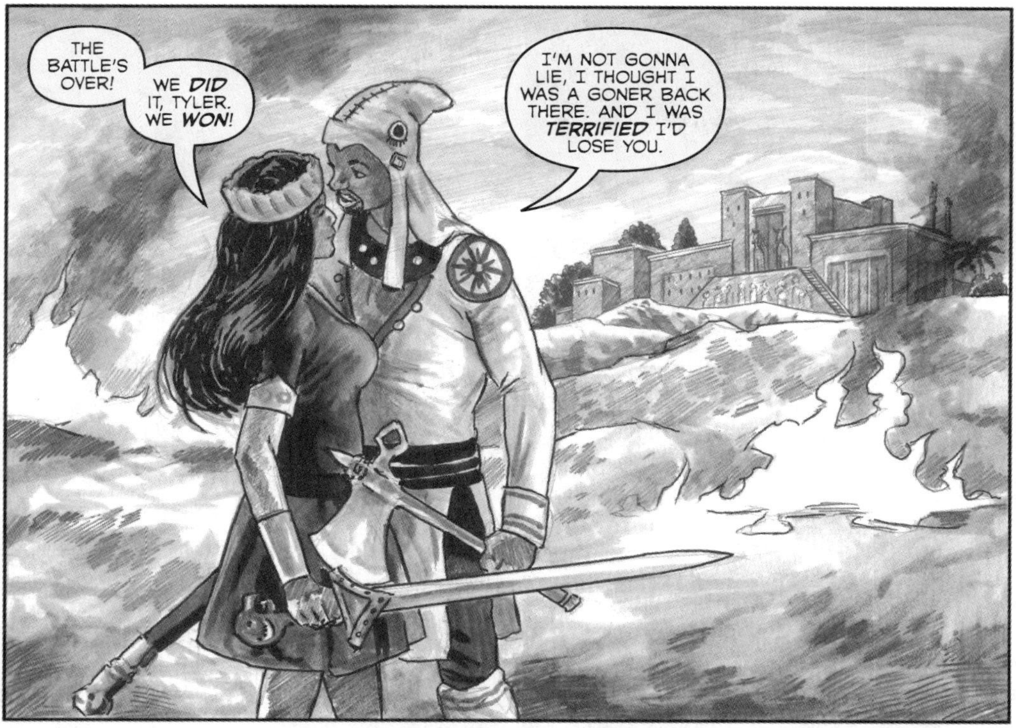
THE BATTLE'S OVER!
WE DID IT, TYLER. WE WON!
I'M NOT GONNA LIE, I THOUGHT I WAS A GONER BACK THERE. AND I WAS TERRIFIED I'D LOSE YOU.

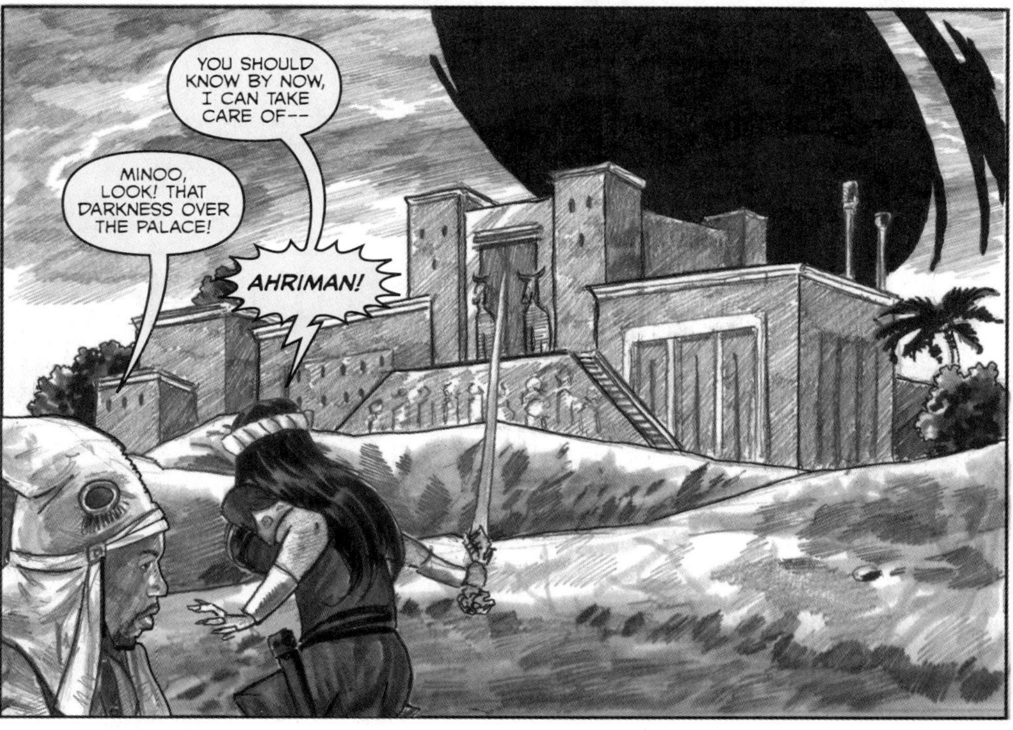
YOU SHOULD KNOW BY NOW, I CAN TAKE CARE OF--
MINOO, LOOK! THAT DARKNESS OVER THE PALACE!
AHRIMAN!

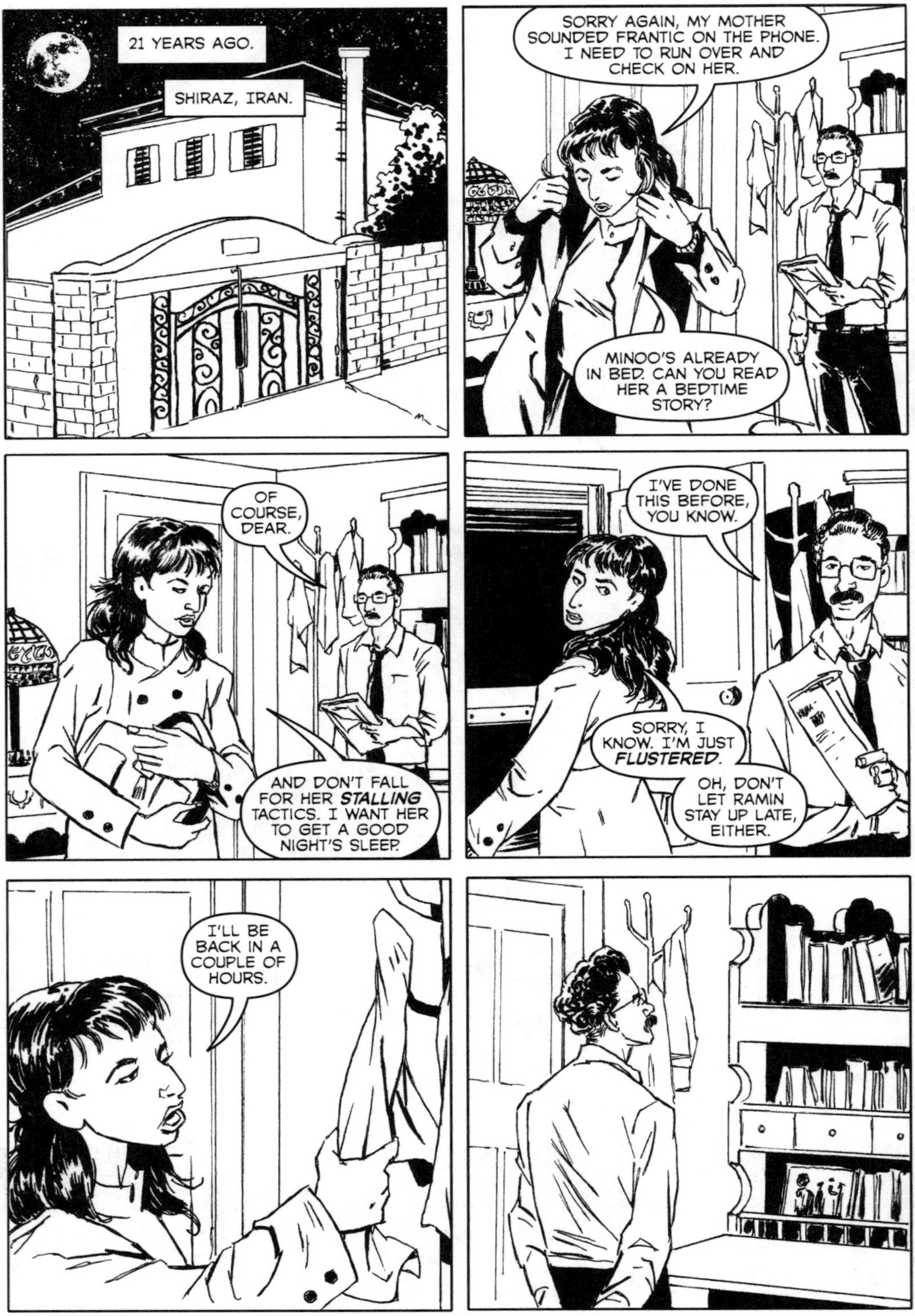
21 YEARS AGO.
SHIRAZ, IRAN.
SORRY AGAIN, MY MOTHER SOUNDED FRANTIC ON THE PHONE. I NEED TO RUN OVER AND CHECK ON HER.
MINOO'S ALREADY IN BED. CAN YOU READ HER A BEDTIME STORY?
OF COURSE, DEAR.
AND DON'T FALL FOR HER STALLING TACTICS. I WANT HER TO GET A GOOD NIGHT'S SLEEP.
I'VE DONE THIS BEFORE, YOU KNOW.
SORRY, I KNOW. I'M JUST FLUSTERED.
OH, DON'T LET RAMIN STAY UP LATE, EITHER.
I'LL BE BACK IN A COUPLE OF HOURS.

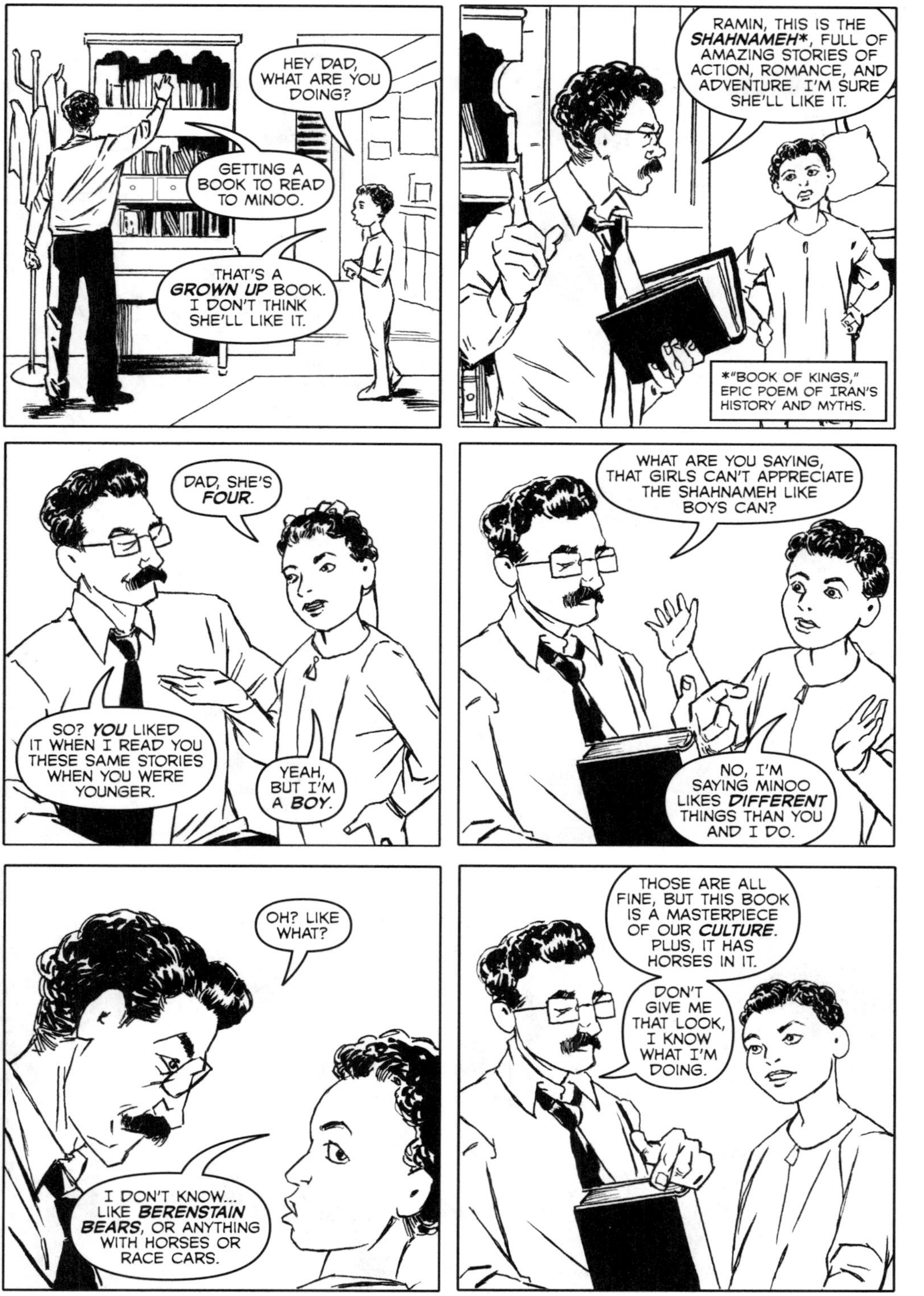
HEY DAD, WHAT ARE YOU DOING?
GETTING A BOOK TO READ TO MINOO.
THAT'S A **GROWN UP** BOOK. I DON'T THINK SHE'LL LIKE IT.
RAMIN, THIS IS THE **SHAHNAMEH***, FULL OF AMAZING STORIES OF ACTION, ROMANCE, AND ADVENTURE. I'M SURE SHE'LL LIKE IT.
*"BOOK OF KINGS," EPIC POEM OF IRAN'S HISTORY AND MYTHS.
DAD, SHE'S **FOUR**.
SO? **YOU** LIKED IT WHEN I READ YOU THESE SAME STORIES WHEN YOU WERE YOUNGER.
YEAH, BUT I'M A **BOY**.
WHAT ARE YOU SAYING, THAT GIRLS CAN'T APPRECIATE THE SHAHNAMEH LIKE BOYS CAN?
NO, I'M SAYING MINOO LIKES **DIFFERENT** THINGS THAN YOU AND I DO.
OH? LIKE WHAT?
I DON'T KNOW... LIKE **BERENSTAIN BEARS**, OR ANYTHING WITH HORSES OR RACE CARS.
THOSE ARE ALL FINE, BUT THIS BOOK IS A MASTERPIECE OF OUR **CULTURE**. PLUS, IT HAS HORSES IN IT.
DON'T GIVE ME THAT LOOK, I KNOW WHAT I'M DOING.

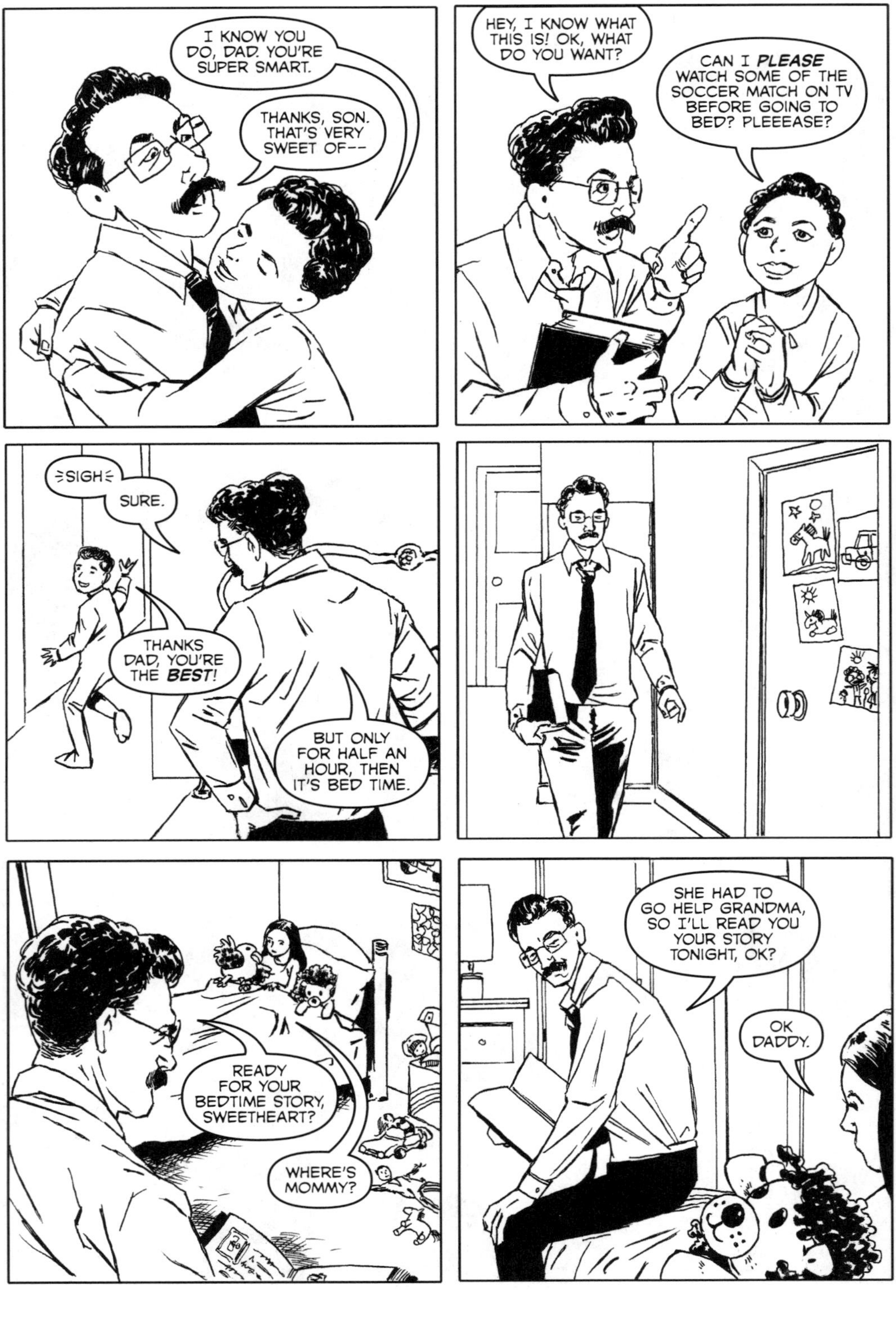
I KNOW YOU DO, DAD. YOU'RE SUPER SMART.
THANKS, SON. THAT'S VERY SWEET OF--
HEY, I KNOW WHAT THIS IS! OK, WHAT DO YOU WANT?
CAN I *PLEASE* WATCH SOME OF THE SOCCER MATCH ON TV BEFORE GOING TO BED? PLEEEASE?
SIGH
SURE.
THANKS DAD, YOU'RE THE *BEST*!
BUT ONLY FOR HALF AN HOUR, THEN IT'S BED TIME.
READY FOR YOUR BEDTIME STORY, SWEETHEART?
WHERE'S MOMMY?
SHE HAD TO GO HELP GRANDMA, SO I'LL READ YOU YOUR STORY TONIGHT, OK?
OK DADDY.

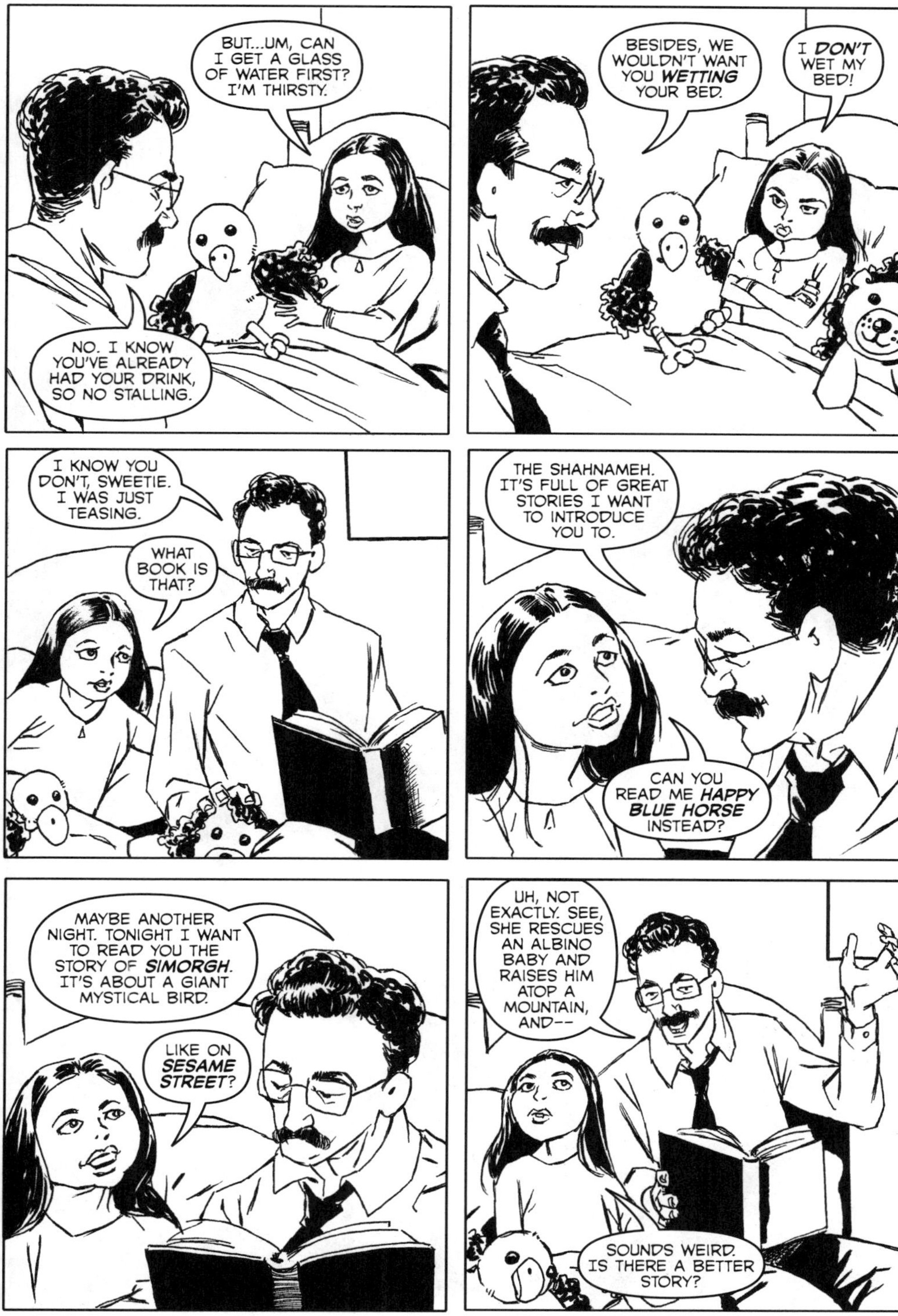
BUT...UM, CAN I GET A GLASS OF WATER FIRST? I'M THIRSTY.
NO. I KNOW YOU'VE ALREADY HAD YOUR DRINK, SO NO STALLING.
BESIDES, WE WOULDN'T WANT YOU **WETTING** YOUR BED.
I **DON'T** WET MY BED!
I KNOW YOU DON'T, SWEETIE. I WAS JUST TEASING.
WHAT BOOK IS THAT?
THE SHAHNAMEH. IT'S FULL OF GREAT STORIES I WANT TO INTRODUCE YOU TO.
CAN YOU READ ME **HAPPY BLUE HORSE** INSTEAD?
MAYBE ANOTHER NIGHT. TONIGHT I WANT TO READ YOU THE STORY OF **SIMORGH**. IT'S ABOUT A GIANT MYSTICAL BIRD.
LIKE ON **SESAME STREET**?
UH, NOT EXACTLY. SEE, SHE RESCUES AN ALBINO BABY AND RAISES HIM ATOP A MOUNTAIN, AND--
SOUNDS WEIRD. IS THERE A BETTER STORY?

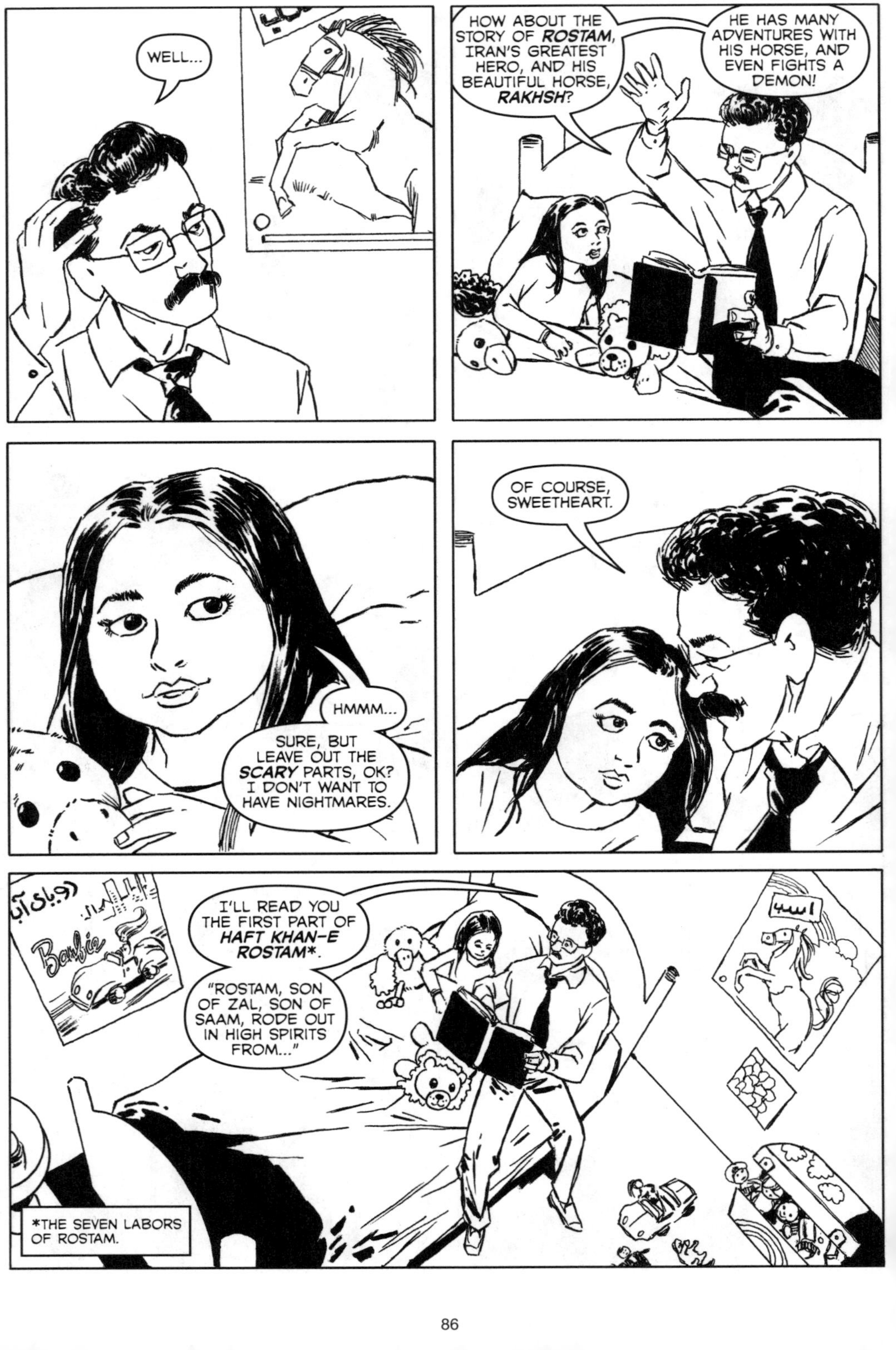
WELL...
HOW ABOUT THE STORY OF ***ROSTAM***, IRAN'S GREATEST HERO, AND HIS BEAUTIFUL HORSE, ***RAKHSH***?
HE HAS MANY ADVENTURES WITH HIS HORSE, AND EVEN FIGHTS A DEMON!
HMMM...
SURE, BUT LEAVE OUT THE ***SCARY*** PARTS, OK? I DON'T WANT TO HAVE NIGHTMARES.
OF COURSE, SWEETHEART.
I'LL READ YOU THE FIRST PART OF ***HAFT KHAN-E ROSTAM****.
"ROSTAM, SON OF ZAL, SON OF SAAM, RODE OUT IN HIGH SPIRITS FROM..."
*THE SEVEN LABORS OF ROSTAM.

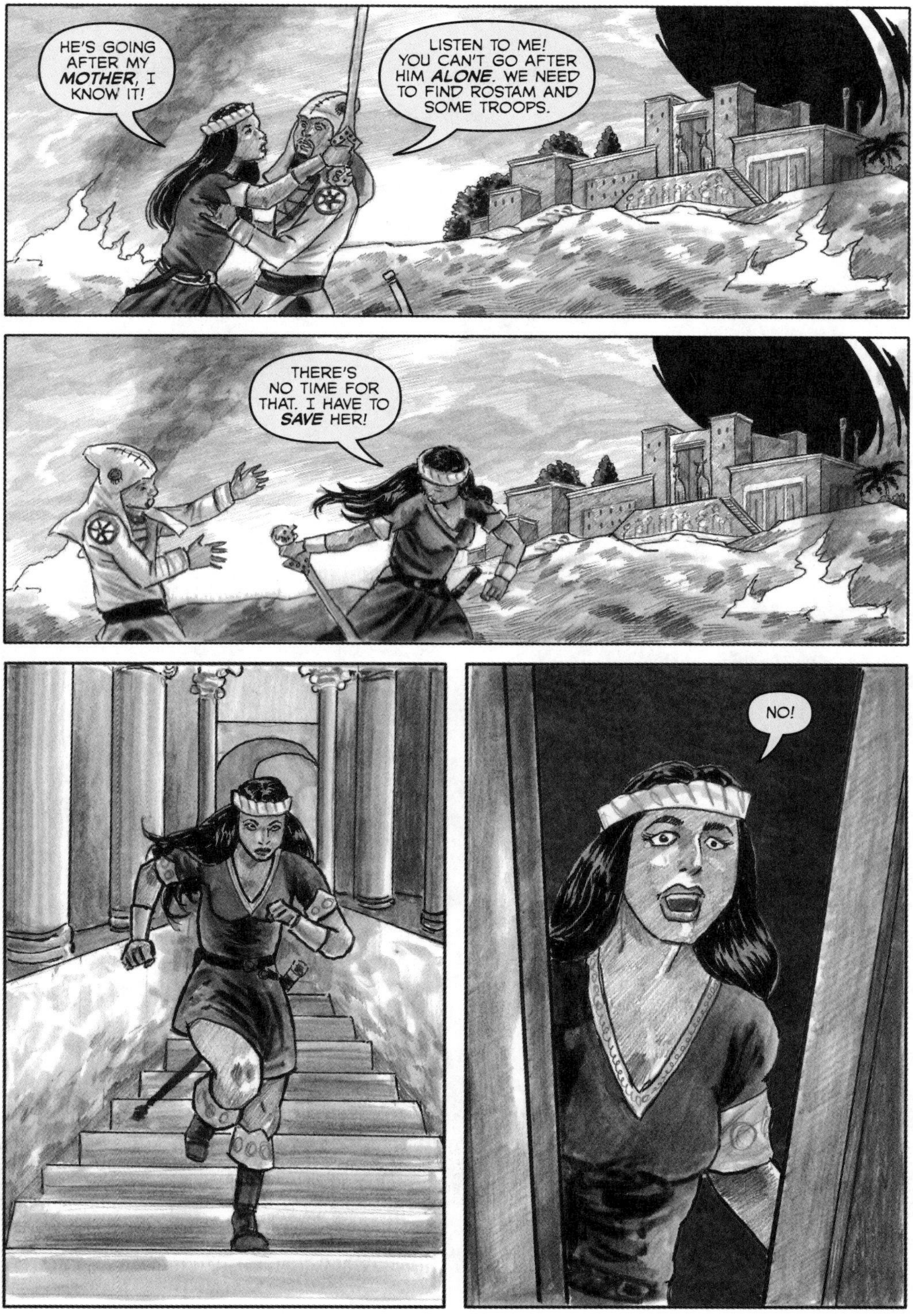
HE'S GOING AFTER MY **MOTHER**, I KNOW IT!
LISTEN TO ME! YOU CAN'T GO AFTER HIM **ALONE**. WE NEED TO FIND ROSTAM AND SOME TROOPS.
THERE'S NO TIME FOR THAT. I HAVE TO **SAVE** HER!
NO!

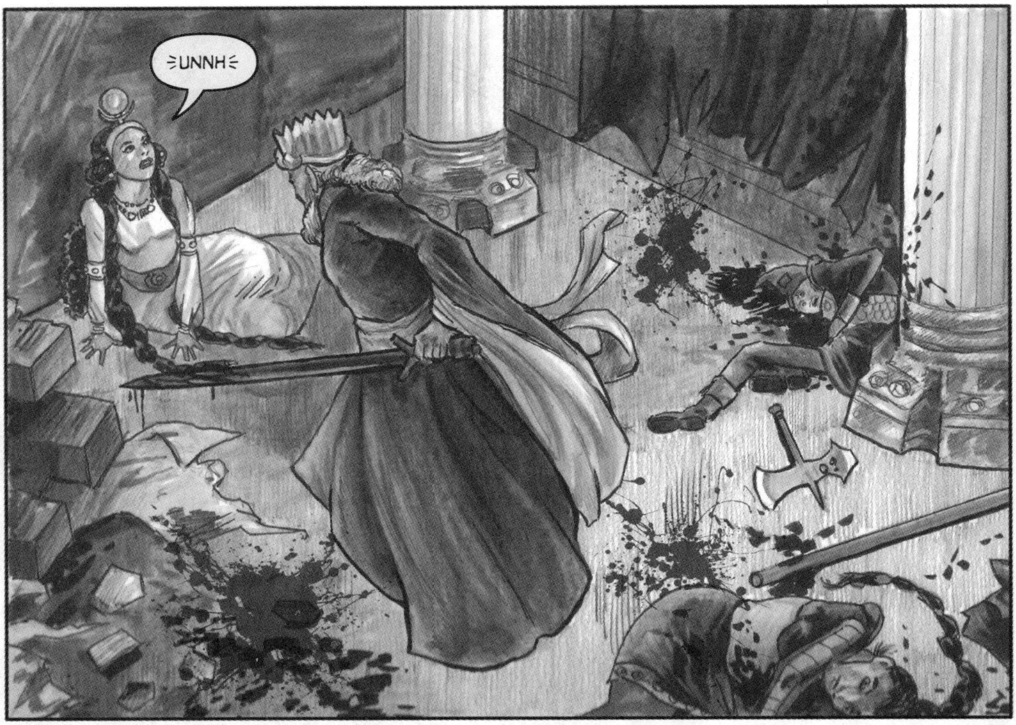
UNNH

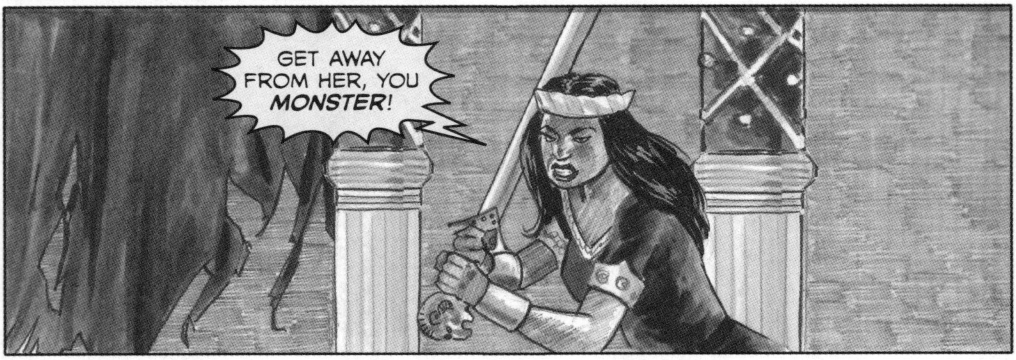
GET AWAY FROM HER, YOU *MONSTER*!

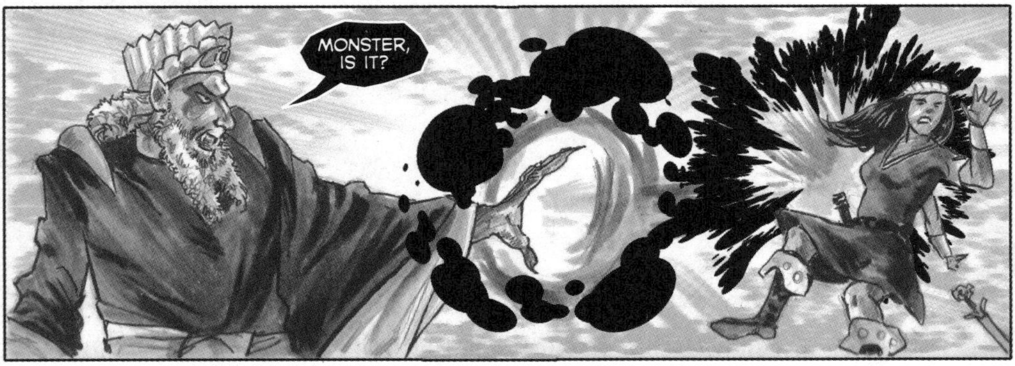
MONSTER, IS IT?

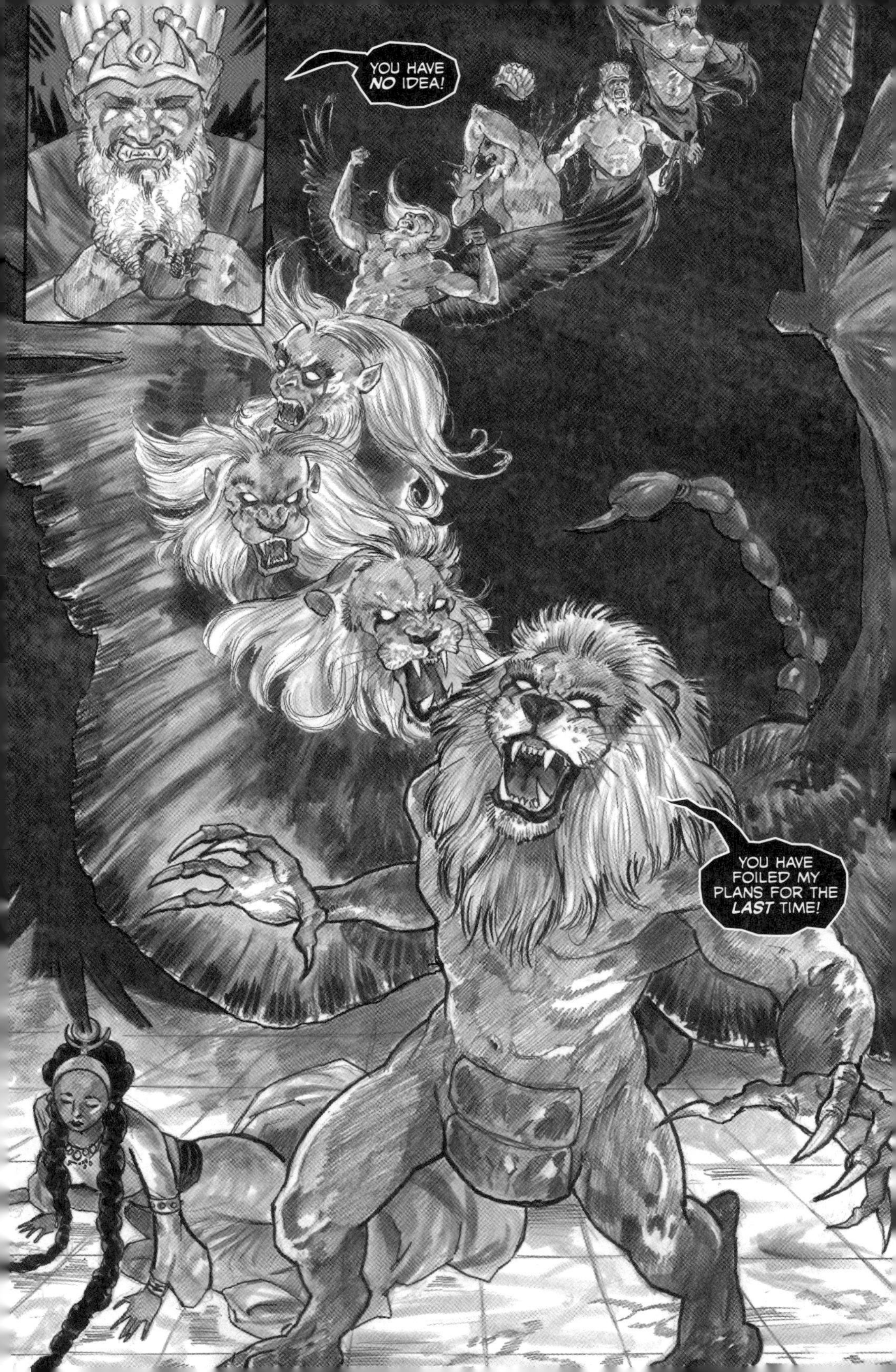
YOU HAVE NO IDEA!
YOU HAVE FOILED MY PLANS FOR THE LAST TIME!

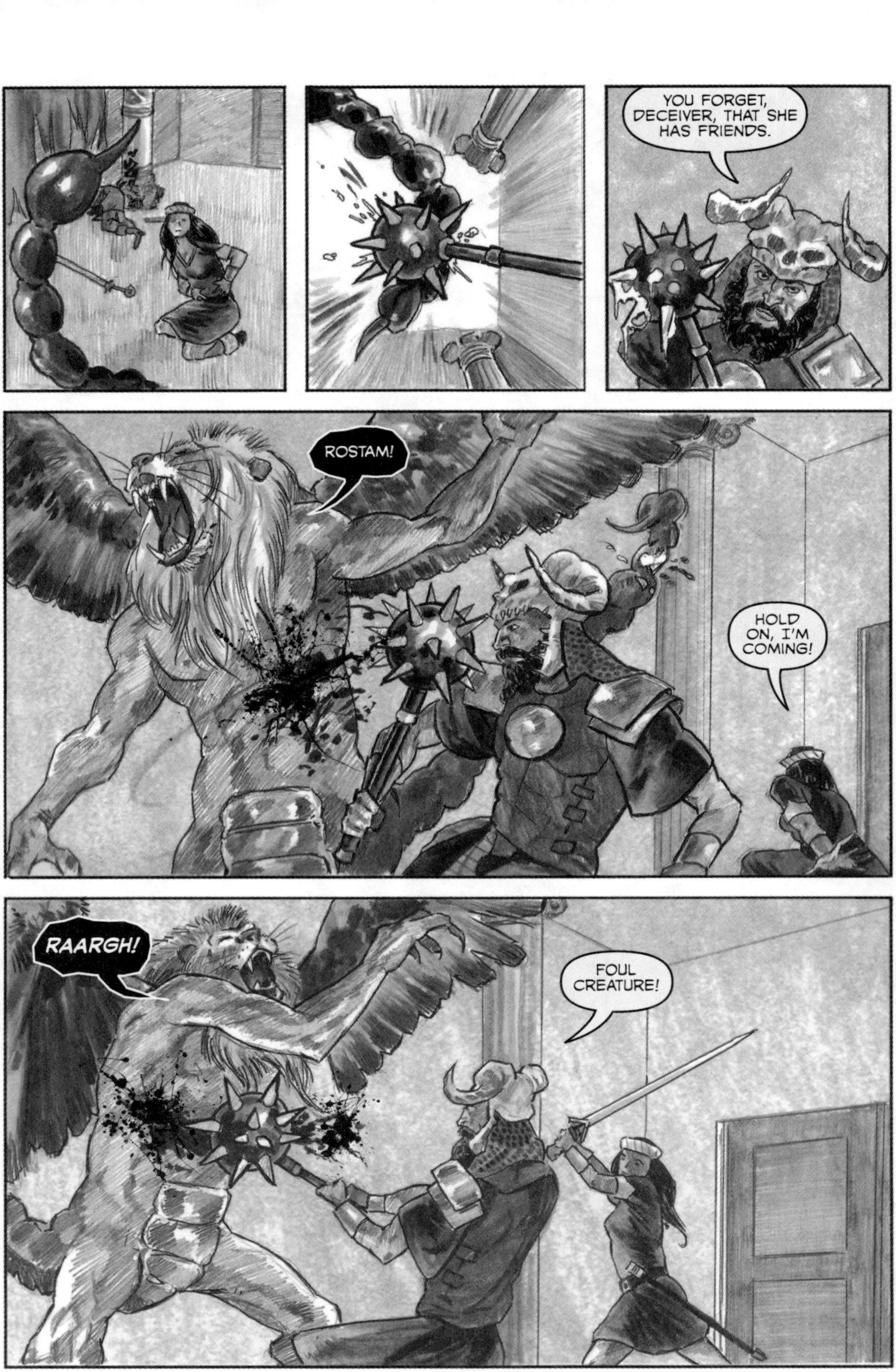
YOU FORGET, DECEIVER, THAT SHE HAS FRIENDS.
ROSTAM!
HOLD ON, I'M COMING!
RAARGH!
FOUL CREATURE!

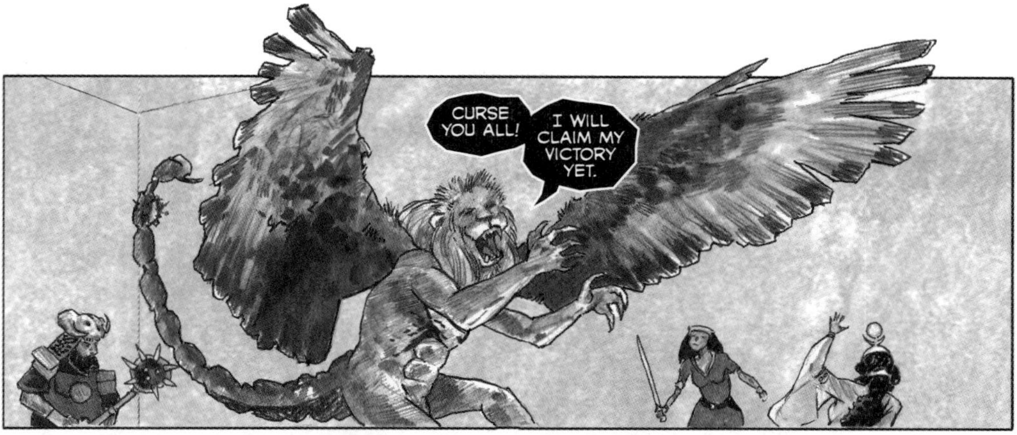
CURSE YOU ALL!
I WILL CLAIM MY VICTORY YET.

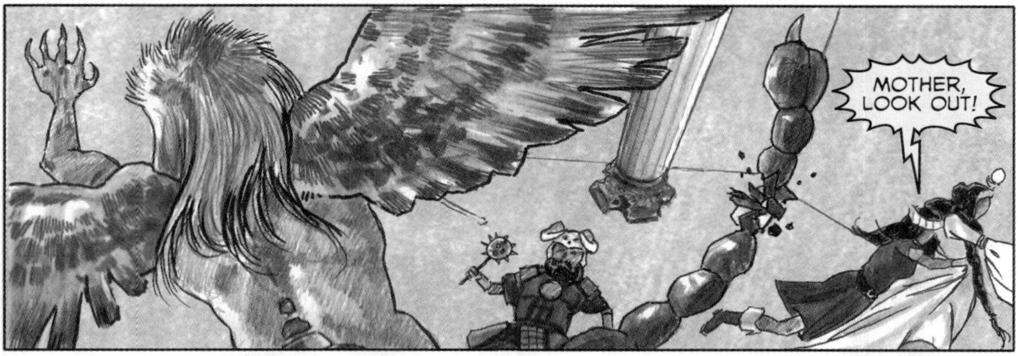
MOTHER, LOOK OUT!

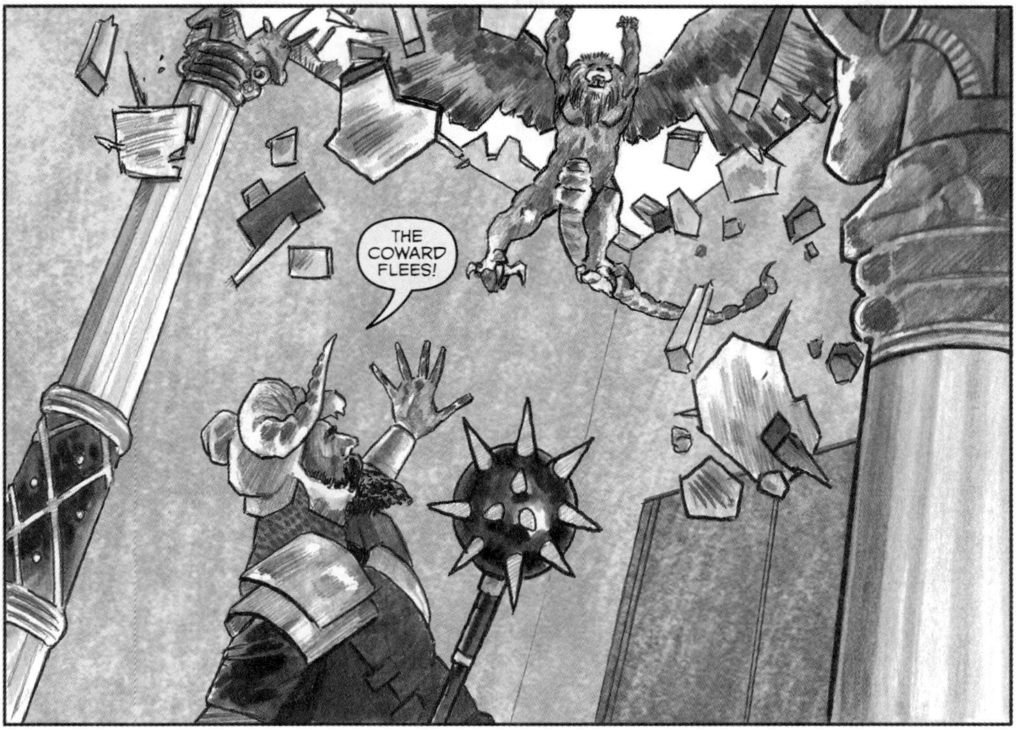
THE COWARD FLEES!

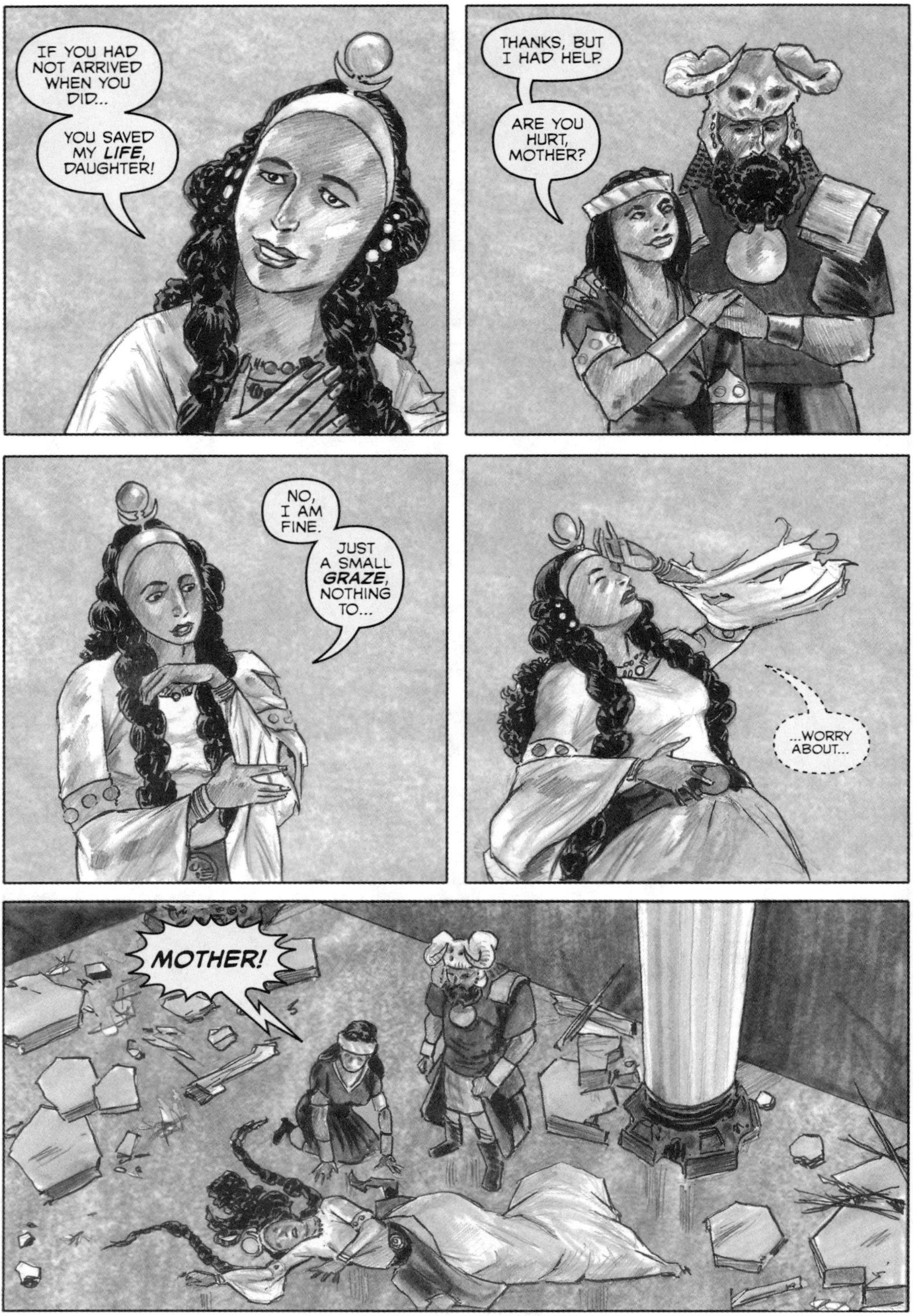
IF YOU HAD NOT ARRIVED WHEN YOU DID...
YOU SAVED MY LIFE, DAUGHTER!
THANKS, BUT I HAD HELP.
ARE YOU HURT, MOTHER?
NO, I AM FINE.
JUST A SMALL GRAZE, NOTHING TO...
...WORRY ABOUT...
MOTHER!

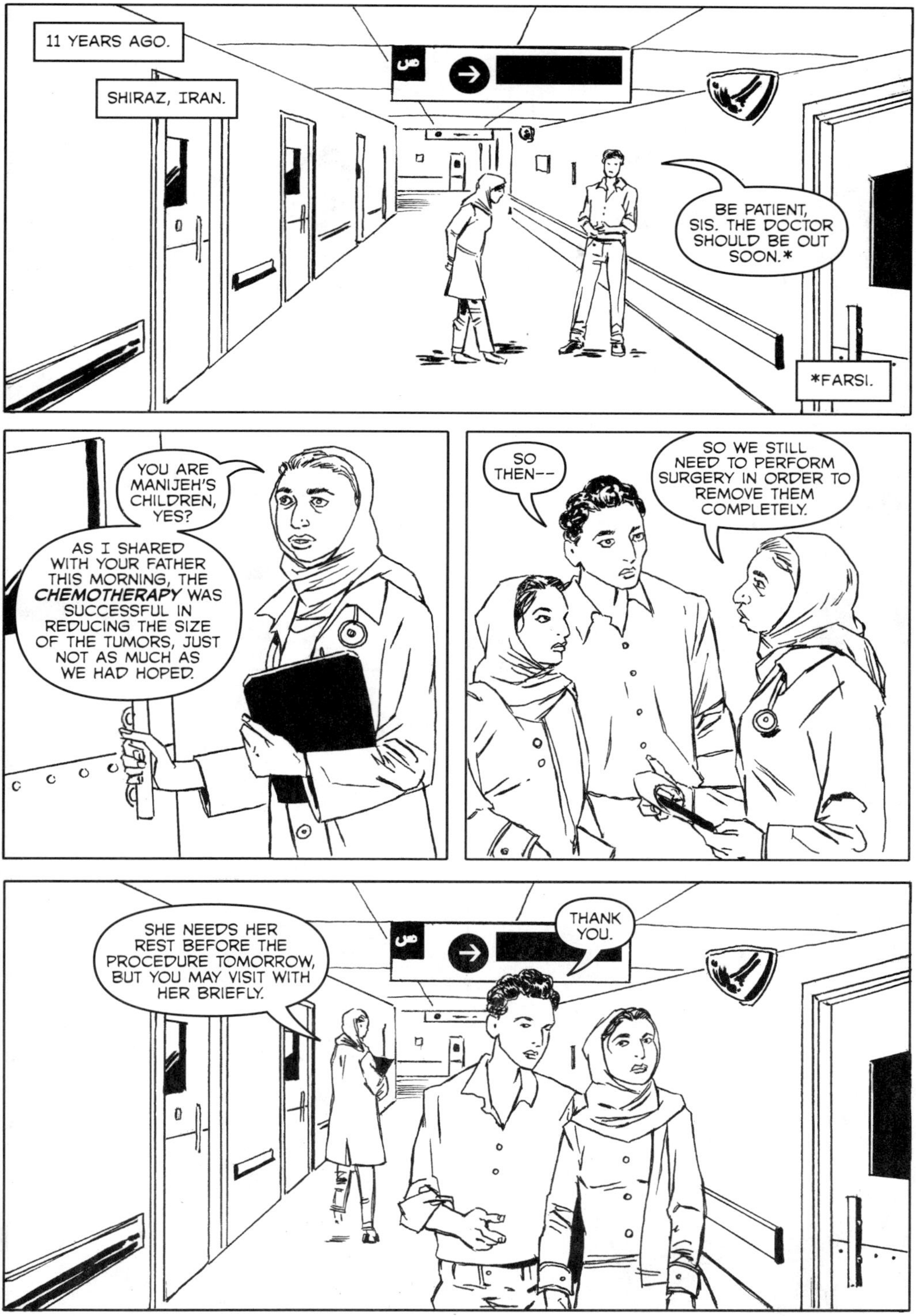
11 YEARS AGO.
SHIRAZ, IRAN.
BE PATIENT, SIS. THE DOCTOR SHOULD BE OUT SOON.*
*FARSI.
YOU ARE MANIJEH'S CHILDREN, YES?
AS I SHARED WITH YOUR FATHER THIS MORNING, THE ***CHEMOTHERAPY*** WAS SUCCESSFUL IN REDUCING THE SIZE OF THE TUMORS, JUST NOT AS MUCH AS WE HAD HOPED.
SO THEN--
SO WE STILL NEED TO PERFORM SURGERY IN ORDER TO REMOVE THEM COMPLETELY.
SHE NEEDS HER REST BEFORE THE PROCEDURE TOMORROW, BUT YOU MAY VISIT WITH HER BRIEFLY.
THANK YOU.

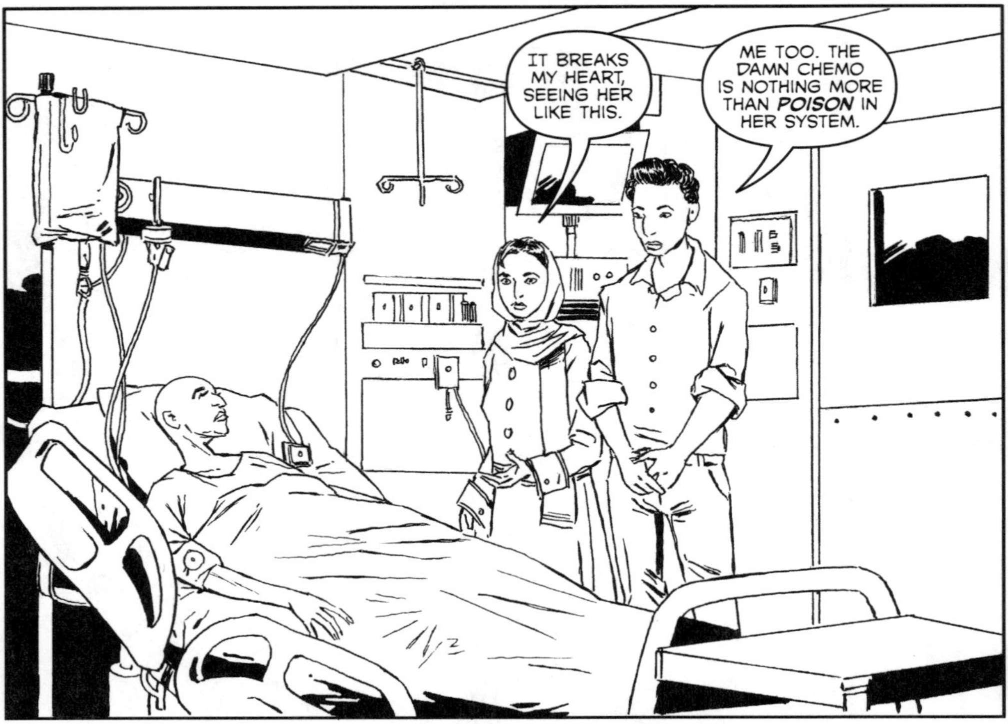
IT BREAKS MY HEART, SEEING HER LIKE THIS.
ME TOO. THE DAMN CHEMO IS NOTHING MORE THAN **POISON** IN HER SYSTEM.

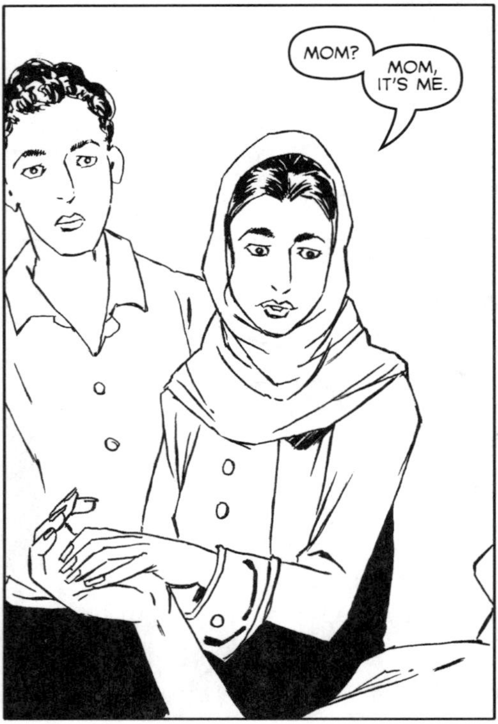
MOM?
MOM, IT'S ME.

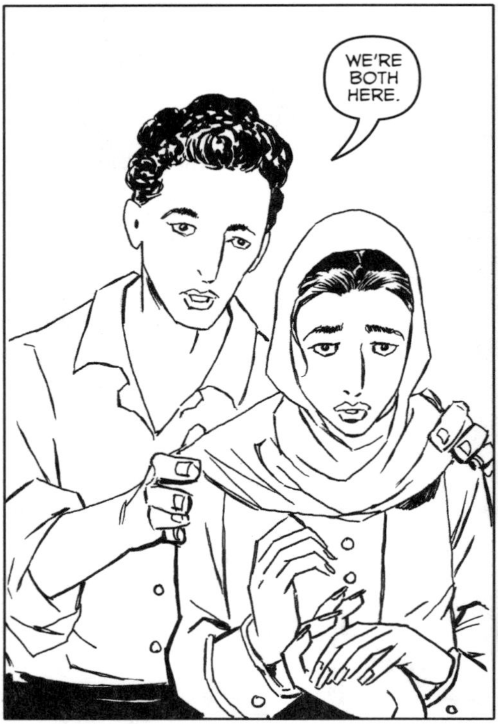
WE'RE BOTH HERE.

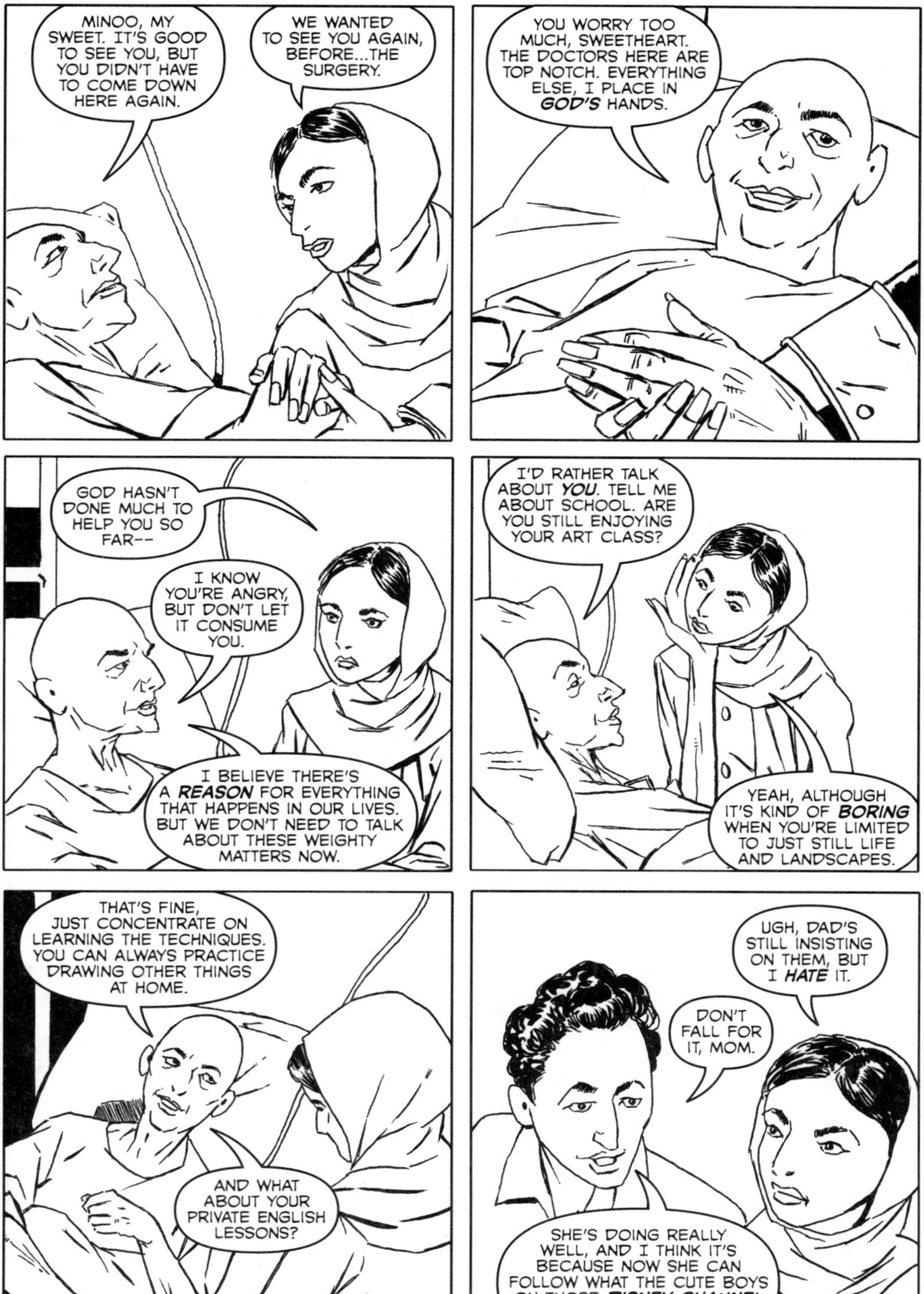
MINOO, MY SWEET. IT'S GOOD TO SEE YOU, BUT YOU DIDN'T HAVE TO COME DOWN HERE AGAIN.
WE WANTED TO SEE YOU AGAIN, BEFORE...THE SURGERY.
YOU WORRY TOO MUCH, SWEETHEART. THE DOCTORS HERE ARE TOP NOTCH. EVERYTHING ELSE, I PLACE IN ***GOD'S*** HANDS.
GOD HASN'T DONE MUCH TO HELP YOU SO FAR--
I KNOW YOU'RE ANGRY, BUT DON'T LET IT CONSUME YOU.
I BELIEVE THERE'S A ***REASON*** FOR EVERYTHING THAT HAPPENS IN OUR LIVES. BUT WE DON'T NEED TO TALK ABOUT THESE WEIGHTY MATTERS NOW.
I'D RATHER TALK ABOUT ***YOU***. TELL ME ABOUT SCHOOL. ARE YOU STILL ENJOYING YOUR ART CLASS?
YEAH, ALTHOUGH IT'S KIND OF ***BORING*** WHEN YOU'RE LIMITED TO JUST STILL LIFE AND LANDSCAPES.
THAT'S FINE, JUST CONCENTRATE ON LEARNING THE TECHNIQUES. YOU CAN ALWAYS PRACTICE DRAWING OTHER THINGS AT HOME.
AND WHAT ABOUT YOUR PRIVATE ENGLISH LESSONS?
UGH, DAD'S STILL INSISTING ON THEM, BUT I ***HATE*** IT.
DON'T FALL FOR IT, MOM.
SHE'S DOING REALLY WELL, AND I THINK IT'S BECAUSE NOW SHE CAN FOLLOW WHAT THE CUTE BOYS ON THOSE ***DISNEY CHANNEL*** SHOWS ARE SAYING.

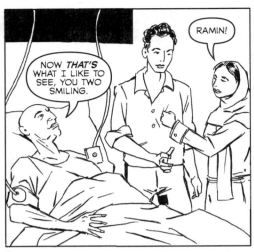

NOW *THAT'S* WHAT I LIKE TO SEE, YOU TWO SMILING.

RAMIN!

AND WHAT ABOUT YOU, SWEETHEART? HOW'S SOCCER?

GREAT, MOM. I HAVE A GOOD SHOT AT MAKING ONE OF THE AMATEUR CLUBS.

I'M GLAD.

I KNOW THESE PAST FEW MONTHS HAVE BEEN REALLY DIFFICULT FOR YOU GUYS, WITH ME IN AND OUT OF THE HOSPITAL, AND YOU HAVING TO MOVE BACK IN WITH YOUR DAD.

BUT I HOPE YOU REALIZE HOW MUCH HE *LOVES* YOU BOTH, AND IS DOING HIS BEST, GIVEN THE CIRCUMSTANCES.

WELL, HE--

WE KNOW, MOM. DON'T *WORRY* ABOUT US.

YOU JUST WORK ON GETTING BETTER.

I'VE BEEN BLESSED WITH THE TWO *BEST* CHILDREN.

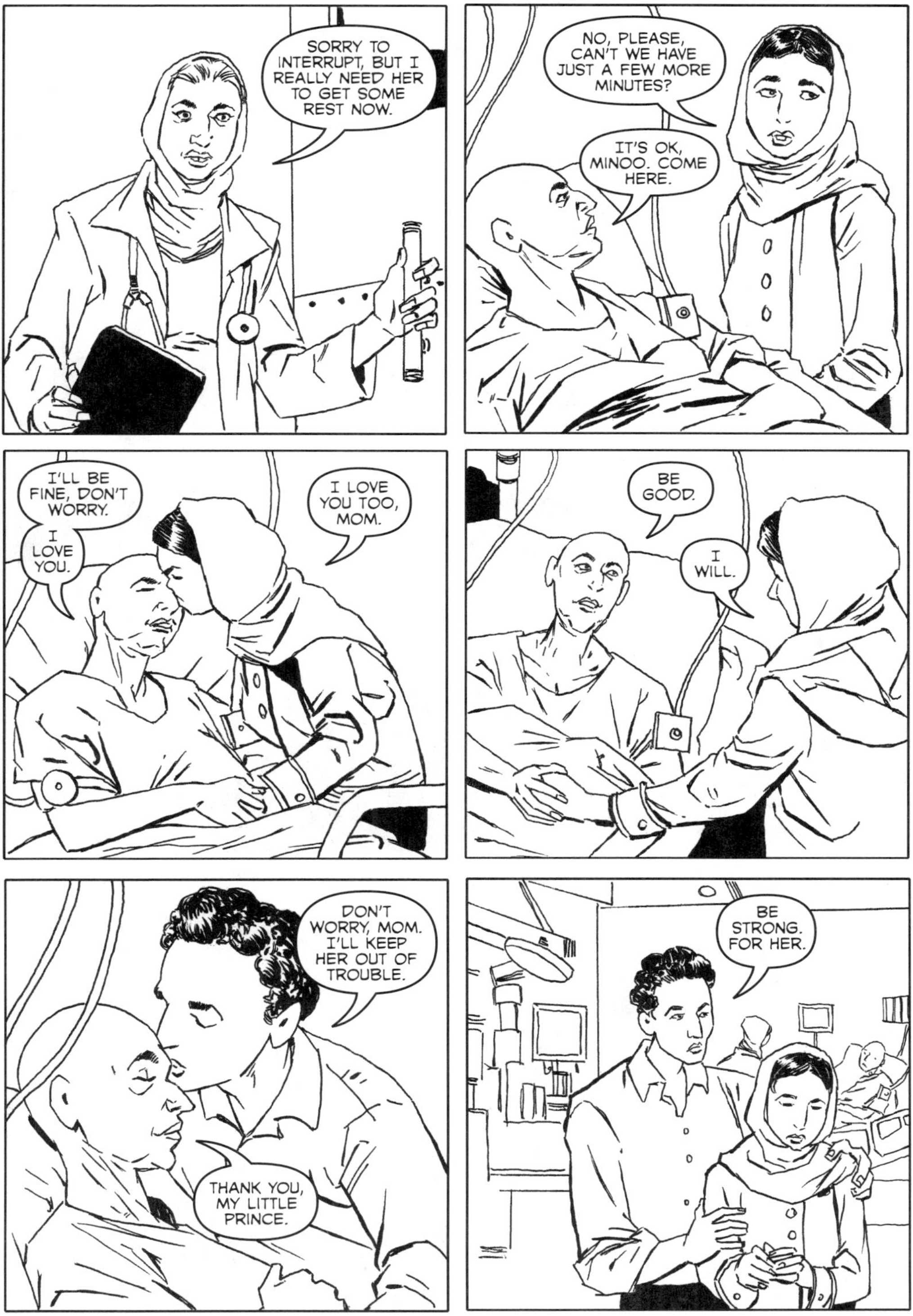
SORRY TO INTERRUPT, BUT I REALLY NEED HER TO GET SOME REST NOW.
NO, PLEASE, CAN'T WE HAVE JUST A FEW MORE MINUTES?
IT'S OK, MINOO. COME HERE.
I'LL BE FINE, DON'T WORRY.
I LOVE YOU.
I LOVE YOU TOO, MOM.
BE GOOD.
I WILL.
DON'T WORRY, MOM. I'LL KEEP HER OUT OF TROUBLE.
THANK YOU, MY LITTLE PRINCE.
BE STRONG. FOR HER.

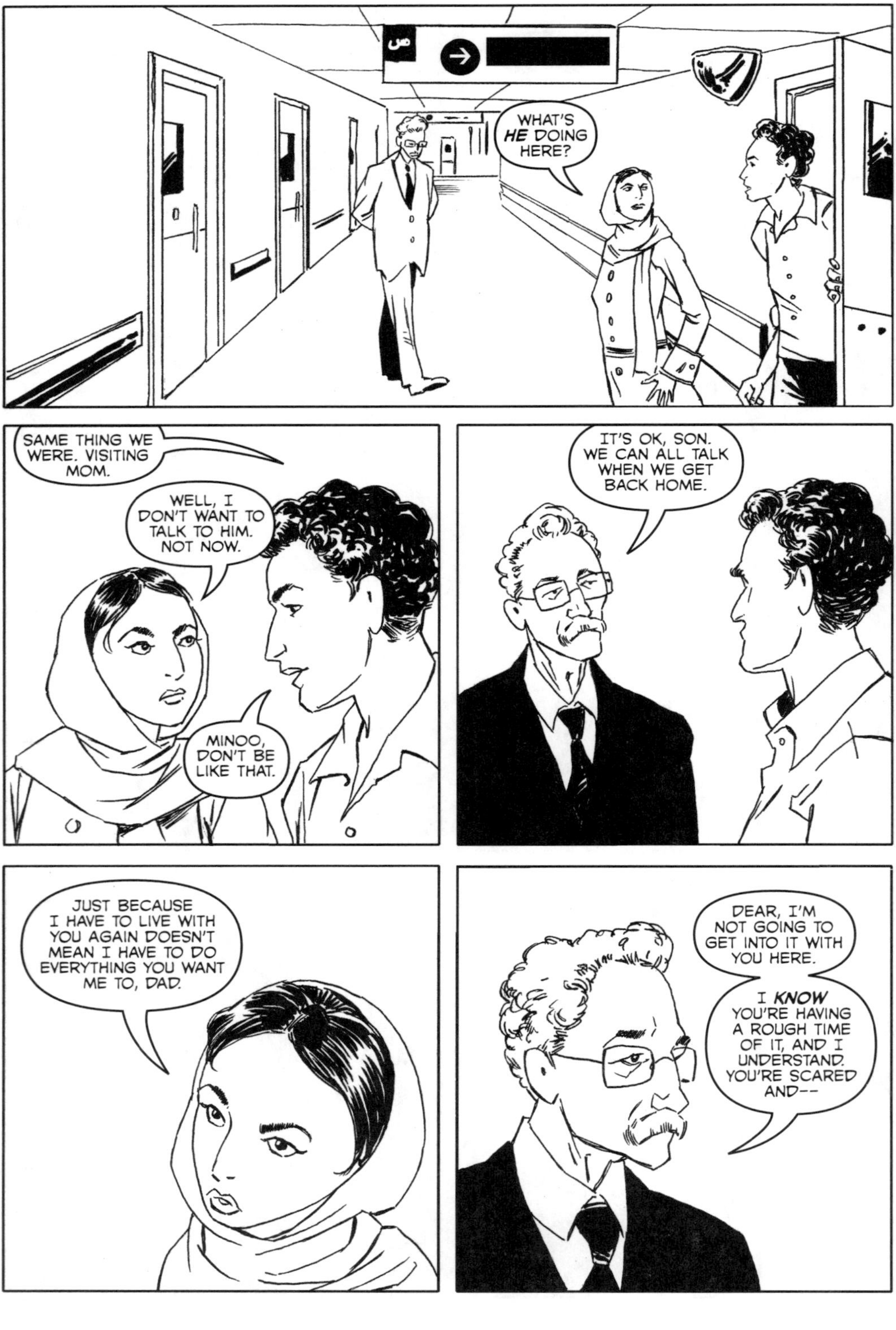
WHAT'S *HE* DOING HERE?
SAME THING WE WERE. VISITING MOM.
WELL, I DON'T WANT TO TALK TO HIM. NOT NOW.
MINOO, DON'T BE LIKE THAT.
IT'S OK, SON. WE CAN ALL TALK WHEN WE GET BACK HOME.
JUST BECAUSE I HAVE TO LIVE WITH YOU AGAIN DOESN'T MEAN I HAVE TO DO EVERYTHING YOU WANT ME TO, DAD.
DEAR, I'M NOT GOING TO GET INTO IT WITH YOU HERE.
I *KNOW* YOU'RE HAVING A ROUGH TIME OF IT, AND I UNDERSTAND. YOU'RE SCARED AND--

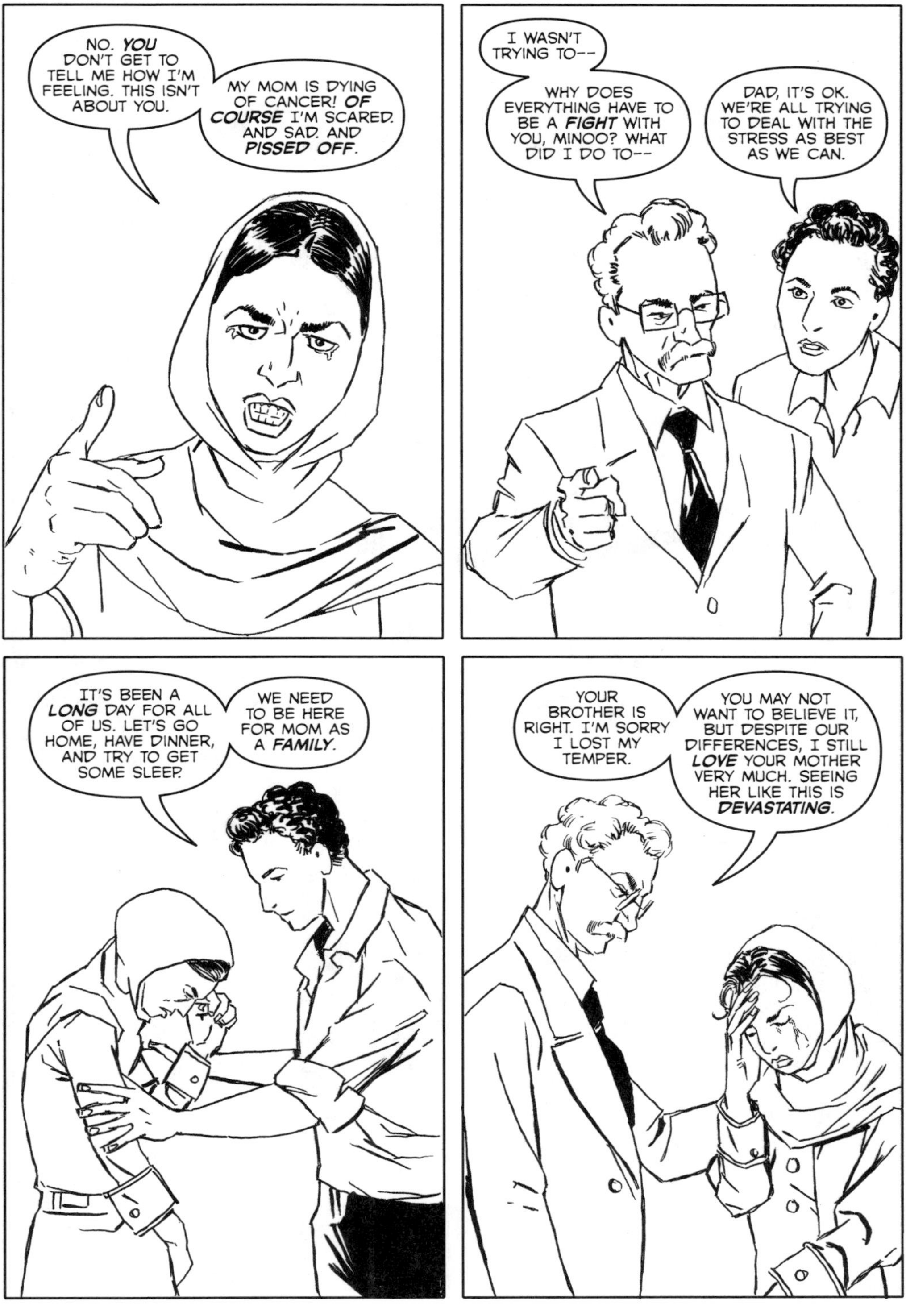
NO. YOU DON'T GET TO TELL ME HOW I'M FEELING. THIS ISN'T ABOUT YOU.
MY MOM IS DYING OF CANCER! OF COURSE I'M SCARED. AND SAD. AND PISSED OFF.
I WASN'T TRYING TO--
WHY DOES EVERYTHING HAVE TO BE A FIGHT WITH YOU, MINOO? WHAT DID I DO TO--
DAD, IT'S OK. WE'RE ALL TRYING TO DEAL WITH THE STRESS AS BEST AS WE CAN.
IT'S BEEN A LONG DAY FOR ALL OF US. LET'S GO HOME, HAVE DINNER, AND TRY TO GET SOME SLEEP.
WE NEED TO BE HERE FOR MOM AS A FAMILY.
YOUR BROTHER IS RIGHT. I'M SORRY I LOST MY TEMPER.
YOU MAY NOT WANT TO BELIEVE IT, BUT DESPITE OUR DIFFERENCES, I STILL LOVE YOUR MOTHER VERY MUCH. SEEING HER LIKE THIS IS DEVASTATING.

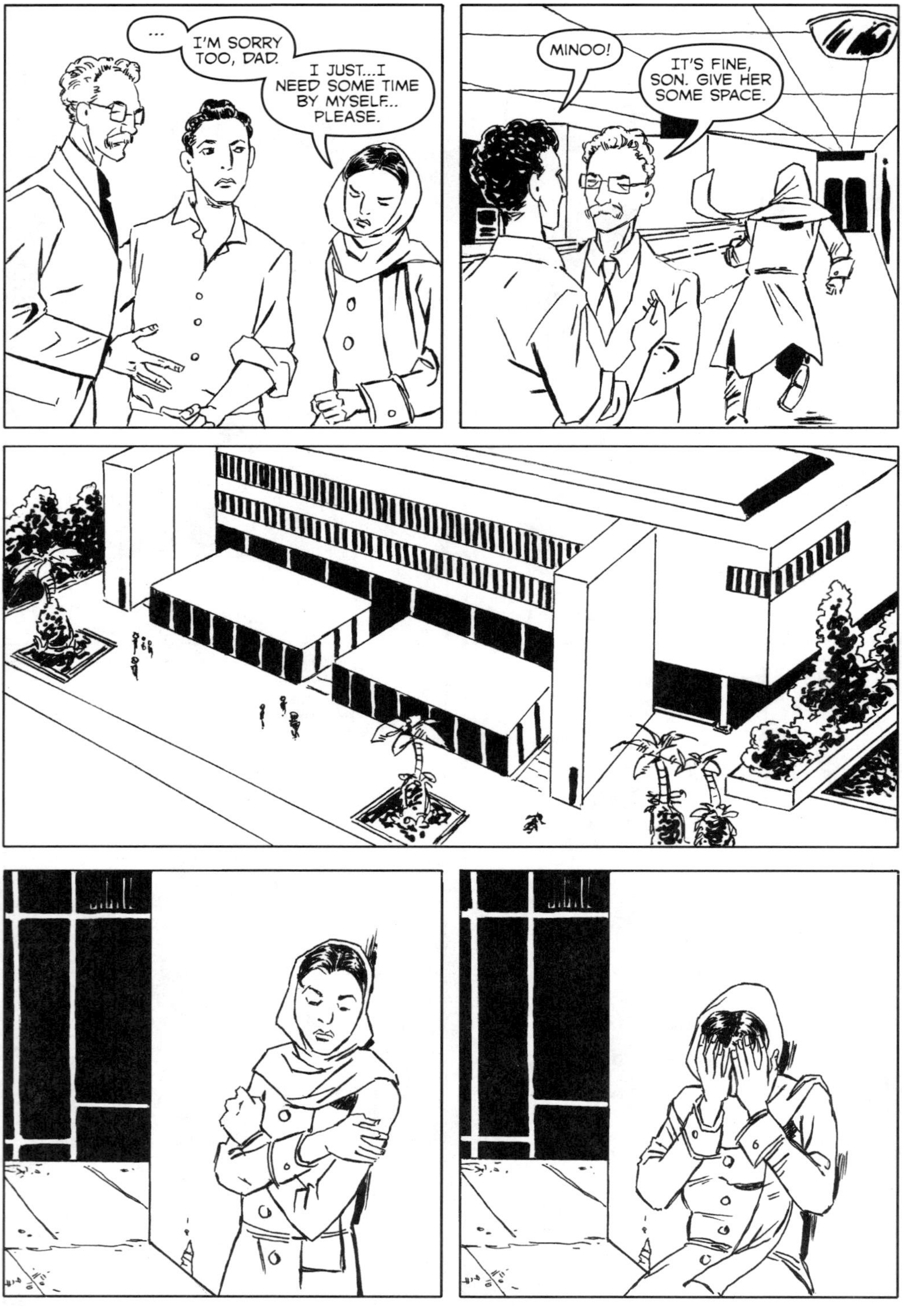
...
I'M SORRY TOO, DAD.
I JUST...I NEED SOME TIME BY MYSELF... PLEASE.
MINOO!
IT'S FINE, SON. GIVE HER SOME SPACE.

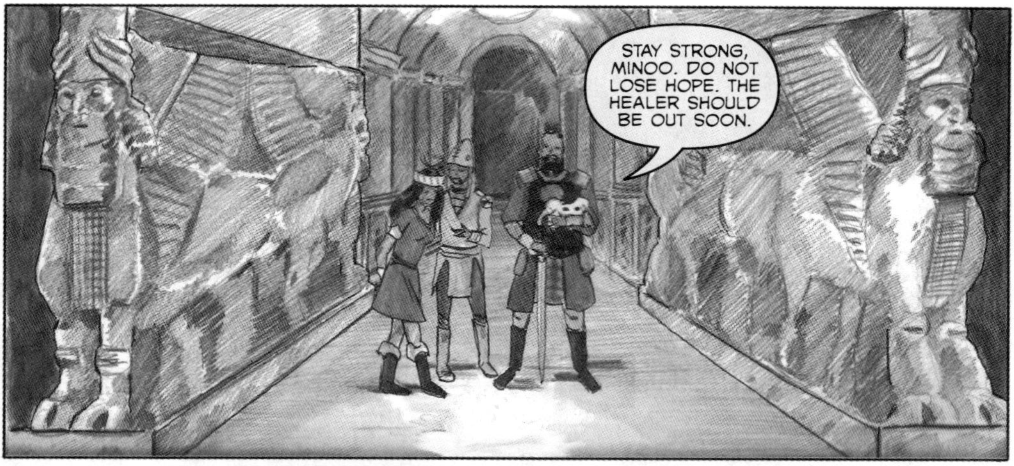
STAY STRONG, MINOO. DO NOT LOSE HOPE. THE HEALER SHOULD BE OUT SOON.

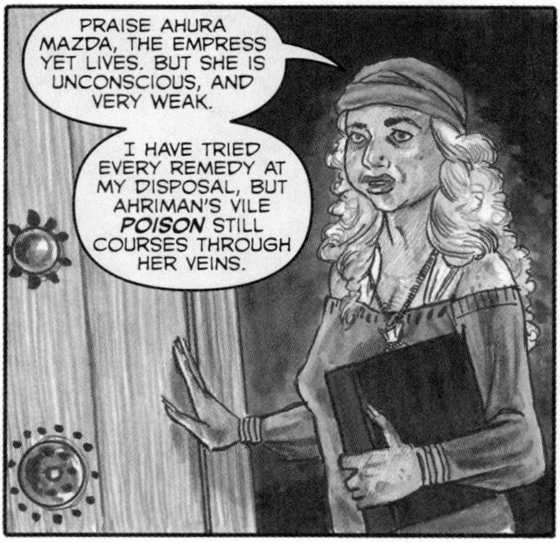
PRAISE AHURA MAZDA, THE EMPRESS YET LIVES. BUT SHE IS UNCONSCIOUS, AND VERY WEAK.
I HAVE TRIED EVERY REMEDY AT MY DISPOSAL, BUT AHRIMAN'S VILE POISON STILL COURSES THROUGH HER VEINS.

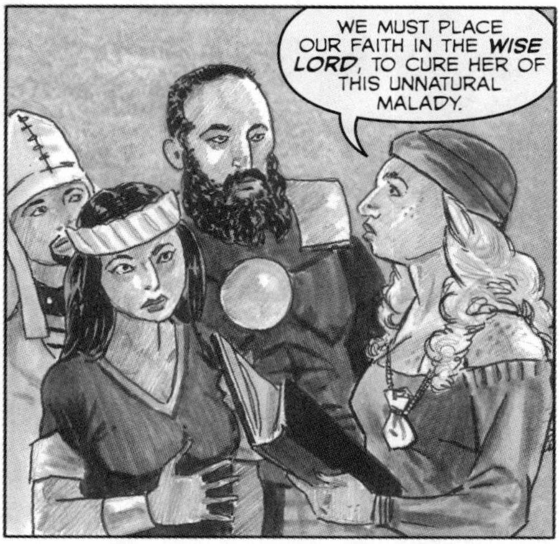
WE MUST PLACE OUR FAITH IN THE WISE LORD, TO CURE HER OF THIS UNNATURAL MALADY.

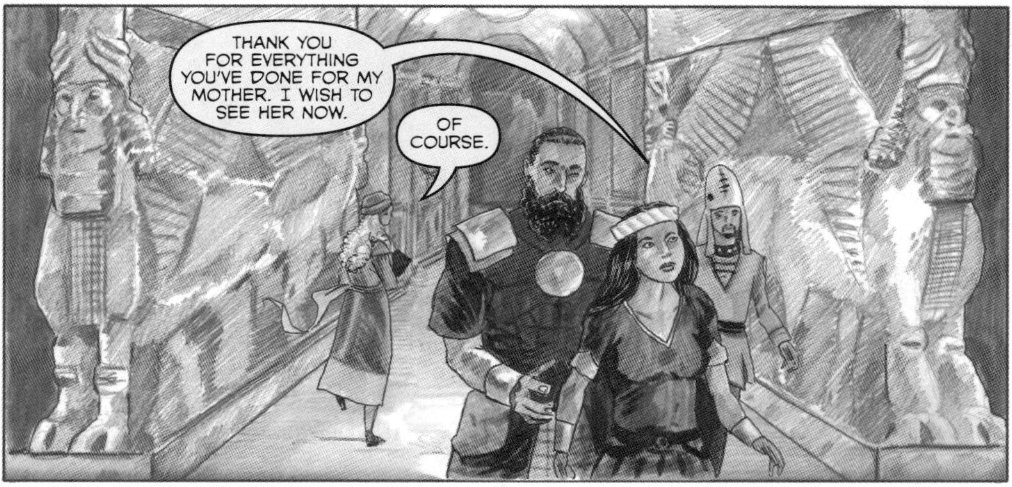
THANK YOU FOR EVERYTHING YOU'VE DONE FOR MY MOTHER. I WISH TO SEE HER NOW.
OF COURSE.

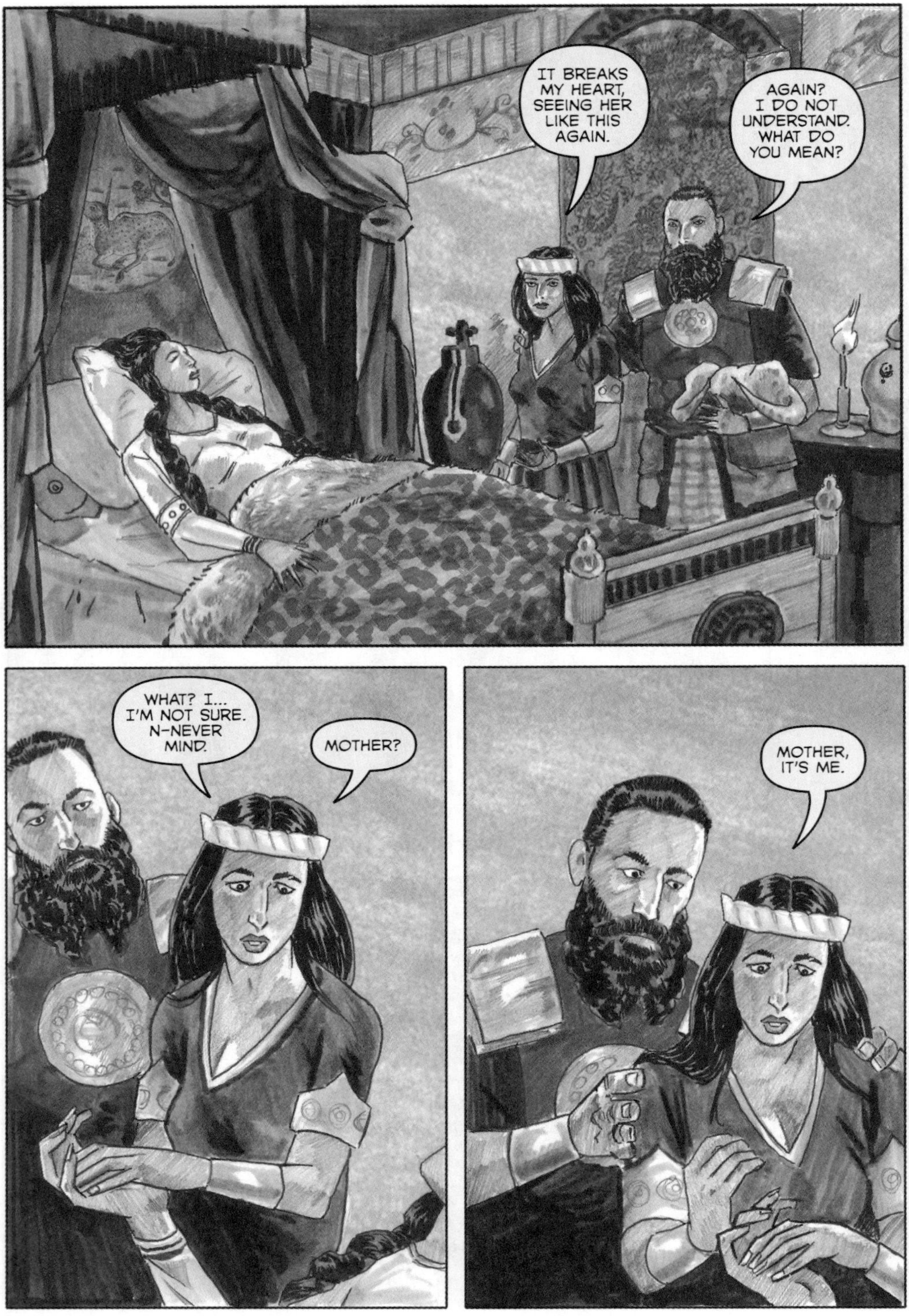
IT BREAKS MY HEART, SEEING HER LIKE THIS AGAIN.
AGAIN? I DO NOT UNDERSTAND. WHAT DO YOU MEAN?
WHAT? I... I'M NOT SURE. N-NEVER MIND.
MOTHER?
MOTHER, IT'S ME.

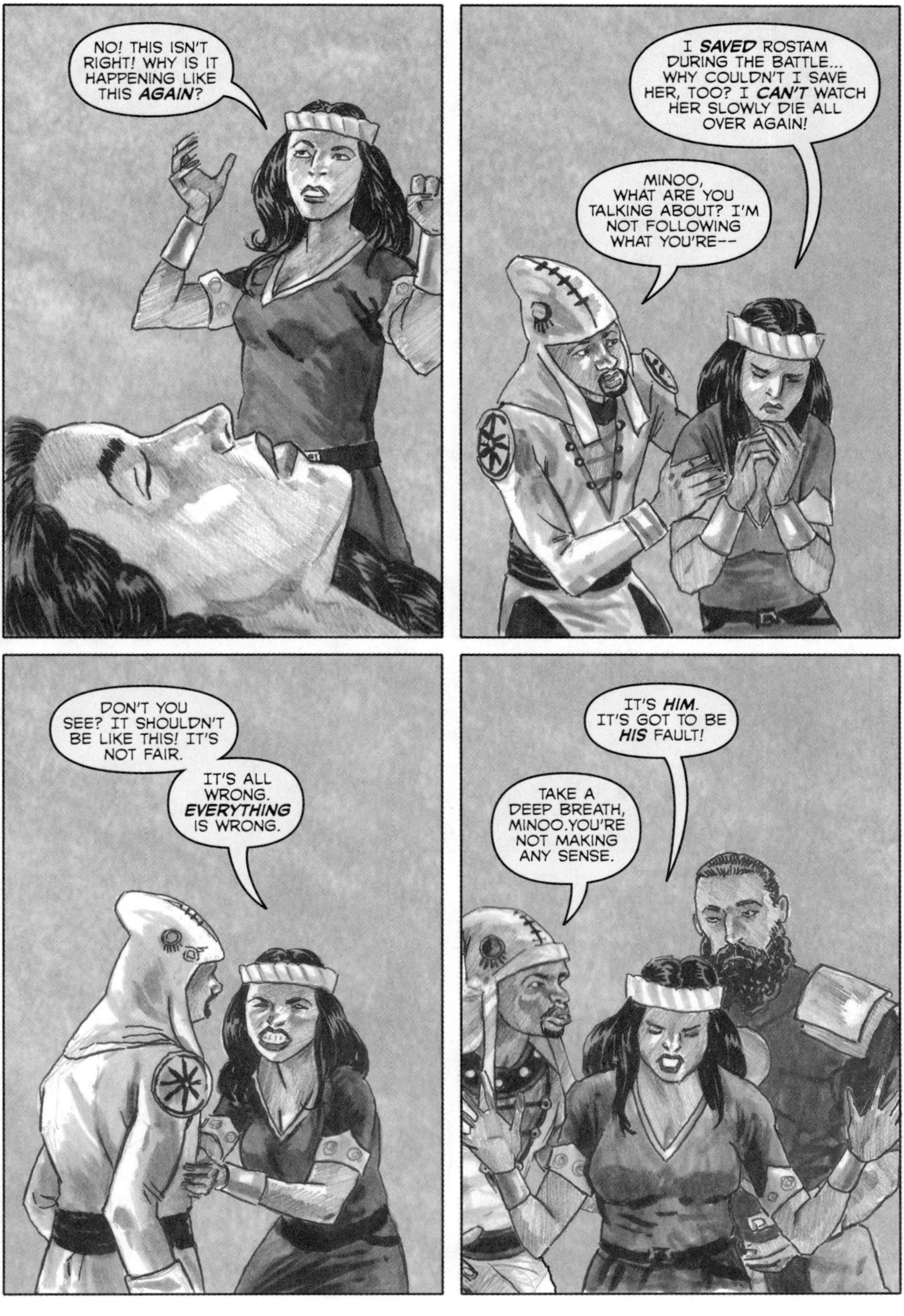
NO! THIS ISN'T RIGHT! WHY IS IT HAPPENING LIKE THIS AGAIN?
I SAVED ROSTAM DURING THE BATTLE... WHY COULDN'T I SAVE HER, TOO? I CAN'T WATCH HER SLOWLY DIE ALL OVER AGAIN!
MINOO, WHAT ARE YOU TALKING ABOUT? I'M NOT FOLLOWING WHAT YOU'RE--
DON'T YOU SEE? IT SHOULDN'T BE LIKE THIS! IT'S NOT FAIR.
IT'S ALL WRONG. EVERYTHING IS WRONG.
IT'S HIM. IT'S GOT TO BE HIS FAULT!
TAKE A DEEP BREATH, MINOO.YOU'RE NOT MAKING ANY SENSE.

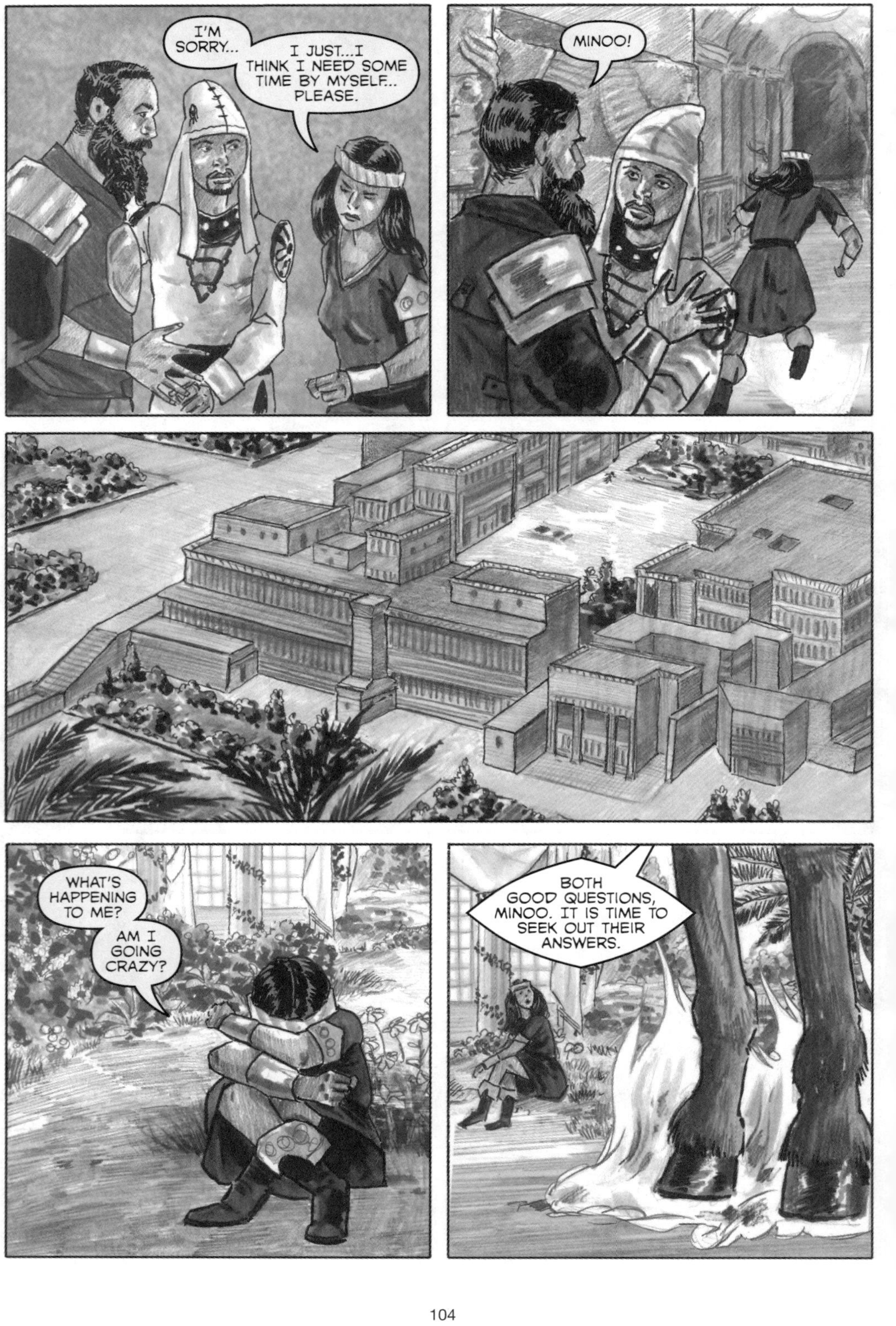
I'M SORRY...
I JUST...I THINK I NEED SOME TIME BY MYSELF... PLEASE.
MINOO!
WHAT'S HAPPENING TO ME?
AM I GOING CRAZY?
BOTH GOOD QUESTIONS, MINOO. IT IS TIME TO SEEK OUT THEIR ANSWERS.

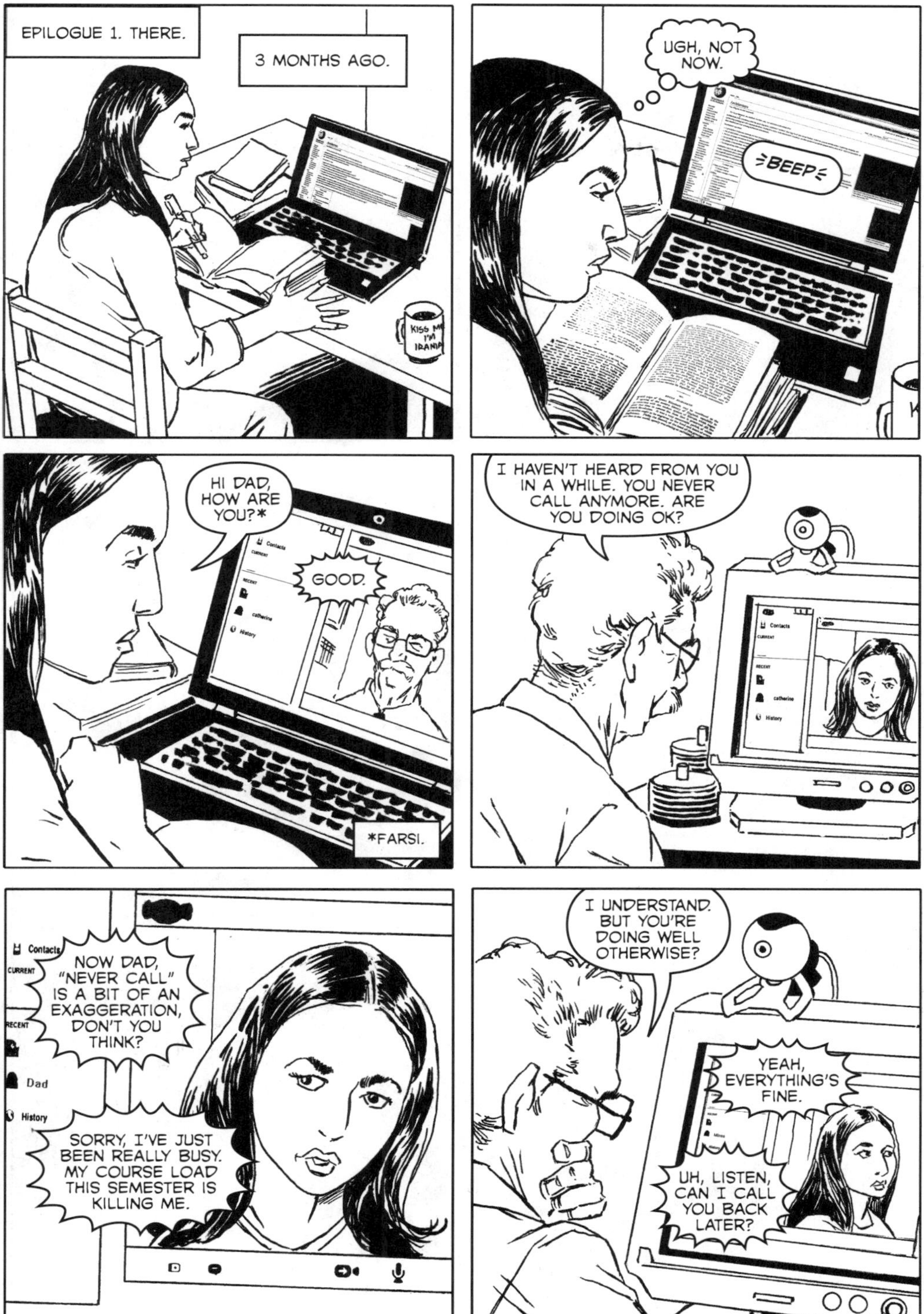
EPILOGUE 1. THERE.
3 MONTHS AGO.
KISS ME I'M IRANIA
UGH, NOT NOW.
BEEP
HI DAD, HOW ARE YOU?*
GOOD.
*FARSI.
I HAVEN'T HEARD FROM YOU IN A WHILE. YOU NEVER CALL ANYMORE. ARE YOU DOING OK?
NOW DAD, "NEVER CALL" IS A BIT OF AN EXAGGERATION, DON'T YOU THINK?
SORRY, I'VE JUST BEEN REALLY BUSY. MY COURSE LOAD THIS SEMESTER IS KILLING ME.
I UNDERSTAND. BUT YOU'RE DOING WELL OTHERWISE?
YEAH, EVERYTHING'S FINE.
UH, LISTEN, CAN I CALL YOU BACK LATER?

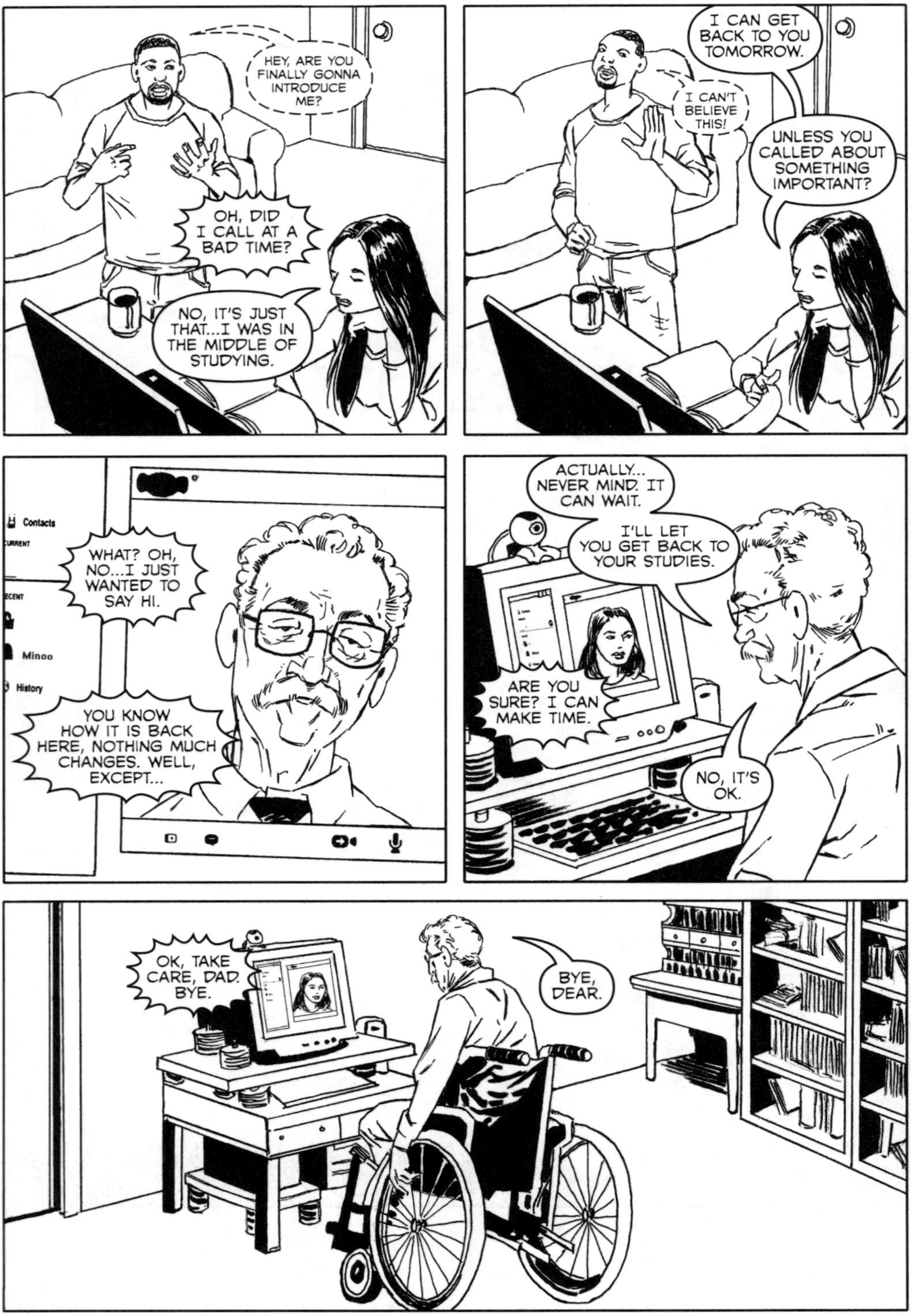
HEY, ARE YOU FINALLY GONNA INTRODUCE ME?
OH, DID I CALL AT A BAD TIME?
NO, IT'S JUST THAT...I WAS IN THE MIDDLE OF STUDYING.
I CAN GET BACK TO YOU TOMORROW.
I CAN'T BELIEVE THIS!
UNLESS YOU CALLED ABOUT SOMETHING IMPORTANT?
Contacts
Minoo
History
WHAT? OH, NO...I JUST WANTED TO SAY HI.
YOU KNOW HOW IT IS BACK HERE, NOTHING MUCH CHANGES. WELL, EXCEPT...
ACTUALLY... NEVER MIND. IT CAN WAIT.
I'LL LET YOU GET BACK TO YOUR STUDIES.
ARE YOU SURE? I CAN MAKE TIME.
NO, IT'S OK.
OK, TAKE CARE, DAD. BYE.
BYE, DEAR.

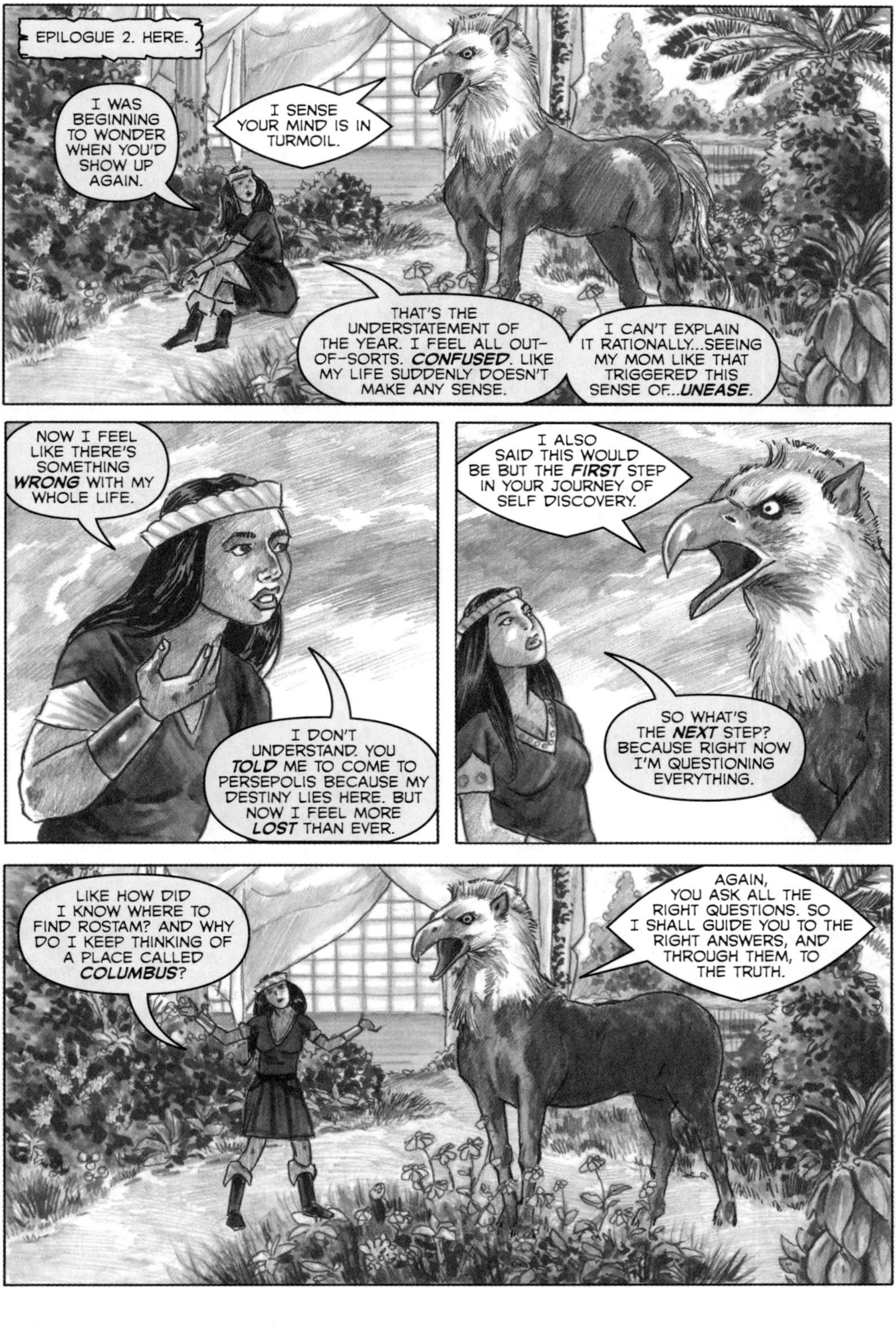
EPILOGUE 2. HERE.
I WAS BEGINNING TO WONDER WHEN YOU'D SHOW UP AGAIN.
I SENSE YOUR MIND IS IN TURMOIL.
THAT'S THE UNDERSTATEMENT OF THE YEAR. I FEEL ALL OUT-OF-SORTS. CONFUSED. LIKE MY LIFE SUDDENLY DOESN'T MAKE ANY SENSE.
I CAN'T EXPLAIN IT RATIONALLY...SEEING MY MOM LIKE THAT TRIGGERED THIS SENSE OF...UNEASE.
NOW I FEEL LIKE THERE'S SOMETHING WRONG WITH MY WHOLE LIFE.
I DON'T UNDERSTAND. YOU TOLD ME TO COME TO PERSEPOLIS BECAUSE MY DESTINY LIES HERE. BUT NOW I FEEL MORE LOST THAN EVER.
I ALSO SAID THIS WOULD BE BUT THE FIRST STEP IN YOUR JOURNEY OF SELF DISCOVERY.
SO WHAT'S THE NEXT STEP? BECAUSE RIGHT NOW I'M QUESTIONING EVERYTHING.
LIKE HOW DID I KNOW WHERE TO FIND ROSTAM? AND WHY DO I KEEP THINKING OF A PLACE CALLED COLUMBUS?
AGAIN, YOU ASK ALL THE RIGHT QUESTIONS. SO I SHALL GUIDE YOU TO THE RIGHT ANSWERS, AND THROUGH THEM, TO THE TRUTH.

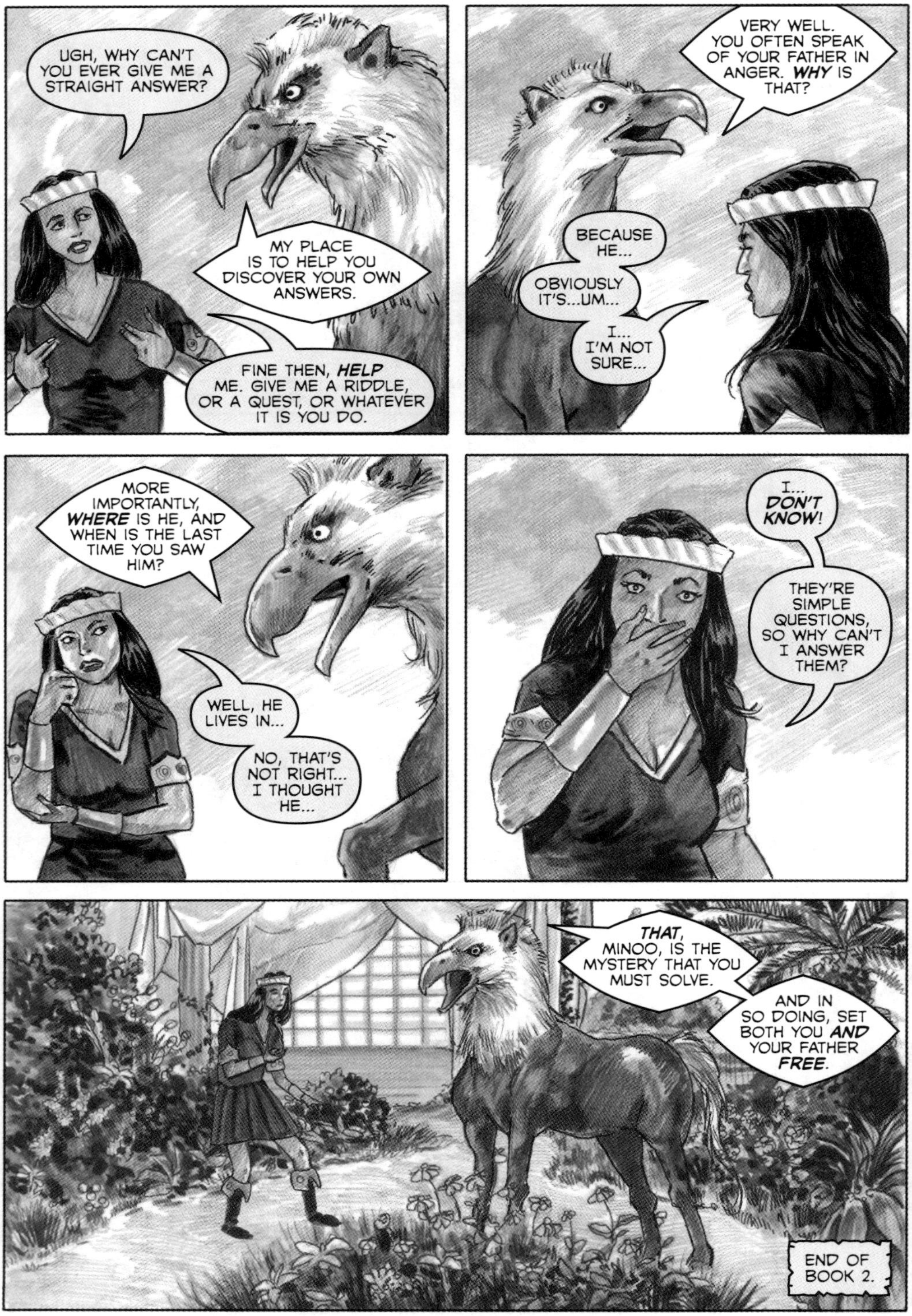

UGH, WHY CAN'T YOU EVER GIVE ME A STRAIGHT ANSWER?
MY PLACE IS TO HELP YOU DISCOVER YOUR OWN ANSWERS.
FINE THEN, ***HELP*** ME. GIVE ME A RIDDLE, OR A QUEST, OR WHATEVER IT IS YOU DO.
VERY WELL. YOU OFTEN SPEAK OF YOUR FATHER IN ANGER. ***WHY*** IS THAT?
BECAUSE HE...
OBVIOUSLY IT'S...UM...
I... I'M NOT SURE...
MORE IMPORTANTLY, ***WHERE*** IS HE, AND WHEN IS THE LAST TIME YOU SAW HIM?
WELL, HE LIVES IN...
NO, THAT'S NOT RIGHT... I THOUGHT HE...
I... ***DON'T KNOW***!
THEY'RE SIMPLE QUESTIONS, SO WHY CAN'T I ANSWER THEM?
THAT, MINOO, IS THE MYSTERY THAT YOU MUST SOLVE.
AND IN SO DOING, SET BOTH YOU ***AND*** YOUR FATHER ***FREE***.
END OF BOOK 2.

Dedicated to my family, for their support and inspiration, and to the memory of my mom, for a lifetime of love.
--Dara

Thanks to my parents for encouraging my talent and all of my teachers for expanding it. Thanks to my wife and kids for giving me the time to draw, and being patient while I was away downstairs doing work. Thanks to Dara and the folks at NBM for taking a chance with me. And a special thank you to our fans, both old and new. The support you've given this project has been fantastic and keeps inspiring me to do my best work.
--Brent

Dara Naraghi was born in Iran and educated in the United States. An Ohio State University alum, he works in the information technology field, but his passion is for the comics medium. His graphic novels include Persia Blues vol. 1, Lifelike, Terminator Salvation official movie prequel, and Witch & Wizard: Battle for Shadowland (of which the latter two were New York Times Bestsellers), as well as works for Image Comics, IDW Publishing, Dark Horse, and DC Comics. Dara lives in Columbus, Ohio with his wife, daughter, and the world's sweetest hound dog and craziest corgi.
www.DaraNaraghi.com

Brent Bowman is a graduate of the Columbus College of Art And Design with a degree in Illustration. A lifelong comics fan, Brent has been drawing since he was old enough to pick up a pencil. His work has appeared in publications by Image Comics and Caliber Press, as well as the collectible card game Age of Empires. He's a contributing member of PANEL, a local comics collective that publishes two anthologies a year. Brent has been nominated for the small press SPACE prize in 2008, 2010 and 2011 for both his PANEL work and his own original self-published comics. He lives in Columbus Ohio with his wife and two boys.
www.PersiaBlues.com

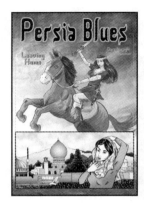  

Also available in this series:
Persia Blues, vol. 1, Leaving Home

Also available from Comics Lit:
Lulu Anew
Stressed out Mother takes off unannounced for personal
time on the seashore, leaving all perplexed.
Story of Lee, two volumes
A Chinese girl meets a Scot, they fall in
love only to face culture clash.

We have over 200 titles.
See our complete list, Naraghi's blog and order at:
NBMPUB.COM

NBM Graphic Novels
160 Broadway, Suite 700, East Wing,
New York, NY 10038

Catalog available upon request.